Getting off
the Ground

Getting off

George Vecsey & George C. Dade

E. P. Dutton • New York

the Ground

The Pioneers of Aviation Speak for Themselves

For information contact:
E. P. Dutton, 2 Park Avenue, New York, N.Y. 10016

Library of Congress Cataloging in Publication Data

Vecsey, George.
Getting off the ground
1. Aeronautics—United States—History.
2. Air pilots—United States—Biography.
I. Dade, George C., joint author. II. Title.
TL539.V4 1979   629.13'092'2 [B] 78-13106

ISBN: 0-525-11333-9

Published simultaneously in Canada by
Clarke, Irwin & Company Limited, Toronto and Vancouver

Designed by Nicola Mazzella

10 9 8 7 6 5 4 3 2 1

First Edition

Contents

Acknowledgments

The authors would like to thank the following persons who helped make this book better through their friendship, advice, knowledge, technical skill and other assets:

Marie Bellon, an excellent copy editor disguised as a typist; Anthony A. Bitetti; Julie Caffrey; Col. E. F. Carey, Jr., (U.S.A.F.-Ret.), International Aerospace Hall of Fame, San Diego; Katherine Constant; John Drennan; Garner Emerson; Joseph Gaeta; Paul Garber, Historian Emeritus, National Air and Space Museum, Smithsonian Institution; Mary Girelli; Mary Hardiman; Dr. David D. Hatfield, Aviation History, Northrop University; Carl (Slim) Hennicke; Captain James and Maxine Hix; Erwin Hoenes; Gerard H. Hughes; William K. Kaiser, Curator, Air and Space Collections, Nassau County Museum; Alastair Mackintosh; Sally Chin McElwreath, United Airlines; William McKenzie; Mary Louise Matera, Nassau County Museum Librarian; Nat Quinn; B. C. Reynolds, Archivist, San Diego Aero-Space Museum; Carol Rullan, Eastern Air Lines; Robert Ryan; William A. Schoneberger, Northrop Corporation; Mrs. Irwin Smith, Garden City Public Library; Frank Strnad; Frank G. Tallman; William Wagner; Richard A. Winsche, Historian, Nassau County Museum.

We would also like to thank Paul De Angelis, a skillful and enthusiastic editor with E. P. Dutton.

And finally we give thanks to Edith Dade and Marianne Vecsey for their support in so many ways.

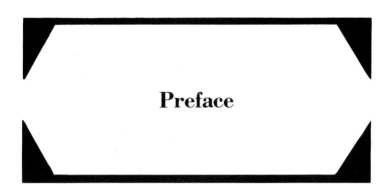

Preface

A few years ago I wrote a newspaper article about a group of aviation buffs who were renovating Charles Lindbergh's first airplane in the basement and garage of a private home.

At first I thought it was merely a pleasant story about a mini-factory in suburbia, complete with duty rosters on the wall, coffee breaks and work benches, and individual parts merging slowly toward a completed airplane.

After a couple of visits to this Santa's Workshop, I realized something deeper was happening at the home of George Dade. These men and women, members of the Long Island Early Fliers Club with long careers in aviation, were trying to re-create, with their hands and minds, another era that had been more fulfilling, more exciting to them.

It seemed that if they kept talking about the old days, and fashioning wing struts for Lindy's plane, it was just possible that Bert Acosta might materialize out of the mists, hung over but willing to fly anything with an engine and a couple of wings, or one of those doomed May Flies of the first decade, Cal Rodgers or Lincoln Beachey or Arch Hoxsey, would flit over-head just one more time, to thrill and inspire the crowd below.

Even club members who had recently piloted a 747 jet from San Juan or helped build a fighter for the Shah of Iran grew more animated when they talked about their first solo or hanging from a wing. When Edith Dade passed around the cider and doughnuts at ten o'clock, the stories seemed to stretch back in time. Everybody in the shop seemed to know somebody who had met the Wright brothers or worked for Glenn Curtiss or visited Louis Blériot or flew with Baron von Richthofen, yet most of them had "folded their wings" (or "headed west"), as aviators sometimes put it.

I felt a compulsion to meet these old-timers—if they were still around. When I wrote articles about the Appalachian coalfields, the most interesting people I met were the old ones, who could remember what the mountains were like before industry ruined the land and the spirit. It became apparent to me that pioneers could also still be found in the field of aviation.

To test the kind of stories these memories might provide, I visited a fellow named Charles Fity, who lives a few miles from my home on Long Island. When he told me how his flying career came to a premature end in 1910, I didn't know if I wanted to laugh or cry. He could recall young women fliers named Moisant and Quimby who were learning at the same time he was. Later I discovered these were well-known pilots of that time; Fity had been present at a small part of history. With the wonder of a child, I begged him for more stories, more stories.

Eventually, George Dade and I decided to write a book before the old-timers totally faded away. George has been associated with aviation since 1921, when his father went to work for Glenn Curtiss on the flatlands of Long Island. As a boy, Dade watched a young pilot named Lindbergh prepare to fly the Atlantic; later George flew solo at the age of sixteen, made a career out of shipping aircraft, and has been an active collector of aviation artifacts. His home is the closest thing to an aviation museum on Long Island, which he and many other people like to call "The Cradle of Aviation."

We divided our book this way: George would track down the old-timers, and I would interview them and write about them. (Several of his own adventures are included in this book.) Our goal was not a definitive history, but an enjoyable oral history of the first few generations of aviators. I wanted to hear flying anecdotes from people who had lived their adventures; I also wanted to see what had become of the old aviators, what they thought about themselves, about aviation, and about the world that has evolved.

We found a model for this book in Larry Ritter's *The Glory of Their Times*, a classic series of interviews with old-time baseball players. Larry Ritter is a friend who gave me some advice about how to compile this book; I acknowledge his help here. We also received help from historian Frank Strnad, who checked our facts as a labor of love, and whose kindness we strongly appreciate.

The chapters are arranged in a rough chronological strand. I found it fascinating, as the interviews piled up, to note the overlapping influences: Fully half a dozen of our old pilots had been influenced by the same barnstormer, Lincoln Beachey. Some of the people in this book knew each other at one time or another. There is one mysterious little feud between two of them, and a couple of jealousies, which you will discover for yourselves, I am sure.

I had a side benefit from this book, which I hope the reader will share. For the past eighteen months I have been associating almost entirely with people whose ages range from sixty-five to ninety-three. They kept appointments with me in over thirty cities in the United States and France. They met me at airports and hotels, fed me, escorted me to museums and meetings, found other subjects for me, and taught me most of what I know about aviation.

Some of these aviators suffered from physical problems and many had outlived their closest friends over the years, yet their kindness and strength pulled me through my busy year. They made me increasingly aware of the active life you can lead in your seventies, eighties, and nineties. In thanks for their friendship, I dedicate this work to the men and women of this book.

George Vecsey
Port Washington
Long Island

I
Early Days

For thousands of years, kings and artists, scientists and jesters tried to break the hold of gravity on their bodies and their imaginations. The sketches of da Vinci in the sixteenth century are often taken as the first indication that the human race would somehow learn to fly, but it was not until 1783 that the first human lifted off the ground in a hot-air balloon designed by the Montgolfier brothers in France.

In the nineteenth century, designers grappled with powered air machines while balloonists propelled themselves around Europe and the United States. Most of the visionaries are known only to historians now—Henson, Cayley, Chanute, Stringfellow, Ader, Lilienthal, Mozhaisky, Langley.

The Wright brothers, who ran a bicycle shop in Dayton, Ohio, became interested in aviation from a number of stimuli—adventures with kites, stories about the hang-gliders of Otto Lilienthal in Germany, correspondence with Samuel Langley in Washington, a toy helicopter from France. They built a powered flying machine in their shop and took it to the sand flats of Kitty Hawk, North Carolina, where they made the first powered, controlled, sustained flight in history on December 17, 1903.

Because of the Wrights' secrecy and official skepticism regarding the flight, few people knew about the Wrights' feat. On October 23, 1906, a tiny French-Brazilian playboy, Alberto Santos-Dumont, performed the first powered flight in Europe in a machine of his own design, unaware—according to legend—that the Wright brothers had beaten him by nearly three years.

For a while, France was the center of aviation progress. The Wrights opened a shop there, and in 1909 the Frenchman Louis Blériot made the first important long-range flight, across the English Channel.

In that first decade of the Wright brothers, dozens of inventors and would-be pilots started from the same minimal point: knowing man could fly, but knowing little more. A motorcycle racer, Glenn Curtiss, encouraged by Alexander Graham Bell, developed stabilizing devices and amphibious aircraft that made him a rival of the Wrights. But two young brothers, Henry and Will Newell, who had the same ambitions as Curtiss and the Wrights, recall in the first chapter the fate of their modest, homemade plane.

In Czechoslovakia, a young science student read about the Wright brothers and decided to move to America to join the move into the sky. Anthony Stadlman recalls in chapter 2 how he helped organize one of America's leading companies.

There were magnificent adventures in those early years, like the first cross-country journey by Calbraith Perry Rodgers, who crossed the United States in forty-nine days in 1911. In an open field in Parsons, Kansas, a youth vowed he would follow Rodgers westward into the sky. That boy, Claude Ryan, tells in chapter 3 how his love for aviation developed into the skill that would build an airplane for Charles Lindbergh.

The first act killed most of its players; thirty-seven prominent pilots died in 1910 alone. Most of the pilots were men, but there were enough women that their ability was proved quickly. One of the epic women in aviation, a carnival parachutist, Tiny Broadwick, tells in chapter 4 how the airplane and the parachute were introduced to each other.

Luck played a major role in the fate of the early pilots. Charles Fity notes in chapter 5 that if he had not drawn a large crowd with his acrobatics one Sunday afternoon, he might have had a long, distinguished career in aviation.

What was on the mind of the daredevils of the first generation? Harry Bruno, an important figure whom we will meet later in the book, has discovered a quote from a doomed pilot named Ralph Johnstone, three days before Johnstone's own fatal crash in 1910:

It's going to get me some day. It's sooner or later going to get us all. Don't think our aim is the advancement of science. That is secondary and is worked out by the men on the ground. When you get into the air, you get the intoxication of flying. No man can help feeling it. Then he begins to flirt with it, tilt his plane into all sorts of dangerous angles, dips and circles. This feeling is only the trap it sets for us. . . . The non-man-killing airplane of the future will be created from our crushed bodies.

1

Henry and Will Newell

Alexandria, Virginia

There are airplanes everywhere: Air Force fighters slashing low across the horizon, helicopters droning into a base along the Potomac, private craft flitting over the suburbs of Virginia, a jet trail thirty thousand feet high, and a technicolor parade of green and red and blue and silver 727 jets coming and going at National Airport.

"We haven't seen the Concorde," Will Newell says, "I guess the pattern from Dulles just doesn't take it this way."

Even without the Concorde, Henry and Will Newell can spot more horsepower in one glance than they ever dreamed possible when they were in their second decade and aviation was in its first. Like other young men of that time, they flocked to the fields when the first airplanes were built, but the Newell brothers also founded one of the first aviation clubs, the Aero Club of Long Island. There was a time when they might have dreamed of being the second famous brother team of aviation.

Now they sit on the eleventh-story promenade of a plush Episcopal retirement home, remembering a world when there were no powered aircraft. Henry is the spokesman for the group, eight-eight years old, trim and peppery and quite formal in his gray business suit. He insists his younger brother's memory is fading, and he grows exasperated when Will fumbles for a name or a detail. At the age of eighty-four, Will is the perfect kid brother. He is bigger, less intense, yet his frequent smiles and winks indicate he is not very much out of the picture.

"Before 1903, it was all gliders," Henry says, evoking the memory of inventors around the world who first attached wings to their arms and backs, and later built craft that could soar with the winds.

"We were more interested in radios. My folks gave me a Dynamo radio for Christmas, which was based on the Morse code. We grew up in Richmond Hill, Queens, near New York City, which was so rural that it didn't have electricity, so Will would crank a bicycle pedal by hand. We could reach a friend about two miles away."

One day the boys cranked up their homemade radio receiver and heard that two other brothers named Orville and Wilbur had—*flown?*

"People didn't believe the Wrights," says Henry, who was fourteen when the first plane flew at Kitty Hawk. "They were so far away, and the only way anybody knew was by telegram."

The Wright brothers had been so secretive that at first few people realized they had flown, but eventually the news got out. The Newells saw their issues of *Scientific American* shift from news about wireless radios to instructions for building airplanes.

"We made models with rubber bands for motors," says Will. "Then we put clock mechanisms in them."

The brothers recall making copies of the Bell tetrahedral kite, a Langley aeroplane, a Martin glider, a Farman biplane, an eight-foot Eddy Kite, and an exact model of a Baldwin dirigible. The two boys were prototypes of the inventive American youth of the time. All around them they saw progress being created by people who liked to work with their hands and their imaginations, and they began haunting the fields wherever people were flying.

The first flight the Newells saw was by Henry Farman, an English-born, French-speaking automobile racer, who turned to aviation, at the Sheepshead Bay racetrack in 1908.

"They used racetracks in those days in case they crashed," Henry says. "They just circled the track."

Farman stayed in the air a few seconds that day, and later they saw Louis Paulhan fly around Jamaica Racetrack twice. Then on November 3, 1908, the brothers traveled to the Bronx to see what was labeled the first public air show in America, at Morris Park. This show was sponsored by the Aeronautic Society, which called itself "the first organization in the world formed for the practical pursuit of the problem of mechanical flight by man."

The wealthy sponsors made it the first club in the world with its own flying grounds, shops and tools, and motors for aspiring aviators like grim little Glenn Curtiss from Hammondsport, New York. On Election Day, the club had promised a display of all the machines built in that year. The only problem was, nobody was ready to fly that day. The crowd of 20,000, including the Newells, had to settle for staring at the planes on the ground. One young man named Lawrence Lesh demonstrated his glider, towed by a horse and automobile, but when he cut the towline he fell to the ground, breaking his right ankle. The Aeronautical Society showed its compassion,

The first public air show in the United States was held November 3, 1908, at Morris Park, New York. No powered airplane managed to fly that day, but the elegant spectators gaped at the new machines, as well as the balloons and gliders. (Photo by Henry Newell)

however, and elected him a complimentary member. And so ended the first public air show in the world—not much show, but enough to inspire the Newells to follow Curtiss out to the spacious flatlands on Long Island.

Curtiss had quickly realized that his home base in upstate New York was neither flat enough nor temperate enough for year-round operation, so he had moved to the Hempstead Plains, a great flat space east of Mineola, Hempstead, and Garden City, in Nassau County, on Long Island.

This flatland would later be divded into several fields, and bear many names—Mitchel Field, Hazelhurst Field, Curtiss Field, Roosevelt Field. When the Newells began visiting it, the area was generally known as Mineola Aviation Field.

Many famous pilots touched down on the Hempstead Plains after 1908, but the most important was Curtiss, a former motorcycle racer turned pilot-inventor. Curtiss' legal battles with the Wright brothers and his pioneer work with planes that could land on water also demanded his time, but in 1909 his main preoccupation was the June Bug, with its stabilizing rudders (ailerons) built into the wings. On July 17, 1909, Curtiss circled the field for half an hour, thus winning a prize of ten thousand dollars for the first flight beyond twenty-five kilometers. Quickly, other would-be aviators rushed to the Hempstead Plains to learn from Curtiss, and utilize the open space.

"They only flew at dawn or at dusk because the wind wasn't as strong," Henry recalls. "We would get on our motorcycle at four in the morning

and ride out to Mineola. We'd stand as close as they would let us. The planes all used castor oil in those days—it was the only lubricant around. When I'd get home, my clothes were so full of fumes, my mother wouldn't let me in the house."

The brothers recall watching Curtiss give ground lessons to Charles Willard, the first aviation student in history.

"They only had one-seaters in those days," Henry says. "So Willard had to make his first flight by himself.

"I remember in the early days, all the planes were started by hand. They'd turn the propellers clockwise. One fellow could start a twenty-five horsepower engine, but when it grew to seventy-five, you needed two fellows gripping hands to pull it."

The brothers offered to help once in a while, to hold a plane during a gust of wind or to push it to its moorings, but mostly they stood at the edge and observed, taking pictures with a bellows-operated Kodak, four feet by four feet, that had belonged to their grandmother.

"It was a gosh-darn good lens," Henry says, "but brother Will took it to Mexico in 1914 in service against Pancho Villa, and lost it."

Sitting in the parlor at their retirement home, the brothers take out boxes of old snapshots that Henry has often displayed at lectures in the Washington area. He passes around pictures of Captain Thomas Scott Baldwin's biplane *Red Devil*, one hundred-feet in the air, being observed by gracious-looking women in long skirts, circa 1910. He shows snapshots of Charles K. Hamilton and Claude Graham-White, two of the more famous pilots of that first decade. Another shot of Baldwin in his dirigible.

As octogenarians, the brothers are valuable historians. But when they

The first rival to the Wright brothers was Glenn Curtiss of Hammondsport, New York, who began building planes such as the "Model F" flying boat. This picture was probably taken at Lake Keuka in upstate New York around 1908, shortly before Curtiss moved to the plains of Long Island. (The Garden City Archives)

were in their teens, they didn't want to be spectators. They wanted to get out and fly like the pioneers just a few years older than they.

In the winter of 1908–1909, the Newell brothers and their friends proposed forming a club to talk about aviation, and to pool their resources, with the goal of getting themselves into the air. They had no shop, no parts, no field, hardly any money; just the name of the club and the dream.

"We couldn't afford an engine, so we decided to build a glider that could accommodate an engine later," Henry says. "We designed it ourselves. It was going to be twenty-six feet long and twenty-six feet wide."

The brothers had no car, but little brother Will was in charge of bringing back four eighteen-foot pieces of Oregon spruce from a lumber yard in Manhattan.

"I carried them over the Brooklyn Bridge, then to the Long Island Railroad terminal in Brooklyn," Will says. "I had to wait for a baggage car. Then I carried them from the railroad track to our home."

He estimates he carried the wood on his shoulders for at least eight miles.

The boys constructed the glider themselves, with the help of the big saw at a lumber yard. They stretched unbleached muslin over the wings, sprayed them with a mixture of wax and kerosene. Then they realized the finished plane had become bigger than the individual parts they had carried into their third-story workroom. It was the aviators' version of painting themselves into a corner.

"We had to take out part of the window and use a block and tackle to get it down from the third floor," Henry says.

The next problem was getting into the air. With no car, they couldn't

9

Above: The Aero Club of Long Island built a "fan-cycle" to see how much propeller power Joe Post could generate. Right: Henry and Will Newell built this glider in their home in Richmond Hill, New York, but never managed to attach an engine to it. Fred Rockstroh, sleeves rolled up, tried to control the glider on a golf course hill one day. Henry Newell is to the far right. (Photos by Will Newell)

tow the glider, as others had done, so they carried it several miles to the Richmond Hill Country Club, which had a few timid slopes.

In July of 1909, with Joe Post, the smallest of the club members, seated at the controls, the club members pushed and pulled the glider until it fluttered away from the slight incline. The breeze caught under the spruce wings and Joe Post was airborne, maybe a few feet, maybe twenty, as Henry recalls today.

"But it was too heavy to give a good flight," Henry says. "It was built for a motor, and it was just too solid to glide very well."

By this time, it was apparent the boys would need a wealthy benefactor to subsidize a motor, as the Aeronautic Society had subsidized Glenn Curtiss. There were none to be had, but in good-fashioned Tom Swift–Hardy Boys style, the Newell brothers incorporated the Aero Club of Long Island on August 20, 1909, with the intention of doing it themselves.

"In August we built a four-foot wooden propeller and attached it to the rear end of a bicycle," Henry says. "We used gears from an old ice-cream freezer. The bicycle chain turned, the gears cranked the propeller instead of the back wheel. We were not trying to get the bicycle off the ground, but to see how much power we could create. We took turns racing the bicycle, and we got it up to twenty-five miles per hour. We called it the 'fan-cycle.' "

Sixty-eight years later, Dr. Paul MacCready of Pasadena, California built a bicycle-plane that another man, Bryan Allen, pedaled above a three-mile course in California, using 1977 lightweight materials. The Newells had none of that in 1909.

In fact, the most successful part of the club was its name, which was coveted by John Moisant, the dashing aviator who had fought in jungle wars in Central America and was competing at Nassau Boulevard field in Garden City.

"He tried to use the name of our club, but our lawyer advised him against it," Henry recalls.

It was one of the few triumphs the Aero Club of Long Island would ever enjoy.

"Our friend Francis Willson was building a biplane in the Grand Central Station area," Henry recalls. "But one day a train crashed through a barrier, hit a gas tank, and the plane was destroyed."

Another club member, Charles Wald, sought out the Wright brothers in Dayton for lessons. Later he operated an air ferry across Long Island Sound. Aviation was moving forward, but the Newells had to stand and watch.

"In 1912 our father moved us to a farm in Lanesboro, Massachusetts," Henry says. "We didn't have any more meetings of the Aero Club. We put the glider in a boxcar and shipped it to Lanesboro, to store it in the family barn. With all the hills up there, it was possible we could have launched the glider, but our parents were against it."

"My mother stopped all the action," Will recalls "She said, 'If you go up in that plane, you won't go to college!' "

One day the father was stacking hay, and the rickety old barn collapsed under the weight of the brothers' airplane. Only then did the craft achieve the soaring heights of its makers' ambition: a trail of smoke from a funeral pyre in the updraft of a Berkshires breeze.

The two brothers went off to pursue their careers—Will in the shipbuilding business in Newport News, Virginia; Henry in banking in Jamaica, New York. Neither of them got both feet off the ground until the 1940s, when they made airplane trips to Florida. But they have always remained close to aviation: Henry occasionally gives talks in the recreation room at Goodwin House, showing the slides and pictures they have accumulated in the past seventy years. The brothers have reproduced the letterheads from the Aero Club of Long Island and use them for their correspondence.

"We had a very practical vision of airplanes," Will says softly. "I believe I would have had great moments in aviation if my mother hadn't spoken to me."

2

Tony Stadlman

Anaheim, California

Tony Stadlman can remember the last days of 1903. He was already seventeen years old, a student of sciences in Prague, Czechoslovakia, when he picked up the Czech science magazine *Epocha* one day and read an article about flying machines.

He was not surprised by the news, since the scientific journals had been full of reports about men trying to fly—in gliders, in powered balloons, and most recently in machines that would lift themselves off the ground. Month by month came the reports, particularly from France and America; the seventeen-year-old in Prague knew enough not to be skeptical.

"I said to myself: 'This is for me,' " Tony Stadlman recalls.

Many people rushed to get in on the dream when they realized what the Wright brothers had done on December 17, 1903. Tony Stadlman even left his homeland and rushed to America, where he later became an early associate of three historic figures: the Loughead brothers, Malcolm and Allen, and John K. Northrop, who founded two of the world's giant aircraft builders.

I met Stadlman at a convention of the Early Birds of Aviation—pilots who made a solo flight before the thirteenth anniversary of the Wright brothers' first flight. When the organization was founded on December 3, 1928, there were 588 Early Birds, but by 1977 they have dwindled to seventy-one. Seventeen of them have been able to attend the convention at a motel next to Disneyland, where these sober old pilots in jackets and ties seem as incongruous as owls in a picnic of cuckoos.

13

Grown men wearing cutoff Bermuda shorts and Mickey Mouse T-shirts amble through the lobby as the Early Birds talk about events sixty and seventy years earlier. Tony Stadlman, who is the oldest Early Bird at the convention, is also the most suave, with his European manner and his trim moustache. He wears a three-piece suit and his thick hair is more black than gray. He is philosopher of the group. From time to time, he will announce that he has had a good life, but that it serves no purpose since he does not believe in an afterlife. His companions flutter at this dangerous talk and insist Tony doesn't really mean what he is saying, but when Tony says it, he means it.

Flying, for example. Not worth the risk. The man who was enthralled by machines in 1903 has come down by bus from his home in San Francisco, because he does not care for flying anymore.

"I was in three crashes in one year, they almost killed me, so in 1916 I promised my wife I would always keep one foot on the ground after that," he says.

"For fifty-seven years I did not get in a plane, but in 1973 Lockheed induced me to fly in their new 1011 Tristar Jet. They kept asking me until finally I said all right. We got up there and all these officials are coming around saying, 'Isn't this wonderful, look how high we are, look how fast we are.'

"I said, 'Don't kid an old man. It's not so wonderful. I look out at thirty-five thousand feet, at such speed, it's not even like having speed. It might as well be an automobile map down there, things are so small. When I could go sixty miles an hour and twelve feet high, now that was exciting. This is boring.' "

Tony Stadlman chuckles at the memory of his being so brusque to all those eager officials from Lockheed, so proud of their new hardware.

For him, the best days began when he was a boy in Prague, being told the legends of Icarus and Daedalus, who dared to fly. Then he read reports about man trying to fly, as he worked with his father at an inn.

"My father let me set up the daily papers on the racks," he recalls, "so I could learn the titles and the headlines. The papers were there for the guests to read. They would sit and read for hours. In those days, no one ever hurried to finish."

When he was seventeen, he read in *Epocha* about the Wright brothers, and he realized that a new day in technology had arrived.

"I studied every report for the next two years," he recalls. "Do you know we got better reports about aviation in Europe than you did in America? It's true. The United States ignored the Wright brothers. They were not recognized for several years, but in Europe we knew all about them."

The controversy over the Wright brothers is recalled by another ninety-one-year-old man sitting in the chair next to Stadlman. Glenn Osborn, now from Malibu, California, was a teen-ager in Dayton, Ohio, in 1903—studying Latin under Miss Catherine Wright, and getting his bicy-

Inventing the airplane had its advantages. Orville Wright got a lift from his mechanic, William Conover, to a flying boat the Wrights had built on the Miami River near Dayton in 1913. (Anthony Stadlman)

cle repaired at the Wright shop. Osborn never became a pilot, but because he knew the Wright family, he is welcomed whenever the Early Birds meet.

"I knew the two brothers," Osborn says. "I even have a receipt for getting my bicycle fixed at their shop. It is initialed, 'Paid—O.W.' I just wish I had asked him to sign his full name.

"Catherine Wright sent me a postcard when she joined her brothers in Europe. Nobody gives her enough credit because she supported them by teaching Latin to us.

"There was a newspaper in Dayton that didn't believe the story out of North Carolina. I remember a headline in the paper said, 'Man Can't Fly.' You know, in later years, they organized a club in Dayton called the 'Man Can't Fly Club.' "

For some reason, Europe paid more attention to the Wrights in those early years, allowing Stadlman to read a good deal about their flying machines while he was still living in the traditions of an old world.

"When I was a boy in my Czech country, it was traditional to celebrate the end of our harvest," he says. "Our observance was not just one day, but would last weeks. We would walk from village to village, just to taste the different feasts of the table. Not only did we walk—so did the poor bird. Flocks of geese would be driven to market, but they wore tar shoes. The feet would be dipped in warm tar, then into a sandbox, over and over until the proper protection was built up for the long trek. No table was complete without a fine fat goose. Anyway, our own feet would give out long before the invitations. It just occurs to me as I am talking that perhaps that is where I learned to be a freeloader."

He recalls deciding to leave his homeland when he became old enough to be drafted.

"I didn't want to go into the army," he says. "I would have been dragged in. Czechoslovakia was under the Austrian government; it had been subjugated for three hundred years. All the time we tried to get out from under, but I wanted to work with airplanes. I wanted to go to America. In 1905 I left and I never saw my parents again.

"In my first few years in this country, when my letters were mailed from here and there and everywhere, they thought of me as a gypsy or a wanderer. Our letters were bitter. I remember writing them in length that I would never disgrace them, and finally our letters carried the warmth of a better understanding."

His parents lived long enough to revel in the success of another son, who became the first violinist in the Czech National Symphony, but Tony never wrote them about his accomplishments in aviation.

Why? "It never seemed important at the time."

Stadlman was supposed to see his brother on an orchestra tour of America in 1938, but Hitler's invasions changed all those plans. Only recently have his younger relatives known that Tony Stadlman was a pioneer of aviation, and they know this only by mail.

"I have never been back," he says. "Today everybody says Europe is so exciting, but I say, 'Don't tell me about Europe, I was born there, I am glad to come to the U.S. This is where I get my chance.'

"When I came to the U.S. in 1905, I was handicapped with my language and I wound up working in the shop at the Morrison Hotel in Chicago. When I started to speak English, I found out my job was called 'grease monkey.' "

He tried writing to the Wrights to see if they had a job for him, but they never answered. One day the *Chicago Tribune* ran an advertisement for the Chicago School of Aviation. Stadlman had saved one hundred fifty dollars from his hotel job, so he enrolled in the course, but soon discovered you didn't just rent a plane and take lessons: You had to build the plane first.

"The others in the school were farmboys from the Midwest. They were eager but they didn't know about machinery, but they had three hundred dollars to pay for the course. The school said it would teach you how to 'build a machine.' I'd seen a few sketches of a Curtiss plane. The time came when I was the only one working on the machine. I became such a leader that when my one hundred fifty dollars evaporated, he said, 'Forget the one hundred fifty dollars, just carry right on. You are the only guy I can depend on.' I found myself an airplane constructor."

Shortly thereafter, Stadlman met a man who would be vital to his career. It happened on a cold January day in 1911, when he went to the Hawthorne Racetrack in Chicago to watch two young pilots try to fly a Curtiss biplane.

"These daredevils tossed a coin to see who went first," Stadlman recalls. "The first flyer barely got off the ground—a hop or two, then the plane sputtered to a stop. But the second flyer took off with verve and made a beautiful circling flight.

"As he landed, we all dashed to the ship to shake the hand of this daring young and successful conqueror of the sky. It was the handshake that was to last fifty-seven years. His name was Allan H. Loughead."

Loughead—who later simplified his name to "Lockheed"—was a native of Santa Barbara, California, now flying and teaching in the Chicago area. He persuaded Stadlman to join the International Airplane Company, owned by an automobile dealer on Michigan Avenue. Stadlman was in charge of building planes, usually some version of the Curtiss-type pusher biplane. There was no such thing as mass production; all parts were made by hand.

After joining that firm, Stadlman recalls meeting both Wright brothers in "a simple exchange of greetings" at Grant Park, introduced by the secretary of the Aero Club of Illinois. Eight years later, he says, he met Orville Wright at the Lockheed plant in Santa Barbara.

"I recall that Orville's attitude about the military use of aviation matched mine. It was not as we dreamed, the way to bring mankind together. Of course, the Wright company was in that type of production, but that was after he sold the company."

Later in 1911, Stadlman moved to another company in Florida, and the next year wound up building a hydroplane on Lake Winnebago in Wisconsin. Also in 1912, in Milwaukee, he repaired a Curtiss-type pusher, a skeletal craft with no external protection from any obstacles it might meet.

"It was an old trap," Stadlman recalls, "but when I finished fixing it, somebody said, 'Even you could fly this.' "

Stadlman had never flown solo in his life, but he snapped back, "Do you think so?" And he hopped in the pusher and made a successful tour of the field. That would have been fine, but he tried it again a few minutes later and found the open craft swerving around a windmill, losing altitude toward a thick woods.

"I could feel the plane go into the tree, but I still had my hand on the stick, so I thought I was all right. But then I realized the rest of the plane was behind me, in the branches of the tree, and I had no airplane with me, just the stick. I was still going forward, but the rest of the plane had stopped. It's comical in memory, but it wasn't funny at the moment.

"I grabbed a few branches, whatever I could, and landed in the underbrush. I started to do this"—with his vibrant ninety-one-year-old body, he starts doing arm calisthenics—"trying to convince myself I wasn't hurt. Then I looked around and realized this farmer was watching me. I was embarrassed."

If there is one common thread that links early aviators, it is the survival of crashes in which their planes were totally demolished. Hundreds of pilots were killed in those days, but the speeds and heights were not so awesome that with luck, a healthy body could not spring out the wreckage of a flimsy little machine. So the early aviators are not merely chronological survivors; almost all of them are physical survivors of crashes that cannot be duplicated today because of increased speeds.

"My last crash on Lake Michigan was the worst," Stadlman continues. "It was a Sunday, beaches loaded with people, sunset, evening coming on. I took off over Lincoln Park, water intake system broke down. Three miles offshore, trying to land, two or three little powerboats right in my path. I thought I'd wreck myself rather than hit them. I went up, trying to land toward the horizon, the lake was like glass. You know, it's hard to judge altitude when you're flying over water. We learn by experience, hard to tell how close you are, I plunged right in.

"Everything smashed in front of me, I swam out under the water, no fear, no struggle. When you are drowning, nothing is disagreeable. This was my second experience with drowning. The first was when I nearly drowned on the Moldau River in Prague when I was a little boy. I just slipped in this pool in the river, with an iron railing around it. You know, I remember there was no anxiety except, 'What will my mother say?' I was unconscious when three men happened to see the color red under the water, and it was the color of my bathing suit. They pulled me up and worked over me.

"I lived through that and my crashes, but after Lake Michigan I decided I wouldn't fly anymore," Stadlman recalls. "I told the other guys, 'I prefer to be a live coward than a dead hero. I'll build the planes—you crash 'em.'"

Convinced that his future lay on the ground, Stadlman went to work for a company seeking wartime contracts with the government. In 1918 he was in Washington, D.C., when he ran into Allan Loughead again, who had made so much money flying tourists at the 1915 San Francisco Fair that he and his brother, Malcolm, had their own airplane shop back in Santa Barbara.

"Allan already had a contract in his pocket," Tony recalls. "The next day the government said all contracts that had been signed could continue production, but tentative orders such as the one I had were to be negated.

Above: In 1914 Tony Stadlman and several other men collaborated to build the Howell Flying Boat, which Stadlman flew over Lake Michigan. Below: But on June 7, Stadlman crashed off Clarendon Beach, splintering the aircraft and keeping Stadlman out of the air for the next fifty-seven years. (Anthony Stadlman)

Allan said to me, 'I want you to come to Santa Barbara and take care of construction.' "

Stadlman moved to that charming coastal city, where the Loughead brothers were building plywood seaplanes in a garage and trundling them down to the ocean on a wooden ramp.

"Allan was a strange kind of guy," Stadlman recalls. "He would never show up at the plant until one or two o'clock in the afternoon, while I would have been there since seven. But when evening came, and the day should have been over, this night bird would be all full of vim and vigor and was ready to discuss a thousand ideas.

"He was persistent, and at the time I would become really angry with him. With production already on the line, it was impossible to make changes even though many of his ideas were good ones. Finally I would say: 'Allan, that's impossible. We can finish what we have—twenty or so planes—and then start a new series using your ideas.'

"I couldn't help but show my annoyances, but he was a good guy. No matter how angry I'd get, he'd just grin and say, 'OK, Tony, I'll put it in the suggestion box.' "

One of the best moves the brothers made was hiring a youngster out of Santa Barbara High School to help with the engineering. His name was John K. Northrop.

"He was the glue that held that company together," Stadlman says. "He was a remarkable young man. He had no engineering training, but he was an excellent draftsman, and was great at stress analysis."

Most of the Early Birds carry documents and photographs, to show their friends or strangers. Stadlman is more reticent than some, but he has brought along one old contract, which he shows to me. It begins:

"This agreement, made and entered into this twenty-eighth day of July, 1919, between Allan H. Loughead, Malcolm Loughead, John K. Northrop, and Anthony Stadlman, all of the City of Santa Barbara, California, witnesseth: that whereas, the said parties are each and all interested in the development, construction, and use of aircraft and aeronautical appliance of all kinds; are engaged in the business of developing, constructing, and using the same. . . ."

The contract states that if one of them has an idea, he must share it with the others. If at least two of them approve, it will be incorporated into the Lockheed production; if only one likes it, the idea remains his, privately.

"I never like to say, 'I did this' or 'I did that' because we worked as a team in those years," Stadlman says. "If I had an idea, somebody else would add to it, or if somebody else had an idea, I would add to it. We had a small shop and we were not schooled. We were just like the Wright brothers, practical men. We were innovators. It's like the Lockheed Vega. They call me a designer, but it was a joint effort. It's not from any one of us."

The Lockheed Vega is now famous for its simplified body structure

Anthony Stadlman and Malcolm Loughead (the original family spelling) on their way from Santa Barbara to San Francisco for an air show in 1920. They are pulling the S-1 Sport Biplane, which Stadlman helped construct for the emerging Lockheed firm. (Anthony Stadlman)

that John K. Northrop describes in a later chapter. While the contract made them equal partners in the creation of the Vega, undoubtedly they had private versions of how the plane came to be designed and built.

Stadlman remembers how it got its name:

"I said: 'How about naming it "Vega?"' They all looked puzzled, but I said, 'It's one of the brightest stars in the constellation of Lyre. It means diving eagle. What could be more appropriate?' There may be many people who take credit for this particular bit of history, but later they named their planes after stars—Polaris, Sirius, Altair, Orion, and now they have the Tristar."

The names of Lockheed and Northrop belong now to major corporations that build space-age projectiles, employ thousands of people, and exert their influence in dozens of countries. Tony Stadlman has no company named after him, and no great financial interest in any of them.

"I like to see my friends succeed," he says with an Old World laugh, brief and controlled. "That way, they do not need my help. You are not happy in this world unless you are sympathetic to those in your circle. You cannot carry a chip on your shoulder.

"It is not my wish to rake over old ashes caused by the fires of disillusionment," Stadlman says. "There have been several occasions in the last ten years that I have seen Jack Northrop. I did not wish to get involved with polemics, and I have offered my hand in friendship.

"I deeply regret that I did not keep letters that I wrote, or that I didn't keep a daily log. It could spin a tale of adventure. We were all characters of sorts.

"There was a time when we all lived on the same block in Santa Barbara—I mean, Jack and I. My wife, who was an exceptional cook, always had a filled cookie jar. I believe she was the most popular of all with the children. Our old family albums show the two families in many happy occasions. For many years our relationship was very cordial, but as in all lives, disagreements mar the harmony of a once-pleasant friendship."

The coolness is apparently mutual. Before I ever heard of Tony Stadlman, I paid a visit to Jack Northrop, who still lives in Santa Barbara. The famous designer talked for over an hour, as described in a later chapter, but mentioned Stadlman only obliquely, and never by name.

The four-way arrangement among the two Lougheads, Stadlman, and Northrop broke up when the Lockheed company had an "unfortunate financial period in 1923," as Stadlman puts it. Stadlman worked for Douglas from 1923 to 1926, rejoined the Lougheads in Burbank, supervising the construction of the Vega, then joined the Alcor Company in 1929. He worked for North American Aviation during the war, and then retired in San Francisco.

"Allan and I remained friends until his death. His children and my two children had been the best of playmates. It is interesting that my 1977 Christmas card from John had this message: "I have at last, at age 62, received my pilot's license. Can't you hear Allan saying, 'What took you so long?' "

A child of the nineteenth century, Stadlman has technically been an old man for a quarter of the twentieth century. Complaining about the food at a recent luncheon, he says: "Maybe the trouble with living so long is that one outlives all the good cooks."

Tony says he enjoys a good bottle of wine and a good book, both with regularity.

"Sure, I enjoy life. I have a good life," he says. "But the way I look at it, when you are born, you are condemned to death like a criminal. We become like fertilizer. All of these [a sweep of the hand indicates the pictures, the documents of the early aviation] are worthless. There is death in everything. No matter what we accomplish, it is worth nothing."

Tony's friend Mary Girelli, an intelligent woman three or four decades younger than he, nudges him with her elbow.

"Come on, Tony, cut the crepe-hanging," she says.

"No, it's true," he says undaunted. "The earth may be like Mars someday. If this earth disappeared in a puff of smoke, the rest of the solar system wouldn't know about it. To me, it is not order. To me, this is disorder.

Left: Anthony Stadlman at his shop in Chicago in 1914. (Anthony Stadlman) Below: Stadlman visiting Frank Tallman's air museum in Orange, California, in 1977. (Photo by David Strick) *New York Times*)

Like the Concorde, that new plane. From an engineering standpoint, they are marvelous. But why do we insist to go so fast to hell?

"It's so fantastic. Half the world is lunatics. Now they want to go to other solar systems. Suppose we receive signals from other planets, trillions of years away. How do we get there? We can't get along on earth. We can't handle our own problems here.

"Let's put all human genius into rectifying all the inequalities. Until we are happy here. Then let's go to Mars."

Tony stops talking for a moment. I mumble something about today's complicated aerospace industry being the logical extension of the simple past.

"The astronauts are well-paid, under doctor's care. They are well-trained. We were starving, but they were thrilling days. We were pioneers, but there were very few worms for the early birds."

He fumbles through his souvenirs, takes out a picture of a handsome young man in a three-piece suit with a moustache that is unmistakably Tony Stadlman, sixty years ago. Standing next to him is a young woman, dark and attractive.

"Let's face it," he says. "This is how I'd like to be today."

3

T. Claude Ryan — I

San Diego, California

The building, just down the road from the airport named after Lindbergh, still has "RYAN" painted across the roof. But the company is owned by a complex called Teledyne now. Claude Ryan keeps an office, with William Wagner just across the hall, where he's been for the past forty years.

"We're retired now," Wagner explains. "We come in on Tuesdays and Thursdays, and we play dollar-a-year man. When Claude sold the company, we kind of moved sideways, all the older guys. That's the way it should be. The older guys don't go out and hustle sales like they did when they were younger."

Only the boss still hustles, just as he did when he built the company that built *The Spirit of St. Louis* in the spring of 1927 for Charles A. Lindbergh.

People in San Diego say it is a shame Claude Ryan doesn't mix more with his old aviation buddies, play some golf, enjoy those retirement years. They talk of him as isolated, withdrawn, but it is hardly the kind of withdrawal staged by another famous old California aviator, Howard Hughes. Bill Wagner says the boss is too busy building a new airplane to gab about the past.

But on the last morning of my visit to San Diego, Claude Ryan pokes his head into Wagner's office and says he could give up half an hour to talk about the old days. The real old days. The Lindbergh thing, well, everybody knows that story by now.

As Bill Wagner walks me across the corridor, I wonder if Ryan will be some pale recluse, unable to verbalize his love for aviation. I get a sudden flash of a ghostly old man with long fingernails and stringy hair, sitting in bed eating ice cream, and I remember that the old-timers in Southern California still recall Howard Hughes as one hell of a good aviator, too.

But the man across the corridor is darkly tanned, his healthy smile making him look more like a middle-aged corporation president than a seventy-nine-year-old relic who saw his first airplane in 1911.

As we make some preliminary small talk, I give Ryan every opportunity to chat about the picture on his wall—the airplane with the pebbled silver cowling that flew the Atlantic in that antic spring of 1927. But he prefers to pick up a wide-winged model on a table and fondle it with obvious love.

"They've got this one out in the back hangar right now," he says, holding up the model. "The FAA is giving it a flutter test, all kinds of stresses. They want to make the wings fall off, but they can't."

The newest plane is a glider with a motor, that can take the wind for hours and use fossil fuel only when necessary, he says.

He takes one more look at his newest love, and then launches into a recollection of the first plane he ever saw. He doesn't remember the Wright brothers' first flight, he says, but aviation did not take long to reach the flatlands of Parsons, Kansas, where he was born on January 3, 1898. (He was given the first name Tubal, which he never used.)

"A lot of early flyers came from Kansas, did you know that?" Ryan asks. "It's because the wind blows all the time, so kids all flew kites, and that's how they got interested in airplanes. That's what I always tell people.

"There are long winters in Kansas, too, and kids did a lot of reading. I wasn't always reading in line with my studies. I'd read all the magazines I could get, particularly if they were full of blood and thunder. There was one magazine called *The American Boy*, which has long since disappeared. There was an adventure about an American pilot flying a Blériot airplane. It was written by an American who must have learned to fly in France, but I can't remember his name. They had his picture, with goggles and helmet and long coat.

"His point was that a monoplane was better than a biplane, which must have stuck with me because all the planes I ever had were monoplanes."

Just as people remember their first kiss, Claude Ryan remembers the first plane he ever saw. That plane was one of the most famous of that first decade, putting landlocked Kansas within flying distance of salt water.

In 1911, William Randolph Hearst offered fifty thousand dollars to the first person to fly from coast to coast within thirty days. The challenge was taken up by Calbraith Perry Rodgers who, as the grandson of Oliver Hazard Perry, the naval hero of the Battle of Lake Erie, and the grandnephew of Matthew Calbraith Perry, explorer of Japan, apparently had adventure in his genes.

Cal Rodgers was a former college football player who chewed cigars and stared at the camera with the arrogance of an early Burt Reynolds.

Having purchased a Wright Model B plane for five thousand dollars, Rodgers talked the Armour meat-packing company, which was promoting a new grape drink called "Vin Fiz," into sponsoring a cross-country flight.

With the name of the drink painted boldly on both wings, Rodgers left New York on September 17, 1911, followed by a chartered train carrying his family, his mechanics, and spare parts. He battled his way through New York State, hitting trees and chicken coops and electrical storms every few hours, damaging himself or his aircraft or sometimes both at the same time, but doctors and the mechanics kept him going.

By the time Rodgers left Chicago, it was clear he could not conclude the trip within thirty days, but "Vin Fiz" was still painted on the wings, and he continued to push himself across the wheatfields.

In the modest hamlet of Parsons, Kansas, people read about Cal Rodgers' trip with great interest. Anything different was welcome in that part of the world—snake-oil salesmen, circuses, revival tents, anything to break the pattern of the wheatfields and the tornadoes. The memory of Cal Rodgers still crackles across Claude Ryan's face, sixty-six years later.

"There was great publicity about it," Ryan says. "He was flying a Wright Brothers Model B pusher that cruised at no more than forty-five to fifty miles per hour, so everybody could see the Vin Fiz advertisement. We knew his route was to follow the Katy Railroad south, to avoid the Rocky Mountains.

"Rodgers had so many rebuilding jobs and so many crashes that he had to raise money," Ryan recalls. "He'd charge five hundred dollars to fly on your town, but our city fathers were too chintzy for that. Still, his advance agent said he needed to land anyway, so he asked the city fathers to pick out a good field for him to land in. We collected bedsheets to mark the field, and the whole town came out to see him."

It was like Christmas Eve in Kansas in October of 1911, when Claude Ryan's father took a picture the son still has today—two boys in their long coats with old-man caps pulled down over their heads, their hands in their pockets, huddled against the open Kansas wind, waiting for Cal Rodgers to come swooping down out of the sky.

"He wasn't too high," Ryan recalls, "but he never came near the field. He flew over the center of town, where people there saw him better than we did at the field. Then he flew straight on to Pittsburg. That was his revenge on Parsons, I guess."

Young Claude was not discouraged by Rodgers' spurning of Parsons, Kansas. He followed the progress of the aviator until November 5, when Rodgers landed in Pasadena, California—one leg in a cast, using crutches to walk—forty-nine days after taking off, nineteen days too late for the prize. The only original parts of his plane were the vertical rudder and the drip pan, everything else having been replaced on the brutal cross-country flight that consumed eighty-two hours and four minutes of flying time and included sixty-five forced landings, most of them painful.

But Cal Rodgers had linked the two coasts even more dramatically

The Vin Fiz being prepared on Long Island for Cal Rodgers' cross-country attempt in 1911. When Rodgers reached California forty-nine days later, the plane had been almost entirely rebuilt. (Air and Space Collection, Nassau County Museum)

than the stagecoaches and transcontinental railroads had done. His passage presaged the five-hour jet flight; it tied Parsons, Kansas, to New York and Los Angeles. Cal Rodgers' reward for that stunning feat of endurance was a gold medal from the Aero Club of America, and he remained in California to perform stunts for a new audience.

Five months later, flying low along the coastline near San Diego, Cal Rodgers treated the crowds to a classic "Look, Ma, no hands" gesture. The plane dipped slightly, crashing into the shallow surf, and Cal Rodgers died instantly.

"I thought flying was the greatest thing in the world," Ryan says, "but it was also the most dangerous thing man ever did. The life expectancy was extremely short. Still, I remember thinking, if you're going to live a long time and never do anything outstanding, isn't it better to live a short time and do something outstanding? Anyway, you know how kids are. They're not afraid."

Anybody with aspirations of flying was reminded repeatedly of the peril by the newspapers of the time. Most of the famous aviators died young—John Moisant and Arch Hoxsey in separate accidents in the last days of 1911, Rodgers on April 3, 1912, Lincoln Beachey in 1915. They died because they were pushing their machines beyond their known capability, testing the limits for the pilots who would follow.

"The old-time airplanes were more tricky," Ryan says. "Most accidents came from simple stalling. They'd lose flying speed, they'd go down, and they were just sitting there in the front row, and they'd be crushed."

But the pioneers left behind a second wave of airmen, who vowed not to make the same mistakes. Ryan became one of them after his family gave up the laundry business and moved to California and he saw Glenn L. Martin flying around Santa Ana. Martin, in those days a daredevil pilot, was to become one of America's most important air industrialists.

Ryan tried to get a job in the aviation plants that grew during the First World War, but nobody would give a nineteen-year-old the chance to fly. In 1917, Ryan saw an advertisement from a flying school in Venice, California, that charged five hundred dollars for a series of lessons.

"To my surprise, my parents didn't discourage me," Ryan says. "My father borrowed the money.

"The school was in extremely shaky financial shape. When I arrived, they had no flyable airplanes. They had one pusher, the grandfather of the Jenny, but it had just crashed. It had a little engine with not enough power to fly, but if you were real skillful you could get it off the ground. This was the French system—drive it around the ground, teach yourself."

The only problem was, the instructors didn't quite get around to letting the young man solo.

"Then they got a big powerful tractor—eighty horsepower Curtiss engine with dual controls. We started getting instructions every morning when there was no wind. You'd fly real low and still have room to land the plane at the other end. Then you'd get out—the student, never the instructor—and you'd lift it by the tail and turn it around. You'd go back and forth, on the ground.

"See, what had happened, the pilot had been in a crash, and he was afraid to fly any higher. They fired him and got a new feller who claimed he could fly. At least he'd take the plane up higher and learn at the same time you did. Then I met Hawley Bowlus, who suffered with me. We were sharing a tent on the field to save money.

"One morning I was still in the tent and Bowlus and the instructor took off at a low altitude. I looked out the tent and, to my horror, I saw them crack up in the sea. I jumped in my Model T Ford, still in my pajamas, and when I got to the seawall, they were just sitting there, all soaked. And I still hadn't flown by myself.

"Well, we repaired the airplane again and I got a new instructor, Al Wilson, who was later a wing-walker in the movies. He encouraged me to taxi at high speed across the field. I could see the school was about to close up, because the deputy sheriff was hanging around, so I figured, 'This is my chance to solo.'

"I gave it the gun and took off. I got about thirty feet off the ground and I pulled the throttle back. The plane just kind of settled down, broke its struts, fell forward on its nose, and broke the propeller. That's kind of a rough way to solo, I guess. Oh, that also put the flying school out of business."

4

Tiny Broadwick

Long Beach, California

In the old adventure books, it was always the boys who ran away to join the circus. *Toby Tyler* was one book, and there must have been a hundred like it, stories about boys who slipped out of the house at night because they had heard the whoop of a calliope or the rumble of a circus train.

Tiny Broadwick was only fifteen when she joined a carnival, but she was already a mother and a widow. She didn't take off to sell popcorn, or curry the manes of show horses, or follow a handsome roustabout, or anything within the feminine tradition. She left home in 1908 to make parachute jumps at a time when most people were convinced humans could not, and should not, even leave the ground.

She jumped two thousand times in her life, at first from balloons, later from airplanes, and she was probably the first person, man or woman, to make a free-fall parachute jump from an airplane. She was a pioneer, demonstrating her parachutes to the U.S. Army during World War I, but then she slipped into a relative obscurity that lasted nearly half a century.

It was not until Tiny Broadwick was "adopted" a few years ago by James and Maxine Hix, a retired pilot and his wife, that aviation people came to grip with how much she had accomplished. The Hixes chauffeured Tiny to aviation banquets in Southern California, where old-time flyers seem to congregate.

Tiny was even accepted into the Early Birds, the club for people who made their first solo flight before 1917. They knew she had never touched the controls of a plane—but jumping out of one, in a rudimentary parachute, well, what could be more of a solo flight than that?

The Hixes, a friendly couple with Arkansas still rich in their voices, made Tiny Broadwick's life more important than it had been for fifty years. They kept her legal matters straight, made sure she got medical help, visited her apartment, where she lives alone, brought her corsages every time they took her out, and screened her visitors to make sure she was not exhausting herself.

One afternoon the Hixes give me directions to Tiny's apartment, on the condition I promise not to wear her out. Wear her out? When I get to the ground-floor apartment, Tiny is clenching her fists and looking ready to go fifteen rounds with Ali. She has just had a fight on the telephone with a doctor, a young one, who had no idea what the other doctors had been prescribing for her heart condition.

"I've already got pills five times a day," she says, pointing to five tiny paper cups in the kitchen. "There's my morning pill, my noon pill, my afternoon pill . . . and they don't even tell you what they're for. I'm so mad, I could punch 'em right in the nose."

Zip. She takes a little uppercut with her right fist, destroying an imaginary doctor. I comment that she must be feeling pretty good if she's acting so feisty. Feisty. The word is pure southern, and Tiny responds like a true daughter of the Tar Heel State. Darn right she's feisty, she says with a grin.

"What would you like to drink before we talk? Tea? Are you sure? Are you sure you don't want anything stronger? Well, I'm having something stronger. That doctor made me so mad, I'm having a Scotch."

She hobbles around the small kitchen, ignoring the aluminum walker sitting in the corner. She's not going to use that thing around the house, she informs me. You get used to it, start relying on it, and you start getting old fast. She broke her leg in a fall last year, she says, but she's feeling better. I look at pictures of her from a year or two ago. She seems to have got even tinier since her fall, but she's still feisty. We sit on the couch with our respective refreshments and Tiny picks up the first photograph on the pile, a snapshot taken a few weeks ago at a dinner out in the San Fernando Valley. There is Jimmy Doolittle, the leading social lion of all aviation dinners, bending over Tiny, and she is giving him a kiss on his smooth, bald head.

"The idea of Jimmy Doolittle saying hello to me," she says in her thin voice. "Why, that man is one of our biggest heroes. You know, a lot of people used to avoid me at these dinners. They never thought I was important because I worked in a carnival. But Jimmy Doolittle and his wife always made a point of coming over to say hello. They don't know how much it means to me.

"It's the same thing back home. It took me four trips back home until the old-timers would talk to me. See, I was a disgrace to the whole family for going into show business. Those old-timers, people as old as I am, they still think 'Little Georgia Tomboy went into show business, when she was young, and left her baby.' That's all they think of.

"Georgia, that's my real name, Georgia Ann Thompson. But they called me 'Tiny' 'cause I was so small when I was born. I wasn't but four feet eight and weighed about eighty pounds when I left home. We had a big family, my mother and father and seven girls, and all of us had to work because we were poor. We raised pigs and chickens and my mama was a great cook and manager, but my father seemed to leave everything up to her.

"My first job was working in the tobacco fields, picking the worms off the leaves. Then I got married and had a baby and my husband died, so I had to go work in the cotton mills. I was breast-feeding my baby, so I had to go home at ten o'clock to feed her, and then I'd go home at noon for dinner. In North Carolina you call it dinner in the middle of the day. Anyway, at three o'clock I'd go back to feed my baby, but my breast-feeding did not agree with my baby, on account of my walking back and forth to the cotton mill. Well, I didn't want to live any more in that part of the country. My mother was a better mother that I ever could be. I was too young. Women couldn't do the things they can do now."

One day—just like in the old adventure books—the carnival came to town. The Johnny J. Jones Carnival, at the North Carolina State Fair in Raleigh. The young mother, on her only day off from the cotton mills, went over to watch the carnival acts, but the only act she saw was the balloonist, who called himself Charles Broadwick.

Broadwick had a canvas balloon, ninety-two feet high, fifty-two feet wide, open at the bottom. He would build a huge fire in a pit three feet deep, and the hot air would rise into the balloon, lifting it off the ground. When he was high above the fairgrounds, Charles Broadwick would slip into a parachute harnessed to the bottom of the balloon and float off into the air. It was known as a "free act," designed to attract crowds to the other events at Johnny J. Jones' carnival. Not Georgia Tiny Thompson. She stayed and stared at Charles Broadwick and his two "French" balloonists, Lola and Mademoiselle Theresa.

"Something told me that was what I wanted to do," Tiny says. "I just stayed there until he was done, and I told him I wanted to join up with him. He said I looked so little. I said, 'Well my daddy passed away and my mama will take care of my little girl for me.' That almost put the whole thing in the ground right there, that I had a little child. But I said, 'You talk to my mother.'

"My mother said, 'Well, she's so young, I don't know if she should go.' And he said, 'I'll take good care of her and if she don't make good on her first jump, I'll send her back with some money.'

"I wasn't afraid to jump. I think he could sense that. I told him I was a tomboy, Georgia Tomboy, always playing with the boys, climbing trees and falling out of trees. To him, I wasn't a girl, I was a tomboy, so he taught me all I knew, and he had confidence that I would make good."

After instructions on the ground that week, Broadwick decided his new charge was ready for her first jump. The balloon went up above the fairgrounds, Tiny strapped herself into the chute, and let herself go.

"All I can tell you is that first jump was beautiful. I could see barns
and trees and roads and people. Just beautiful. Dad Broadwick was a good
teacher and I was never afraid. I felt such a comfort coming down. I was in
God's care. I just knew I was going to be safe. And everything came down
perfect, as though I had been doing it all my life.

"I never worried about the chute opening because I never knew
enough about it to worry," she says. "Coming down, you can steer the
parachute by raising or lowering the sides of the wooden ring, which holds
the seat. If you see a barn coming, you just wiggle the rings a little, and
you may miss it. You pick out the trees rather than the ground. You pick
out these things on the way up, and you try to pick up the wind currents,
as they change. Then he would fire a pistol on the ground, so I would know
when to jump.

"When it was over, we packed up the balloon and moved on to the
next town, because it was the last day in Raleigh. Whatever they wrote in
the Raleigh newspaper that day, I'll never know, because I never got to see
that paper. I do know that my family never did think much of my joining
the carnival, but I didn't do anything but to make a living."

The year was 1908. Tiny was now in the care of a man who billed himself as a "Famous French Aeronaut"—the French having developed ballooning during the reign of Louis XVI. Broadwick's real name was John
Murray, and he was from Michigan. He had learned ballooning from Captain Thomas Scott Baldwin, one of the first American balloonists.

"How he got his name, I never questioned," Tiny says. "I was just a
youngster, enjoying being in a carnival, and his past history was something
else. I finally met his mother in Detroit and realized his name was Murray,
but that still didn't click in my little mind. I was just a child. He always
called me 'Punk' and told me I didn't know nothing, and I called him 'Dad'
and felt such confidence in him."

If Broadwick could change his own name, he could certainly change
hers, too. His advance posters began to advertise "Miss Tiny Broadwick,
World's Most Daring Aviatrice—Parachutist. A Tiny Chance-Taking Slip of
a Girl in the One Feat Requiring the Maximum of Nerve, Skill, and Daring."

The posters also called her "The Doll Girl."

"That always used to burn me up. I dressed like a toy doll—you've
seen some of my white uniforms, and they tacked that name on me. I had
to wear ruffled bloomers, with ruffles way up to here, and when I fell in a
tree, all this modesty came up, and you could see too much of me so they
put an elastic band around the dress. This was all right until I hit the
water. I didn't know how to swim in those days.

"Charles Broadwick told me, 'Every aeronaut in the game has three
falls a season,' " she says. " 'Unless he has them, he is bound to be worried. If he crawls out of them alive, he knows he is safe for that season.' "

"One time at six thousand feet, the first two sections of the chute
failed. I wanted to pray, but all I could think of was that when I got killed,

I wondered who they would blame. I hit an old mill and suffered a broken arm, a dislocated shoulder, and a banged-up ankle, and that was all. That was the worst injury. Another time I went through the back window of a train and dislocated my arm and acquired a few cuts and bruises. But I never got hurt serious.

"I had enough close calls to learn how to handle the chute. If I had trouble, I would work it out myself. Anybody can tell you what to do on the ground, but when you are in the air, you have to work it out for yourself. I didn't talk about danger in those days. If you talked about it, danger would confront you all the time. I thought about the excitement as the people gathered around to watch. The applause was grand."

The carnival worked state fairs all over the East; it was a big event in 1908, when carnival performers were taken as seriously as television personalities are today. When Tiny came to town, reporters and fans would be waiting to talk to her, a prospect more frightening to Tiny than jumping out of a balloon.

"They came to see the monkey that was doing it," she says. "That aggravated me, and I used to hide. When they would ask to interview me, I would go for a Coke, or to the animal tent. I never talked with people because I didn't have an education. It's only since I changed from that exciting life, to a life that I considered like everybody else, that people accept me as I am. I can sign my name, you see, but I can't write 'Best wishes' or 'Happy landings' unless you spell it for me. Still. I'm still that way. That's why I was so bashful."

Tiny was so young that she accepted Coca-Cola and sandwich money as her pay—"and I was kid enough to enjoy it." Finances didn't get better when Tiny and Charles migrated to Venice, California, in 1913.

"I didn't know nothing about sheiks at that time, but, boy, he was a sheik. He was a fine-looking man, Dad Broadwick was. He'd go out and pick out the best-looking women and take 'em to dinner. That was his excitement, aside from working with the balloon and me. I've seen him take four beautiful women into the Ship's Café, down in Venice. Four. Yes. I've been trying to figure out, all of my late years when I know the score, why he took out four of them. He had a complex. He'd pick out the most beautiful women in town and take 'em to this famous place. When I asked for money for the baby, he would spend it on the women, and then we'd have to go out and make some more."

Even with Broadwick spending up all the profits, Tiny felt life in California was "better and cleaner," working the county and state fairs rather than the carnivals. Also, aviation was booming there, and it was inevitable that the parachute and the airplane would be mated.

"My first airplane ride was at Dominguez Field, near L.A., where they had the first air meet in the U.S. I was doing hot-air balloon, and we got a second current, and it carried me so far that I would have had a hard time walking back. Howard Gill flew after me, landed on the field, and took me back to the grandstand. It seemed like the most natural thing in the world, to get into a plane."

She got her chance again soon, and not just to fly. On March 1, 1912, Captain Albert Berry had become the first human ever to jump with a parachute from an airplane. Now Glenn L. Martin began experimenting with parachutes, on the theory that a pilot might need an escape one time in a hundred. Martin devised a trap seat, in which the parachutist would sit, unleash the parachute, and then fall softly into space. On June 21, 1913, Tiny became the first woman to jump from a parachute, falling from a height of two thousand feet into Griffith Park, onto what is now the parking lot of the Los Angeles Zoo. She began jumping from airplanes as her act.

"Parachuting from hot-air balloons was a lot rougher than from an airplane because there was no choice of a landing site in the balloon," Tiny says.

After one of her jumps, she was greeted by a thin, serious-looking chap named Wright, from Dayton, Ohio.

"I think it was Wilbur," she says, "although I'm not sure. He stuck his hand out, I stuck out mine, and he said, 'You're awful small to do that.' I said, 'Thank you.' I was too scared to say anything else. I'd been to his bicycle shop in Dayton, Ohio, when I was traveling with the carnival. Now I wish I'd talked to him more."

Small or not, Tiny became the country's leading parachutist after Broadwick designed a packaged parachute that could be strapped on an aviator's back. They called their creation a "life preserver of the air." In 1914, Tiny was asked to demonstrate the "Broadwick Coatpack" to General George P. Scriven, chief of the Aviation Bureau of the army.

"There was no interview from any of the army personnel," Tiny recalls. "The men was on the ground, and people frightened me anyway. Dad Broadwick did all the talking and sometimes you'd like to give him an extra cup of coffee to shut him up, in front of those army people, so educated."

With Oscar Brindley as the pilot, the first three jumps went normally—the parachute billowing out before she released herself from the trap seat—but on the fourth trial, the static cord became entangled in the underside of the plane.

Tiny says she didn't want to risk loosening the parachute and having it still be tangled, so she severed the static line, hurled herself out of the trap seat, completely free of the plane, and then pulled the remaining end of the static line—what today is called the rip cord. The parachute emerged from its pack, and Tiny had performed the first free-fall parachute jump.

After Tiny survived the 1,400-foot descent, the San Diego *Union* quoted General Scriven as saying to her: "I certainly admire your pluck."

That jump was on September 13, 1914. Several books, including *Rip Cord*, written by Lloyd Graham in 1936, have listed the first free-fall jump

as having taken place on April 28, 1919, by Leslie L. Irvin, in a parachute designed by Floyd Smith for the Army Air Service.

"Irvin got his ideas from Dad Broadwick," Tiny says. "He was a balloon man with Red Unger, a gas man who used a balloon on a cable. Irvin worked for him. When we were in hot balloons at Ocean Park, he would help out as a ground man. When he went abroad, there was such a demand for parachutes that he copied some, because he was so smart, and we're glad, because it's been a lifesaver to people.

"Later, we had all those lawsuits between Irvin and other people, and of course Broadwick was in the hospital. All I had was the original parachute that I jumped with from the airplane. This is the Japanese silk, the original. These are the samples that Irvin. . . . See, Irvin's name was on there, because he made these up for me. We was friends up until the end, but he didn't like Dad Broadwick."

There seems to be no doubt that Irvin's jump did take place in 1919. Others who have studied parachutes of that era have suggested Irvin was influenced by Broadwick's designs. And Tiny's performance, five years before Irvin's, has been honored by so many aviation authorities in recent

Left: She flew through the air with the greatest of ease. Tiny Broadwick, about to jump from Glenn L. Martin's airplane. Right: Broadwick's act had its origins in her carnival stunting days. (American Hall of Aviation History, Northrop University)

years, and documented so often (including an interview with Glenn L. Martin at his Baltimore plant in 1946), that Irvin must be assigned a distinct and distant second.

Tiny's improvisation showed it was possible to jump without elaborate advance preparation. If your engine suddenly died, it was now possible to jump from a plane as long as you had a parachute strapped to your back. This development seemed to herald greater safety for pilots of stricken planes—if the army wanted to use the parachutes. The army did not.

"The army said at the time, 'If you give 'em a parachute, they'll leave the planes and smash up the planes.' Of course, they wasn't thinking about the fellow's life who was flying the plane. They could have saved so many lives if they put 'em in. I think later, Lindbergh had to bail out a couple of times and that give them a little eye-opener."

While pilots were falling to their death in Europe, Tiny and Charles Broadwick had a parting, partially because of his legal and financial troubles. (He died in 1943 in a veterans' hospital.) Tiny soon married a man who didn't care for her jumping out of planes. Besides which, the novelty had worn off and the public would no longer pay to watch. In 1922, she announced her retirement and made her final jump with Clyde Pangborn, a famous stunt pilot, at the controls.

Her husband died a few years later, and Tiny, with no education, took jobs as a housekeeper for elderly people.

"I was working for a widow who wouldn't let me have a boyfriend. On my one day off, I'd go to every movie in Hollywood. I'd get home at eleven P.M. and she'd be waiting there, going 'puff-puff-puff.' I said, 'You're supposed to be asleep,' but she said she was worried about me. Afraid I'd find a boyfriend, that's what. I had to do something with my time, so I collected stamps instead of having boyfriends."

During World War II, Tiny worked in a defense factory and was asked to visit the paratroopers training in the area.

"One boy said, 'We read about you in our training manuals.' Another boy took one look at my old Japanese silk parachute and said, 'Holy smoke. I wouldn't jump off a lockerbox in that rig.'"

Tiny continued to work as a housekeeper after the war and might have settled into further obscurity if she hadn't met Jim and Maxine Hix.

"Maxine got me into the *Guinness Book of Records,* which would never have happened otherwise. They came to my rescue, a terrific rescue," Tiny says.

Even while we are finishing our chat, Maxine Hix calls on the telephone to make sure everything is all right. Tiny tells Maxine "I can't get him to drink anything stronger than tea." Maxine decides Tiny is feeling just fine.

Since the Hixes made her famous again, Tiny has been receiving the latest parachuting magazines, and is welcomed to parachuting contests.

"You put your hand out to show how close you got to a spot," Tiny says with a giggle. "Others land with their boots on somebody's hand. If it was me, I'd kick 'em in the head to get closer.

"There's women parachutists, too. I wish I could leave my accomplishments to them. I was talking to some of them and they said they had to pay for the parachute and also for the airplane ride. I shot off my mouth and said, 'Why, *they* paid *me* in my day.' I felt like a cluck after I said that."

Asked by young parachutists if she ever had a reserve chute, she replied: "Oh, yes, I always had a reserve chute in the hangar in case the one I was using got wet or torn."

Tiny visits North Carolina more frequently now, when friends get her a ticket. Tiny has six grandchildren from her one daughter, and the grandchildren have gone on to produce twelve great-grandchildren, and they two great-great-grandchildren.

"That's the part I like these last few years. I can go back to North Carolina and not have to be ashamed of myself.

"My daughter and I get along just fine," Tiny says. "My mother raised her lots better than I could have. I've talked to God many times about the care my mother took of my daughter. She's a lovely woman, she's got a lovely family and I thank God for that.

"I can go back, and if somebody snubs me, that's the old-timers. You're never respected once you make a mistake with those people. They pin you down and they never forget it. Does that sound too exaggerated? But it's true. What I lived and what they see is real life and there's no camouflage in it. I have held on to respect. I've been married two times—but who hasn't? I can't really care about that sort of thing because I know God has taken care of me.

"I'm not afraid to go. I know I'm in God's hands. If I'm not here the next time you come to Long Beach, you know where I am. I'll be better off there, with God. No, I mean it. I'm not afraid to go. I've had a good life and I was always healthy until I took sick, if you know what I mean.

"If I had my life to live over, I would do it exactly the same way. I wish I were a little girl again. I would be among the first women on the moon."

5

Charles Fity

West Hempstead, New York

Charles Fity reminds me of Marlon Brando. The old man moves around his house with an aluminum walker to take pressure off his arthritic hip, but my mind keeps slipping back to the youthful, brooding Brando in *On the Waterfront*, whose brother asked him to throw the fight. The old man talks in a raspy voice, but somewhere off in the ozone is the slurring lament of young Marlon Brando: "I coulda been a contenduh."

In 1910, Charles Fity was a contender. He flew an airplane at the same field as many famous pilots, at a time when anybody who went up in the air was special. Crowds followed him as he tested the collapsible-wing craft he had designed. The crowds were thrilled by him, but their adulation helped destroy his career before it hardly began.

It was only seven years after the Wright brothers flew at Kitty Hawk, a few months after Blériot flew the English Channel. Those aviators have long been dead, but Charles Fity still putters around the tiny private home he shares with his daughter.

This morning he wears a golf cap to keep the morning sun out of his eyes, but in his snapshots he is wearing an aviator's leather cap and goggles, from when he was a "contenduh."

"There were times when I told myself, 'If I hadn't bombed that plane, I'd be flying today,' " Fity says. "I know during World War One, when I saw people getting rich from manufacturing airplanes, I told myself I could have been a millionaire. The plane I designed could have been used so many ways."

To this day, nobody has built an automobile that can spread its wings

40

and soar off into the atmosphere. Fellini did it in fantasy in one of his films, made a car that soared above a classic Roman traffic jam, but no inventor has perfected a design for the mass market.

Charles Fity got his inspiration for flight in the middle of New York City, where he was raised.

"Where Father Duffy's statue is today, just north of Times Square, that was second base for our baseball games," he says.

Playing baseball in Times Square does date a person. In this case, the date was 1905. Fity (whose name rhymes with "pity") was wandering around near Central Park when crowds started pointing at a man in a balloon—Roy Knabenshue, one of the first American "aeronauts."

Knabenshue, who was known for his flair for publicity, maneuvered his gas balloon into a playground in Central Park, and before the police could chase him, promoted his latest upcoming event. Meanwhile, Charles Fity stared at the balloon.

"It had a bicycle pedal and a chain to propel the machine," Fity recalls from a distance of more than seventy years. "Right then and there, that gave me the idea to fly. I went out and subscribed to the first airplane magazine, and read everything on the subject.

"About two years later, I found a dead sparrow in my backyard. I spread the wings, and that gave me the idea for a collapsible wing."

The nineteen-year-old took the idea to his father, the head chef at the Astor Hotel, a Frenchman whose family name had been LaFitte. In addition to being an excellent chef, the son says, his father displayed two other characteristics of the French: He did not spend money foolishly, and aviation was in his genes. When the son asked for an airplane, Gallic conservatism fought with the Gallic feel for the sky.

"To this day, I don't know why he agreed to put up the money," Fity says. "I would say it wound up costing him ten thousand dollars—a lot of money in those days."

With his father's blessing, the young man went to a patent attorney on Wall Street, and then found a draftsman who could capture his theories in sketches. Then he brought his plans to a metal working factory in Astoria, Queens, whose name he cannot remember.

"The first idea was the folding wings from a bird. The second idea was a two-seater plane. A pilot and passenger seat for a sight-seeing trip. The third idea—four landing wheels, with the rear wheels for steering on the ground. The whole concept of the airplane was, if the pilot had to land far from the airport, he could fold the wings back to the fuselage and use the propeller to thrust the plane forward on the ground, back to the airport.

"The wings were opened and closed by two arm ratchets—one on each side of the pilot. The leading edge of the wing was a pole around six feet long, which was horizontal when the wings were opened, and vertical when they were closed.

"I had an automotive steering wheel as a control stick for the elevator and warping ailerons. The rudder was controlled by two foot pedals. Also, while the plane was on the ground, the two foot pedals acted as a steering guide for the two rear wheels.

"The only two levers in the cockpit were a spark lever and a throttle lever. I had no instruments—just a lot of nerve, heh-heh-heh!"

When the plane was nearly completed, it was trucked to the air field at Nassau Boulevard in Garden City, Long Island—a long-forgotten site now, because Roosevelt and Curtiss fields assumed greater importance after the war. But for a few short years around 1910, Nassau Boulevard was the base for some of America's leading pilots.

Among the pilots Fity can remember from Nassau Boulevard is John Moisant, the soldier of fortune from the Central American jungle wars, who competed in the early air races until he crashed and died on December 31, 1910, near New Orleans.

Fity can also remember the fuss when two of the world's early female pilots, Harriet Quimby and Mathilde Moisant (sister of John Moisant), arrived at Nassau Boulevard.

Women had first flown in France, with the Baroness de Laroche and Hélène Dutrieu gaining their licenses early in 1910.

Later that same year, Blanche Stuart Scott was taking a lesson on the ground at Glenn Curtiss' field in Hammondsport, New York, when a gust of

wind pushed the pusher biplane as many as forty feet into the air. Because Scott's "solo flight" and safe landing were ruled accidental by the Aero Club of America, Bessica Raiche was ruled to be the first American woman to solo when she took off intentionally, two weeks after Scott. By 1911, Scott made a sixty-mile solo that qualified her as the U.S.'s first cross-country flight by a woman.

At the same time, Mademoiselle Dutrieu, fresh from her victory in the first Coupe Femina in Europe, was visiting Nassau Boulevard to encourage Quimby and Mathilde Moisant, and to model her own design of women aviator costumes.

Quimby did not need much help in attracting attention. Tall, green-eyed, slender, and obviously feminine, she was also a "liberated" woman before the term was being used. A drama critic for *Leslie's Weekly*, Quimby had met John Moisant at the opening of a play and had asked him to teach her to fly.

John Moisant was buried in Metairie Cemetery in Louisiana when Quimby took her first lesson in April of 1911 at a school operated by Alfred Moisant at Nassau Boulevard. She received the first license ever issued to a woman in the U.S. (number 37). In her plum-colored satin flying costume of a blouse, knickerbockers, and a monk's hood, always wearing earrings

Left: Nobody knows who built this strange craft, but Long Island historians assume it never flew. (The Garden City Archives) Right: Charles Fity flew this collapsible-wing craft three times—and lived to tell about it. (Charles Fity)

and a necklace, she was a stunning combination of beauty and skill, known as "The Dresden China Aviatrice." Quimby formed an exhibition team with Mathilde Moisant. The next year she became the first woman to fly across the English Channel, but on July 1, 1912, her plane suddenly veered into Boston Harbor, killing her instantly. She was the first woman known to be killed in an airplane accident.

Mathilde Moisant also caused a fuss when she insisted on flying at Nassau Boulevard on Sunday, despite a sheriff's order that she not disturb the sabbath. She was issued a summons, but a justice of the peace in Hempstead ruled flying was a "legal" pursuit on Sundays—which was the day Fity chose to fly.

"Maybe you saw these people and maybe you'd talk to them a little, but there was nobody around to teach you," Fity says. "You were out there on your own."

Charles remembers how another airman, George Beatty, suggested altering the pitch of his propeller, to get more power. Another airman told Fity how to tell if his plane had enough strength to fly—by attaching a rope to a 300-pound tension scale, and gunning the engine. The plane pulled 125 pounds on the scale, enough to get off the ground.

Convinced the plane was ready, the young man drove it around the field in the "grass-cutting" technique, "to make sure everything was all right. I didn't want to go on any fool's errand."

After skimming around for a few weeks, Fity was ready to fly. To most pilots, the first solo is one of the culminating events in life, like going away to school or getting married. Sitting in his living room, Fity tries to recall the details and the emotions.

"Really, all I can remember is pulling back on the stick. I remember I wasn't scared. All my thoughts, as I was taking off down the field, were: 'Would this damn plane ever get off the ground?' I remember it felt like climbing a hill. I didn't have a chance to see the distance. It was too important to watch what was around.

"To my surprise, the plane did take off. I made a left turn because I was afraid to turn right, due to the propeller turning right. I was afraid it would capsize. I just didn't know. That's the way things were in those days. Nobody told you much. I didn't want to take chances, so I kept steering counterclockwise, around the field, fifty or sixty feet above the ground, just above the poles of the hangars."

After about twenty minutes, he made a smooth landing, putting the tiny machine down on the grass field. Fity puts the date as roughly March of 1910.

"I flew around the airport property only. The sensation I had on landing was that the plane was not coming down to earth—rather the earth was coming up to me. Finally, I landed safely with a few bounces, a lot of relief. I would have drunk a Manhattan cocktail if I could have gotten one."

The follówing weekend, he took the train out to Garden City again and flew around the field making left turns.

His third flight was also his last. His father came out that day to examine his investment, but was pressed into physical duty when a mechanic did not show up. They started the engine with an intricate little fandango: twisting the propeller, then dancing out of the way before the activated blade became a modern guillotine.

On the muddy pitch, Fity Père stumbled and nearly fell into the buzzing propeller, setting the tone for the day.

The takeoff and flight were uneventful, Fity recalls, but the longer he stayed up, the more of a crowd collected. It was Sunday, and the airfields were becoming a chief source of recreation for people. Plane watchers would go out to the field much the same way spectators go to automobile races, bullfights, boxing matches, and maybe even missile launchings today—if everything goes well, no problem. If somebody gets destroyed in the process, well, that's an extra bit of excitement, like catching a foul ball at a baseball game.

On this Sunday in March of 1910, Fity recalls, the crowd began surging onto the grassy field as he came in for a landing.

"In order to avoid these nuts, I banked the plane too far to the left, and sideslipped, and stalled the plane, and crashed about one hundred yards from my hangar."

There was no such thing as a seat belt in those days, so the young man was thrown clear of the wreck, bouncing up in one piece. But his plane had two broken ribs, and the propeller and left wing were shattered.

"The propeller hit the ground, broke off, and flew up into the air— several hundred feet, I was told."

Even worse, the "nuts" were swarming all over the plane like ants at a picnic, pulling at souvenirs of cloth and wood. Father and son swatted the pests, and maneuvered the plane back into the hangar. Charles ordered new parts from a mechanic. Then they walked together to the railroad station.

"During the ride back to Brooklyn, not one word was spoken about the plane accident," he recalls.

"But the next morning I took the train back out to repair the plane, and I saw the mechanic sitting on a stool, reading a newspaper. I asked why he wasn't working on the plane, and he just pointed to the hangar. Didn't say a word.

"I looked around, and in one corner of the hangar there were parts of a plane, all chopped up, broken to pieces. I rushed out of the hangar and asked the mechanic, 'What happened?' He said, 'Your father came out to the hangar early in the morning and chopped the plane into small pieces with an ax.'

"My father told the mechanic, 'That's the end of my son's flying career.' "

Charles Fity at the controls of his own aircraft in March of 1910. (Charles Fity)

The young man took one last look at the remains of his airplane, then took the train home and burned all the blueprints, all the documents.

"I never discussed the incident with my father. It was too late. It was all chopped up," Fity says calmly.

"It was his money. He could do what he wanted. I heard he sold the motor to an auto school. I wasn't resentful—but I was real sore. I left home for a month or more, came back and got a job. My father died in 1914 and he never said a word about it."

The young man got a job as an inspector of electrical wiring, and never went back to Nassau Boulevard. He says he volunteered for the Lafayette Escadrille, the first squad of Americans who flew with the French during World War I, but never was called. He would never touch the controls of an airplane again.

The next time Charles Fity set foot in a plane was in the mid-1960s, when his daughter persuaded him to visit the West Coast. Aviation had progressed slightly between flights, but he felt comfortable in the big jet, thirty thousand feet above the continent.

It revived the feeling of 1910, of being a single human being above the ground. When he saw the captains, in their blue uniforms, the old pilot's curiosity was aroused.

Fity at his Long Island home in 1976. (Photo by Meyer Liebowitz)

"I looked in the cockpit and I told them I flew a plane a long time ago. When we stopped in Las Vegas, I told the crew how my flying career ended. Boy, did they laugh!"

Laughing was better than the only other response, which would have been to cry for the broken dreams. When they stopped laughing , the captain of the flight said he would bend the rules in honor of his distinguished guest. When they got over the Colorado River, the captain promised to drop the plane to a lower altitude and dip the wings on the right side, so Charles Fity could inspect the Grand Canyon from only a few thousand feet.

"I told my daughter what he was going to do, but she said I was crazy, it was against all the rules. When we got over the Grand Canyon, the pilot made an announcement that in my honor we were going to take a closer look at the Grand Canyon. I gave my family the razzberry because they didn't believe me."

Since then, Charles Fity has settled into his little house, alone during the day while his daughter works. He does needlepoint, talks to his dog, watches the game shows, and gazes at a few snapshots he inexplicably forgot to destroy in 1910.

His daughter, Roseanna, used to say it was a shame nobody knew what her father had done so long ago. Without her father knowing it, she wrote a letter to Nassau County, suggesting that her father should be included in the prospective aviation museum, since he was perhaps the oldest living pilot on Long Island.

The letter reached William K. Kaiser, an historian with a feel for personal achievement, who made sure the pictures and tape recordings of Fity would be preserved forever. When the county held its bicentennial air show in 1976, Charles Fity was an honored guest.

"This is the first time in sixty-six years that I've been recognized," he says.

In 1977, during the fiftieth anniversary of Lindbergh's flight, Fity was asked how he felt, as somebody who had flown a decade before Lindbergh did.

"When he crossed the ocean, I said to myself, 'That man has courage.' I wasn't jealous. He flew the ocean. I flew around a grass field."

But secretly, deep down inside, didn't Charles Fity feel it could have been he, landing at Le Bourget in the dark, the tickertape parade on Broadway, tracing routes across America? When the greatest heroes of aviation are counted, doesn't he feel he too could have been a contender?

"We'll never know that, my friend—will we?"

II
Birds of Prey

When Teddy Roosevelt took his first flight in 1910, the old Roughrider did not dwell reflectively upon the beauty of the heavens, the freedom of the birds. According to the pilot, Roosevelt shouted only two words throughout the flight: "War . . . bombs . . . war . . . bombs."

Roosevelt was not the first to see the potential of aircraft for military action. Even before the French flew their balloons in 1783, generals and kings had speculated on the ways they could use an aircraft. Eleven years after the Montgolfier balloon soared over Paris, Napoleon used balloons for observation at Mauberge. In 1849 the Austrians staged the first air raid in history, dropping bombs on Venice. Balloons were used for observation in the American Civil War and to carry passengers and mail from Paris during the siege by the Prussians in 1870–1871.

The first airplane ever used in combat was sent by Italy into Libya against Turkish ground forces in 1911, and other planes passed through Balkan skies in 1912–1913. The Americans chased Pancho Villa by airplane in 1913 with about the same effectiveness as their ground forces, but the day of the military airplane was coming fast.

When the so-called Great War began in 1914, aircraft were first used for observation. In the early months, British Royal Air Force observers saw a German front extending from Louvain to Brussels, and alerted Sir John French's troops to stop the flanking movement by General von Kluck. This maneuver was credited with keeping the Germans from reaching the English Channel in the early days.

Pilots were not even issued weapons in the first few months of World

War I, but they soon found ways to shoot an opposing pilot, as Max Holtzem, a former German pilot, recalls in chapter 6. Eventually, pilots carried their own pistols and rifles; then mechanics fixed automatic weapons on the wings or the cockpit. The gunners occasionally shot off their own propellers, until Roland Garros, a French ace, fixed deflectors on his propellers. Later, the Germans learned how to synchronize the automatic weapons with the turn of the propeller, producing excellent hunters such as Baron Manfred von Richthofen, whose life and death are described by Max Holtzem.

Although the U.S. did not join the war at first (there were only 59 airworthy craft in the entire country in August of 1914), idealistic American pilots rushed to fly in Europe. Perhaps the most famous squadron of the war was the Lafayette Escadrille, a collection of adventurers fighting under French command who scored early victories and died young. James McMillen, in chapter 7, tells why he left Wall Street to fly air duels in somebody else's country.

With the war stalled in the trenches, only air battles seemed to produce the kind of heroes the world could admire. Each country had its "aces," to use a French term: von Richthofen led all pilots with 80 confirmed kills, followed by René Fonck of France with 75, and Mick Mannock and Billy Bishop of Great Britain with 73 and 72, respectively. The leading American "ace" was Eddie Rickenbacker, with 26 kills in seven months of fighting, followed by a young crew-cut boy out of Princeton College, George "Bobby" Vaughn, who tells his story in chapter 8.

The war produced a steady escalation of tactics and machinery, putting new pilots at a growing disadvantage. In the latter months of the fighting, men were rushed into combat, as Forrest Wysong and Carl Heinz von Pier describe from opposite sides in chapters 9 and 10, respectively. Anthony H. G. Fokker, a Dutch-born inventor who had offered his services to Britain and France, was accepted by the Germans, and produced such excellent machines that British and American pilots called themselves "Fokker fodder," for good reason. When the war ended, the airplane was a full-fledged killer of human beings, as Teddy Roosevelt knew only too well. His son, Quentin, was killed in France.

Even though General Billy Mitchell of the Army Air Service would be court-martialed in 1926 for advocating stronger military aircraft within the armed forces, the public and the government soon realized the airplane was a new breed of destructive force. Since then, airplanes and their rocket-age relatives have become famous for their work at Guernica, Pearl Harbor, London, Hiroshima, and Vietnam. If there is any consolation, it is that some innovations made in wartime have been applied to peaceful uses later.

6

Max Holtzem

Santa Ana, California

"You Americans call it the flying bug," Max Holtzem is saying. "I think I was taken with the same thing. I may have had it in my blood, like you say. I remember as a child I had this dream, not once or twice but more, that I was sailing through the air.

"I remember very clearly in the dream I was standing at the top of a stairway, a long straight stairway. I spread my arms out, and instead of running down the stairs, I flew down. That may sound ridiculous, but I wanted to fly even before I saw them in books. That was a dream I had as a little child."

When Max Holtzem was a little child, there were no powered aircraft, not in America or in France or in Cologne, Germany, where he was born in 1892. There were, of course, balloons, and it is possible that he gazed up from his baby carriage one afternoon and saw an early German balloonist floating across the sky. Or, perhaps he shared the dream of da Vinci, and the ancient Greeks who told legends of flight, and the Frenchmen who willed themselves into hot-air balloons before the first tumbrel clattered in the French Revolution. But by the time the first rudimentary German airplanes sputtered over Cologne, Max Holtzem was not surprised to see them, but rather he felt fulfilled. It had happened just as he had dreamed.

His flying would be different from the dream in one respect: In the dream, he floated down a staircase; in reality, by the time he was an accomplished pilot, there were French and British pilots trying to blow him out of the sky. By the time he was a man, other men had taken the dream and twisted it into an instrument of warfare, subtle at first, murderous after a short time.

Now he is standing alongside a red Fokker, and it all seems quite distant—more than sixty years since he flew, with the "guns of August" thudding underneath him. The Fokker is a replica of the plane flown by Baron Manfred von Richthofen—the "Red Baron," as people remember him today.

The Red Baron has been cutesey-fied by a cartoon strip about a dog who wears a scarf and goggles and thinks he can fly. The German airline, Lufthansa, advertises itself with a character called "The Red Baron of Lufthansa." But Max Holtzem, who flew loyally for the Kaiser during the First World War, remembers the "Red Baron" as a hunter of human beings who happened to use an airplane.

The red Fokker is standing in the museum put together by Frank Tallman, a movie stunt pilot who keeps his collection of vintage airplanes on the edge of Orange County Airport.

Max has come to the museum with his fellow old-timers, the Early Birds, all wearing the club's black-and-white checkered caps. While they poke around the Nieuports and Spads and Fokkers, Max Holtzem describes how his dream of flying came true.

"I would never have become a pilot if Father had lived—I know that," he says, his accent still thick and bubbling, more than fifty years after leaving his homeland.

"But Mother was already dead when I was nine years old, and when Father died, I could do more or less what I wanted to do, at the age of eighteen or nineteen. I was a student of architecture in college and I should have been a very good architect. But with Father dead, I took lessons in flying from Bruno Berenson and I started building my own plane, but I didn't get very far when I ran out of money.

"So I didn't become an architect, and you ask me would I do it all over again. I think maybe yes, because I did try flying, and I'm still here. And if I had done the other thing, I don't know what would have happened to me. There were two wars, remember.

"In Germany, when they made preparations for the second war, many friends wrote me, 'Max, why don't you come back to us again?' But I had no family left in Germany and I was already married to an Italian lady, who spoke fluent German and she loved Germany, but I said, 'No. I'm an American. I stay here.' And it is a good thing I stayed here, because what would have happened to me under Hitler? The same what happened to Ernst Udet [A German World War I ace who fell into disfavor with the Nazis and apparently committed suicide early in World War II].

"Well, that's how my money went out, before the first war, in building my own planes. I got stuck, and I said, 'Now I become a military pilot. I had the good fortune to pass the medical tests, and now here's the funny thing:

"The first day we newcomers arrive at the station, the inspector comes to the line of newcomers and stops a few persons ahead of me and talks to a civilian pilot whom he knew and who was very enthusiastic. You could tell by the conversation the inspector was in a good mood.

"Now he comes directly to me and looks in my face and he says to me, 'Max, you look exactly like our crown prince. Any relationship?' Everybody laughed at this remark. The officers laughed. I was not supposed to laugh. I was at attention there. I said, 'No, Major. No relationship.'

"The crown prince was known to like women. I understand that. He had children, see. I said, 'No, Major, no relationship.' The whole staff was laughing. He writes down my name and says, 'What brings you here? What do you expect to do here?' I said, 'I hope to become a military pilot.' He says, 'Oh, you have big ambitions. Have you any experience in that?' I said, 'I can drive an auto.' He said, 'Oh, that's very good.'

"I was lucky. There were about a dozen men who wanted to become pilots—but none of them could drive an automobile. It wasn't like in America, where kids learn to drive an auto nowadays. This was in 1912. I wasn't yet twenty years old, but as a young guy I learned to drive a car and had a license for it. That turned out to be a good thing for me.

"So the adjutant writes all this down, and after a few days, instead of getting all the infantry training, I was working in the garage with the automobiles. I even got to drive the commandant's car in my first year, and I could spend the evenings in my own home, much to the anger of the drill sergeants there."

Also, there were airplanes to be explored. And when the war began in August of 1914, Max was put in an unarmed Rumpler biplane to observe the battlefields and spot for the artillery.

"There was no radio. There was only one way for understanding with the ground. There was the flare pistol that shot different colors. I'll tell you how we did our work for the artillery. The night before we would go over the maps. The artillery commander said, 'At six in the morning, you will go there and stay there, over the target, and I will shoot, and you give me the signal.'

"So early the next morning, I flew over him. He laid out the white bedsheet and I flew forward. I shot my flare pistol. He shot his artillery. I shot my red pistol, meaning it was too far. In the planes, we laughed at it when they missed. They had no instruments to measure their distance. We were up two thousand feet in the air and the shell was below us, and we were laughing when he shot, even when he was on our side.

"The antiaircraft shooting of the French was late, and our shooting was wide. We saw the puffs in the air around us, from the French and our own side, and we laughed. It was not like the end of the war. By the end of the war, the artillery had shot down lots of planes, but not at the beginning. No, there was not much danger. Not then."

Airplanes were not considered offensive weapons at the beginning of the war, but were expected to help in surveillance. Pilots were not even issued weapons at the start of the war.

Max Holtzem studies a re-creation of the Fokker DR-1 triplane used when he was a pilot for Germany in World War I. Picture was taken at the Movieland of the Air at the Orange County Airport, California, in 1977. (Photo by David Strick)

"One day I met a Frenchman doing the same artillery correcting. Around noontime, we met many times crossing the front lines. I wave, he waves, I shout: 'You damn Frenchman,' he shouts: 'You damn German.'

"One day I say to my observer, 'Let's scare the Frenchman,' so we look for something to throw at him. Then I get the idea: 'Let's point the flare pistol, not so it points down, but so it points straight at the Frenchman.'

"Even in the sunshine, big smoke and fire came out of the gun. So that day, I flew close to that Frenchman and I let go on the gun and, quick, he dove away like mad. He didn't even come close to me. He must have gone back and told his comrades, 'This crazy German has a cannon on board.' Of course, we had no cannons. We didn't even have a machine gun."

Some historians say the first air duel was between a French Voisin and a German Aviatic, with the Frenchman carrying a machine gun loose in the cockpit. Within five months of the start of the war, the French were mounting machine guns on the upper wings of agile Nieuport biplanes, and pulling the trigger with a string. By then, mechanics on both sides were fighting a duel of ingenuity.

"Roland Garros [a French ace] flew that little monoplane, shot his machine gun through the propeller, but he had no synchronization with his engine," Max says. "He had deflecting blades, metallic blades on the propeller, to deflect his own bullets.

"But even then, he shot holes in the propellers, and some people were killed because of the shots. I mean, one-two-three is still not dangerous, but more bullet holes was like sawing off the propeller, and then it ripped the engine off. They say Immelmann killed himself just like that."*

"But I came back early, before there was really much fighting in the air. I became a test pilot for Pfalz in Bavaria. I was from Prussia but they did away with all those separate units in that war. They put gray uniforms on all of us. I went near Munich and was testing those little Pfalz planes with rotary engines.

"Every morning, I'd fly into the wind, zoom up steep until my feet got cold, push the stick, come down tail first. Those rotary engines, you never knew when one would catch fire. They had no carburetor so you had to mix your own fuel, all with your left hand. It took two separate adjustments for the mixture, and you were flying with your right hand, and never knowing when the engine would explode and come flying right into your lap.

"I was paid five-hundred dollars for every plane I broke in, so every night I bought myself a bottle of champagne and drank the bottle all by myself to make me relax so I could have a good sleep for the next day. I was twenty-two, twenty-three years old, and I didn't know what to do with my money, so I drank champagne every night. I had six students who became aces, but they all got killed by the end."

After two years of testing airplanes and training new pilots, Max Holtzem says he volunteered for the front again. I ask him why, and he shrugs.

"That's a good question, why I wanted to go into combat. Let me say, I had to fly in the war for my wish to sail through the air. I know that sounds silly. In war, you do your duty to your fatherland, and I did, as much as I needed and maybe more.

"In that way, I made good pupils, and later I went to a fighter squadron and wanted to help the war activity more. I had fifteen months in Squadron Number Sixteen, which were half students of mine before, so I was a little king in that squadron. I could do what I wanted.

"I was a good patriot and a good pilot, but I was a poor soldier. I couldn't handle a gun and I wasn't interested in guns. I didn't like fighting. I can brag about that. I became a very, very good pilot."

Early in 1918, Holtzem says he was assigned to the same area of battle as Baron von Richthofen, who had already become the leading ace of the war. Holtzem says the proximity with the Baron made him realize, even more, how little of a killer he was.

"Richthofen comes from the east Prussian region where there are big

* British records document that Max Immelmann was killed by an aerial gunner, Corp. J. K. Waller, not by any malfunction.

landowners of aristocracy, who live like kings, lots of territory. Manfred von Richthofen was the oldest son, and as a young fellow he was trained to go hunting big bears near the Russian front. Big, big forests there. He became that kind of a guy—a hunter, he was a hunter; he was a marvelous marksman. And killing animals, see, that was his life. I wouldn't have taken that kind of life. In South America, they took me hunting for these birds; I felt sorry for these little birds. They get shot at, flop down to the ground, and can't neither die nor fly anymore. This was not my idea. I wasn't that kind of a killer. Of course, you get angry, you feel excited, you want revenge, that feeling when you lose one of your friends.

"I met the Baron during the Marne offensive. I was close to him many times. Now I tell you about his tactics. He was a hunter from childhood, from his young years. He was only twenty-five years when he died. And he was the best hunter. The best. He was the kind of patriot who knew that he would have to die for his country. His pilots were the kind who wanted to get as many victories because they knew they would be dead in the end.

"The Red Baron could choose the pilots he wanted. He had the finest equipment. The best airplane, Richthofen got it. When he had a man he didn't like the first week, he wouldn't last two weeks. He would send him back, choose another one. Richthofen had a special tactic for his pilots. I tell you about it.

"We had eight ships in our squadron but the Baron had eleven. He divided it up into three 'wings.' The upper wing goes up first. Then the Baron waits in the upper altitude until the British comes long. The British is trying to shoot the lower wing. The Baron is up there watching for the Britisher, who is paying all his attention to the lower wing. Then—boom— the Britisher is shot down by Richthofen, because Richthofen is on the hunt, and shoots him down before he knows it.

"Yes, that's right, Richthofen's own man was the pigeon. We all did it sometimes. I did it for my own company, too, but only momentarily. Most of the victims could not defend themselves against Richthofen because he come in protected with left and right wing men. He didn't have to look back behind him to be attacked because he had a wing behind him.

"I hardly talked with Richthofen. I didn't know him, really. I was an acrobat pilot, and he didn't permit acrobats. He said it was an unnecessary risk of your life, and your life had cost the government too much money. Your equipment costs too much money to do acrobatics. It meant nothing to him. The opposite. He prohibited it. I flew many times, but not straight.

"The way I see it, acrobatics saved my life and the life of thousands of others. When a young student came into a spin and didn't know how to get out of it—that was acrobatics. I taught my students to get out of a spin— you release the stick, the plane will come out of the spin by itself. The beginners do just the opposite, they pull back the stick, to get the nose up, and they increase the speed of the spin. And they crash.

"We were different pilots, that's all you can say. At the end of the war, the Germans had parachutes, he wore 'em and I didn't. They were hindering me. I would rather drive through all kinds of tricky flying, but I didn't have parachutes. His own men had to sit, waiting for the call, with the parachute strapped on their body.

"I had seen four guys come down in parachutes, and they were helpless. I could never have done that to a man. My character wasn't like that. Richthofen demanded it. He said, 'If you have a man forced down on our side, *kill him!* Otherwise, he may flee prison, go back to the front, get in a plane, and kill you.' "

Death came for Baron Manfred von Richthofen on April 21, 1918 when he slipped behind an inexperienced Royal Air Force pilot, perhaps counting his eighty-first kill. The official reports say Captain Roy Brown, a Canadian, came in from the rear of the Baron and shot him down, but Australian gunners on the ground also thought they had brought the Baron down, and exuberantly stripped the Baron's plane for souvenirs.

Either way, the British buried the Baron with full military honors and dropped pictures of the funeral into the German camp, to show their respect of him.

The Germans had a third version of the Baron's death. To this day, Max Holtzem isn't sure which version to believe.

"They told us the Baron was on the tail of this Britisher for a long time—two, three minutes. Then the Baron must have had machine trouble, because he finally veered off three miles behind the front line, made a right turn at very low altitude, and nosed into a swamp there.

"The German artillery with glasses saw him climb out of the airplane, safe. They said he was attacked afterward. They saw him land, nose up, tail up, and climb out. The doctors said it was instant death, but how could a man shot between lungs and heart climb out of a plane, unharness himself, if he is shot like that? The Australians say he was shot from artillery. The British say he was shot by Brown. We were told he was shot on the ground, the entrance wounds were from a short distance. Well, how do you know?"

I ask Holtzem: Didn't the pilots know, by the time the Baron died, that flying in that war had become an easy way to die—that technology had caught up with the dream?

"Yes, I think every pilot felt, in the last six months, that they could get killed," Holtzem says. "In the last six months, the average life-span was three months for these young replacement pilots. But I was with Squadron Sixteen from August seventeenth to November eleventh, Armistice Day.

"I was close many times. Once I got hit by a bullet from the trench, and the bullet smashed my belt buckle and went straight up. Lucky it was winter, I was wearing a coat with a buckle, but that is what I mean. Luck."

When the war ended, Holtzem discovered there were hundreds of pilots in Europe with no way to pursue their new skill. He tried to use his acrobatic skills to attract paying crowds in Germany—until he heard of a country where acrobatics had not yet been exploited.

"Argentina," he says. "The Argentina people said it wasn't real—that nobody could walk on wings, do stunts like that. I said to myself, 'Oh, boy, I make money on that idea.' "

Holtzem made a good living in Argentina with his team of male and female daredevils, and he married Olga Oppezzi, an Italian concert pianist. In 1928 he moved to the United States because "I knew aviation would develop very, very fast after Lindbergh's crossing the Atlantic."

At first he was a pilot for Anthony Fokker, the Dutch-born builder who had built such good planes for Germany during the war. After the war, Fokker had come to the United States to build planes for nonmilitary uses.

"He sent me a telegram, 'Max, now is the time we work together,' " Holtzem recalls. "I tested a flying boat for him, and it maneuvered very badly on the water. Fokker was very clever not to fly the first one—only after I did it."

Fokker's fortunes dropped after one of his planes crashed in 1931, killing Knute Rockne, the famous Notre Dame football coach. Holtzem says he still believes the fault was not in the airplane structure, but in the propeller, built by another company.

After leaving Fokker, Holtzem moved to Manhattan Beach, California, where his wife died fifteen years ago.

Many of his best friends are American pilots from World War I, who know he never fought against Americans. Besides, he has been an American citizen for years, and they talk about their adventures with the enthusiasm of survivors.

The last of the survivors, the Early Birds, wander among the museum airplanes, renovated or created for the movies, and their reminiscences seem less glamorous than the Hollywood versions of that war.

"All those fellows who went out to get big victories, they all got shot down," Holtzem says. "If you ask me who were the greatest fighter pilots—the British, the German, the French, the Americans, the Italians—I would answer you, it's the single individual who makes the best pilot.

"If he is a real good acrobat pilot, then he can make air fights. But against a good airplane, it depends on the weather. If the wind drives me to one side or the other, that has much to say about it, no? You say finally, good luck. My good luck was with me. I have been under stress many, many times, but I got to be eighty-four years old, and I will have eighty-five before the year is over. That I never dreamed of."

7

James H. McMillen

Locust Valley, New York

It is not easy to impress members of the Creek Club, a country club so exclusive that most of its windows face the Connecticut hills rather than the bourgeois plains of Long Island. Nevertheless, when James McMillen walks through the Creek Club dining room, subdued voices tell each other: "He flew in the Lafayette Escadrille."

The whispered words conjure up a picture of American volunteers rushing to France to repay the Revolutionary War gallantry of the Marquis de Lafayette, by flying in the most famous squadron of the First World War.

Heads turn as the elderly man takes his table by the window facing Long Island Sound. He lives upstairs, alone, in a small apartment also facing the Sound. Some days he comes down for meals and some days he doesn't. Today, as he escorts George Dade and me to lunch, you can hear people properly pronouncing the French through their nasal passages—"Es-ka-dreeh."

As we begin our meal, McMillen shows us records that indicate he did not technically serve in the "Escadrille" itself—the first squadron of American volunteers—but rather in the overall body, the Lafayette Flying Corps.

"There aren't too many of us left," McMillen says as he orders a daiquiri. "We don't hold any meetings anymore. We're too scattered. Getting too old. I'm eighty-six—be eighty-seven next time around. Hard to believe it was sixty years ago."

From a distance of sixty years, McMillen recalls what put him in a strange machine, high above a foreign country. He had no French ancestry and had never flown an airplane when he made great effort to join the

61

Lafayette Flying Corps in 1917. There were other ways he could have served rather than flying those skeletal machines, so vulnerable to bullets, to fire, to sudden impact with the ground.

"I was working in 'The Den of Iniquity'—Wall Street," McMillen says. "I was already twenty-five years old, and why I joined is a good question. I felt the Germans were wrong and the French were right. That's the only way I can put it. I had sympathy for the French position. There were a lot of bad things going on—the Germans marching through Belgium.

"I weighed only one hundred thirty-two pounds and I wasn't strong enough to be in the infantry, I thought. I had never fired a gun. Somebody suggested I fly with the French. It's funny, but six months after I enlisted, my brother said there was a letter from the army."

The Escadrille had been formed in 1916 by two Frenchmen and seven Americans, as a way for Americans to fly in a war their country had not joined. The Escadrille was given Squadron Number 124. At the luncheon table, McMillen displays the two volumes of the literate and comprehensive history entitled *The Lafayette Flying Corps* by James Norman Hall and Charles Bernard Nordhoff, pointing out his picture and those of his buddies.

According to this history, the group was first called "L'Escadrille Americaine," but since the United States had not officially entered the war at the time, this was a little touchy, so the name was switched to "L'Escadrille des Volontaires" and, finally, "L'Escadrille Lafayette." Only thirty-eight Americans actually served in the Lafayette Escadrille itself, but their quick heroics attracted several hundred other volunteers like James McMillen who formed the Lafayette Flying Corps, the umbrella group.

"I tried to join in New York, but the Germans were sending their people over here to volunteer in the French army. The French finally got wise, and you needed five sponsors to prove you weren't German," McMillen says. "I finally got a visa and tried to enlist.

"The way you did it, you took a train to Newport News, Virginia, to get tested. On the same train was Tommy Hitchcock, who would become an ace, and his father. We got to Virginia, and it was a bad windy day—but that didn't mean anything to me. Three teachers were sitting in the shack and they said, 'Oh, no, we're not flying today. Too windy.' But I said, 'We've come all the way from New York,' and they agreed to give us the test. This was the army, and they were flying Curtiss Jennies.

"This fellow said, 'When I get you in the air . . .' I said, 'Wait a minute, I've never been close to a plane before.' He said, 'What?' I still didn't even realize what bad weather it was. But finally he agreed to give me a test and he passed me in thirty minutes. He didn't pass Tommy Hitchcock for an hour. He sat behind me, he had this thick board and he said, 'If you freeze at the controls, you'll get this right over your head.' Of course he had

James H. McMillen, during his service with the Lafayette Flying Corps in France, 1918. (James H. McMillen)

his own controls. He'd lean forward and show me where to put my hands. It wasn't that hard, really.

"This was February of 1917. I got on a boat and wound up in Paris, reporting to this doctor who was a sponsor of the Escadrille. He referred me to a French army officer. They were so anxious to get me to the front, anybody who had two legs and two arms. They'd give you tests you couldn't possibly fail: They'd ask you, 'At what time does the six o'clock train leave?' "

The recruits were camped at Avord, Russians, French, and Americans in the same barracks. An old Paris bus would pick up the pilots at 4:30 A.M. so they could utilize the least breezy time of the day. They were all transported to the Blériot Field where classes lasted until 8:30. After class, the Americans would stop in the small towns to seek out something more substantial than the French breakfast of coffee and croissants. McMillen's two-volume history tells of a French café operator scurrying around her barnyard for a couple of eggs and holding off the hungry Yanks with a testy "Une petite minute, messieurs."

McMillen received his license on December 3, 1917, but Americans were out of favor at that moment, for some bureaucratic reason, and McMillen's officer kept him standing in the snow, day after day, awaiting an assignment to fly. On March 12, 1918, he was summoned to Spad 38, one of the top squadrons, to be interviewed by Captain Georges Madon, one of the leading French aces.

"What a wonderful guy," McMillen says, his voice full of hero worship, now nearly sixty years later. "Right away, I wanted to work for him.

"He came asking for five pilots to send up. He took a look at five of us. The next day we learned he had turned all five of us down. I was heartbroken because I wanted to work with him. But the next day I was restored to duty. I was told to report at five A.M. to Captain Madon. I almost wet my pants.

"He gave me orders to follow him, but I coudln't get my plane going. I had to get another Spad. I was supposed to meet him at five thousand meters. He said, 'Follow on my tail and make all turns to the right.' But I got the plane up to around fifty meters and couldn't get it up any higher. I didn't know what the devil to do. I decided to follow him even if I couldn't get to that level.

"Way up above me, he got into a fight with Germans. He hit three of them. One of them almost fell on me. This was my first combat. Then we went back to the field. He said, 'I'm going to give you four days in jail. When you can't get up to my altitude, don't stay low like that. Go back.' You see, he had to protect me, to keep an eye out for me and he couldn't do it if I was that low.

"A few hours later he changed his mind about jail. I don't know why he changed his mind because I certainly changed his style of flying that day. Instead of attacking, he had to defend. That was his style. He was a good pilot and he could shoot. Everybody who got to the front could fly, but not all of them could shoot.

"Today you see movies where the pilots are shooting rat-a-tat-tat. That wasn't the case with the good ones. Not them. They could shoot. Bing-bing-bing. Also, the good pilots wanted to be alone, not to be detected. They didn't want to have to protect other pilots. In that first combat, I forgot even to fire, while Madon made three hits.

"On days when I didn't fly with Madon, I had to fly with this other French lieutenant. His instructions were 'Follow me.' One day he took five of us up and ordered us to all 'Follow me.' All of a sudden, he headed back to the field and landed. We did the same thing. He went crazy. 'Why did you land?' he screamed. 'You told us to follow you.' He went crazy. He was a terrible fellow. But Madon was wonderful. A nice guy and a terrific shot."

Every so often the squadron would be given a day off and would head directly to Paris, to a restaurant patronized by René Fonck, one of the leading French aces.

"I never really knew Fonck," McMillen recalls. "Madon and Fonck both went there—but they would never go there at the same time. They didn't want to compete.

"I don't remember a lot about Paris. We would go to Paris and drink wine and make whoopee. That sounds awful, the way I say it, but that's what we'd do. Of course, we were only acting like the French in drinking wine. Everybody drinks wine over there.

"I had a good time with the Frenchmen. I didn't speak a word when I got there, but we got along, most of the time. One night in a restaurant I tried to make conversation with this woman. She tipped her chair back and said, in perfect English, 'Where did you learn that language?' I must have gotten my words slightly wrong and said something terrible.

"For a while, I was the only English-speaking person in my squadron, but then in June, three or four Americans came in."

In his copy of the two-volume history of the Lafayette Flying Corps, McMillen has marked the pages about his friends with "good fellow" or "I know him," or similar expressions. One page that is particularly marked displays a large black man with large round goggles on his forehead. The name printed is Eugene Bullard, but McMillen has inked "Jacques" as a middle name, and at the bottom of the page he has written:

"Adjoining cots at Avord. Good friend—failed on Nieuport. Sent back to Bregeut. Came to New York 1923. Jazz band. Died 1961."

The thumbnail sketch in the history book tells of a proud adventurer who had been wounded four times in the Foreign Legion, and came to the Flying Corps already bearing the Croix de Guerre. The book says Bullard's experience in the Legion helped his fellow squad members get through their early training. He knew how to prepare for inspection; he was already a soldier.

The book also mentions that Bullard got along excellently with American southerners, who recognized a warrior when they saw one, although an officer from Delaware or New Jersey usually jumped up on a chair and sang "Dixie" whenever Bullard was around.

"He got along with ninety percent of the people," McMillen said. "I don't remember much racial stuff, but if somebody kidded him, he'd fight. People didn't know he was a prizefighter. As a youngster from America he was a great prizefighter, and he ended up in England. His first prize, he said, was a pair of yellow shoes with knobbed toes.

"He was a good-looking colored man, and he could fight.

"He loved flying, but he couldn't handle speed, so they gave him slower planes. We teased him about it, but not much. No, I don't remember much racial stuff, but you're talking about sixty years ago. He hit a captain on a train, that's all I remember, and they had to take him out of aviation."

The history book doesn't reveal much more about Eugene Jacques Bullard. I look at the picture again, the erect head, the white scarf; his stance reminds me of Jack Johnson or an African chief.

"He was my buddy," McMillen says.

Now McMillen is talking about flying.

"I had eight *pannes*—breakdowns—but none of them were close to the lines. The pink-and-purple followed us. They were typical Germans. They had to fly at a certain altitude and at certain times. They wouldn't follow you over your lines. They had three squadrons that were offensive, but the others stayed behind the lines.

"Everyone thought the Fokker D-7 was the best plane in the war. It was hard to see and very maneuverable. They'd throw a few planes over Paris to give the Parisians a scare, but they had to follow orders.

"One time we were all making whoopee and this major said, 'Tomorrow, we fly.' It was bad weather, but he took his squadron up anyway. The Germans forced them down, out of gas. The Germans sent back a message saying, 'Thank you for sending us six beautiful planes and their pilots.' The French sent a message back: 'Take care of five of those pilots, but kill that major.' You'd drop notes to each other like that."

George Dade asks what McMillen's main fear was during the war.

"Walking to the airplane," McMillen shoots back. "Once you got in the plane, you didn't think it would happen to you."

But it came close. McMillen says the French were trying to cover two fronts near the end of the war, and he was up near Rouen, taking aerial pictures of German movements.

"We were near the English. One day I dipped my wings to an English pilot and he started shooting at me. Fortunately, he was a bad shot. He was just new, and I guess he was nervous.

"You were young then. You looked forward to it. I was fortunate to get with a good squadron. We had seven aces—you had to get five kills to be an ace. They had to be certified from the ground by two people. It was tough to get certified. Sometimes you'd go around the front lines by car and ask people, 'Get any reports?' But they never did.

"Madon and I flew alone sometimes. One day he saw an American bomber and he started shooting at the tail, drove it to the ground. When I got back to the field, I asked him why he shot at an American plane and he said, 'They were German.' Sure enough, reports from the front said the Germans must have captured this plane. I never knew how Madon could tell the difference.

"I loved every minute flying with him. When the U.S. started flying in the war, they made me a first lieutenant in July, but Madon requested that I stay with him. I returned to Spad Thirty-eight until September twenty-seventh. I didn't see Madon after that. He was killed after the war, flying over a soccer field they named for him in his hometown. A hell of a nice guy."

Most of the aces didn't even survive the war. While McMillen was in France, von Richthofen was killed, as was the most celebrated Lafayette Escadrille pilot of them all, Raoul Lufbery. Lufbery was a French adventurer who had lived in Connecticut briefly as a young man. Known as a fearless pilot, he had always told his friends he would stay with his crippled plane rather than bail out without a parachute. But on May 19 of the last year of the war, Lufbery's plane was hit near Nancy, and he leaped— perhaps aiming for a gentle stream. He landed in a garden. By the time his comrades came for his body, the French villagers had covered him with spring flowers.

The Escadrille was on its way out anyway, since the Americans wanted control over their own pilots.

"When I joined the Americans, I quickly got into trouble," McMillen says. "I was at Issoudun, Field Nine, to prepare others for combat. This American officer told me to salute him indoors with my hat on. I had been told never to do that. Then he said, 'You should never wear your hat inside a building.' I hated him. He told me, 'Go off and find out why we're having so many accidents.' I said, 'I already know. You're taking your turns too flat.'

"After that, they took some of us pilots and used us as guinea pigs for medical research. They wanted to see at what heights we could fly, so they'd take away our oxygen, little by little.

"The niceties of life disappeared during that war. I've seen doctors drop hypodermic needles on the ground, wipe them against their pants leg, and give you an injection."

Long before the war was over, Lufbery and the Escadrille had become legends around the world. The entire Lafayette Flying Corps had been given credit for 199 planes shot down. Of the 267 men who had enlisted, 180 had served at the front in French uniform. Eleven had died of accidents or injuries; another 51 had been killed at the front.

Some survivors tended to blur the distinctions between the Escadrille and the Flying Corps. William Wellman, the film producer, was one Flying Corps member who was often credited with being a member of the Lafayette Escadrille. He helped perpetuate that myth by producing a film about the Escadrille, which carried his name as a member. The French and the Germans, who knew a lot about it from a distance, thought the film was terrific.

James McMillen doesn't promote himself as a member of the original Escadrille; it was quite enough for him to have followed his instincts and fought for the French.

"I came back to the U.S. on the same ship Wilson took over," McMillen recalls. "I was in a hurry to get married and make some money. Don't forget, I was twenty-six, twenty-seven already. I never went back to France, either. I was too damn busy making money in 'The Den of Iniquity.' I never flew again after the war, and I don't believe I ever missed it."

8

George A. (Bob) Vaughn, Jr.

Staten Island, New York

When George Vaughn came back from war, they put his picture on cardboard collecting cards, just like Babe Ruth and Ty Cobb, and they held parades to honor him as America's second-leading air ace.

Sitting on his porch in a rural corner of Dongan Hills, Staten Island, he recounts the story of his thirteen certified kills as if it were just another family anecdote—like the time Cousin Ezra painted himself into a corner, or Aunt Minnie won first prize at the bake-off.

He dwells on how unprepared he was for his first dogfight, on how easily he could have spun out into the French countryside—just another college boy from the States sent into battle before he was ready. He does not stress the medals he received for a war in which successful warriors were called something more than killers.

"It is hard to explain to somebody from your generation," Vaughn says kindly. "People went to all extremes to get in the service."

He guesses that somebody like myself, in his late thirties, has been conditioned more by the Vietnam War than any other conflict. But I want him to tell stories about *that* war. So does his wife, Marian, who sets tea on the table and rigs up her own tape recorder, since "he doesn't tell the stories very often, you know."

Vaughn is one of the last surviving heroes of the First World War, a pilot who was forced to upgrade his skills in the final months of the war, to avoid being obsolete and dead. Now, watching a pheasant poke around on his lawn, he tells about the path from Brooklyn to the skies of France.

The first thing he does is clear up the confusion over his first name, since his scrapbook carries stories about "George" and "Bob" and "Bobby" Vaughn. All the same person, he assures me.

"I was called 'Bobby' as a very small boy, probably because I was a Junior, and my middle name—which is Augustus—was hardly suitable for distinguishing me from my father. 'Bobby' became 'Bob' from school days on, and my family and close friends still call me that."

As he shifted from "Bobby" to "Bob," Vaughn attended school in the Hill Section of Brooklyn and saw his first planes overhead.

"The old Curtiss airplanes used to race to the Statue of Liberty, around and back to Belmont Park. We'd watch them go overhead. This must have been around 1910, when I was thirteen years old.

"I'd watch the planes and make models of them—Wrights, Blériots, Curtisses. Some of them were chosen by Curtiss Aviation Company to be displayed in a department store window. So you can see I was interested in airplanes as a boy.

"When I went to Princeton, there were a lot of people who were interested in aviation so we founded the Princeton Aero Club. We had no airplanes but we subscribed to *Aviation Magazine*. Then the war came and we decided we ought to do something about that, so we got in touch with some wealthy alumni of Princeton and in their patriotic spirit, they decided they would establish a flying club, so you could learn to fly.

"The club rented a field between Princeton and Lawrenceville, bought two Jennies, hired a few instructors and mechanics, and we went out there and learned to fly at the expense of these alumni."

Did Vaughn know that flying an airplane would get him directly into combat?

"That was specifically the reason we joined. Everybody in those days was trying to get into some branch of the service—unlike the wars we've had since."

Can Vaughn give his reasons for wanting to fly in combat? Adventure? Justice? Hatred?

"Oh, I don't know. Don't forget, we were twenty years old. We'd read all the business about the war and its causes. No other ties to prevent us from doing it. Great spirit to serve some kind of uniform. I don't think we went into it to save humanity, that kind of thing. Just one of those things. It was our duty.

"We learned to fly at Princeton from a man named Frank Stanton. After about ten or twelve hours of practice he got out of the front seat and told me, 'Take it up.' That's all you needed in those days. Just take it up. I felt quite confident I could go ahead, and I stayed up fifteen, twenty minutes, a very short flight. No problem at all. As a matter of fact, of those twenty-five people in my group, only one of them ever damaged a plane in all the time we were out there.

"We all got to the point where we soloed once, where they considered us graduates, and we didn't fly anymore after that, but we had learned to fly. Then these same people took us down to Washington the spring of '17 and tried to enlist us all as a unit. They said we couldn't do that. We weren't old enough, then, you had to be twenty-one to be commissioned and furthermore we had no military experience. But they compromised by starting one of the first schools of military aeronautics at Princeton and we enlisted as privates in the Signal Corps.

"After six weeks we were sent overseas right away, because we had already soloed, and there were no combat aircraft in the U.S. to learn on.

"We were sent to Ayr, Scotland, on September seventeenth. They had a school of aerial fighting where we were taught dogfighting, equipped with cameras instead of guns that shoot bullets. When you got down, the films would tell if you had good position for shooting. That was the extent of military training. The rest you had to learn by being there. I guess I had around ninety hours of solo time when I got to the front—and that was a lot. People were going into combat with twenty-five."

Vaughn spent the fall and winter of 1917–1918 in Scotland, but was sent to France in May of 1918. In nearly four years of warfare, aerial fighting had been refined, intensified. The tactics were better, the airplanes were steadier, the margin between novice and veteran was wider.

"I was trained first on a Curtiss Jenny and then on a British Avro, a two-place tandem with rotary engine. Then we went to a Sopwith Pup, which was a single-seater airplane, and then we went to the SE-5, a fighter-type aircraft. That was the kind we flew all the time in combat when I went to the British eighty-fourth Squadron at Amiens, France.

"Of course, the first thing they would do when you went to the front was, somebody would escort you over the front lines, so you wouldn't get lost on your own."

But one day George Vaughn, a year out of Princeton, was alone in his SE-5, flying over the front lines.

"It was very different from training," Vaughn says. "Strangely enough, many people had the same experience the first time they went up. I didn't know there was anybody near me, because until you got used to it, it was very hard to pick up the German aircraft, because they came up so fast behind you, out of the clouds, that sort of thing.

"I never saw the plane. I heard it. Somebody was shooting at me before I ever knew it. The shots went right through the tail of my plane. I heard it go through the fabric. That was the first time in my life I was shot at."

With machine-gun bullets ripping through his airplane a few feet from his body, George Vaughn was in trouble. A hunter-pilot, using tactics that von Richthofen and Madon had perfected, was waiting for him in the hiding places of the sky. This was far different from the training fields of New Jersey or Scotland.

"As soon as I heard the bullets, I went into the routine I learned in Scotland," Vaughn recalls. "It's called 'evasive action' now, but they didn't call it that then. You just squirmed around and got out of the way the best you could. First down. Then up and around. Tight turns, get behind him."

George A. Vaughn, Jr., between air battles in France, 1917–1918. (George A. Vaughn, Jr.)

Sitting on his porch, calmly and impersonally, Vaughn recalls his first glimpse of his hunter—"a yellow Pfalz, with the regular German insignia on the tail, an iron cross. My plane was olive drab. I couldn't see the pilot's face. The Pfalz was a big round thing, and the pilot's head did stick out the top, but you couldn't see him. You had no idea of seeing anybody."

Vaughn recalls being surprised to find himself behind his enemy, just as the instructors had taught him.

"He started to go home as soon as I turned away, because he thought I was hit. He just went east in a straight line. I turned around and followed him, and caught up with him. He was heading east, didn't make any turns. Our planes were about the same speed. I could never have caught him if he had tried to get away. But he was just heading east in a straight line.

"I was around one hundred yards when I started firing. You were taught not to fire further than one hundred yards. Everything I was taught, I remembered. The angle . . . when I first started firing, I was a little below him, aside and below him. I got up to level, and behind him, firing across. You had to allow for deflection when you had a target coming in from the side."

How did Vaughn know he was successful?

"He went down in flames. You could see the smoke coming out of the cockpit. I didn't wait to watch any more because there were others around. My next instinct was to get away. I didn't know it had gone into flames until later. I'd been shot at by others by now. It was time to take care of yourself, not worry about anybody else.

"When I got back to the airdrome, somebody said, 'Vaughn got a Hun.' The commanding officer announced it."

How did Vaughn feel when he heard that?

"I felt quite happy because this was what you were supposed to do, out there. I was particularly happy because he didn't shoot me down first."

Never having been in combat, I ask Vaughn how he felt when he got back safely.

"I had seen enough of my mates shot down. It's a very impersonal situation. No personal feelings about any of it. It's a matter of survival."

Did he ever meet anybody who had second thoughts about shooting down an enemy pilot?

"No, I never heard of it. You've never been shot at. It makes a difference."

The smart pilots learned from that first combat, Vaughn says.

"I was never again fired on by surprise. I always knew where the other planes were. That first time, I was watching the ground, but after that, I kept moving my head, all the time. I learned to be aggressive—to use the sun at my back, where an opponent might be blinded. I learned to come out of a cloud bank, to start evasive action before the other pilot could begin firing at me, to vary my maneuvers so they couldn't tell what I would do next. You learned these things."

The slim, big-eared kid from Brooklyn took the improved technology, the refined tactics, and made six confirmed kills in three months—one of them against an enemy kite balloon, used for observation.

"They were well protected from the ground," Vaughn recalls. "Machine guns all around the bottom. It was frankly a matter of luck if you got through."

After his three months with the British 84th, Vaughn became one of three Americans eligible for the British Distinguished Fighting Cross "for conspicuous bravery."

"He wrote a letter home to his mother," says Marian Vaughn.

The letter said: "I don't have too much to write about just now. But I did get one letter and one medal from His Royal Highness."

Despite the kills and his award, Vaughn says he was never a celebrity in the British ranks. While the French would exhibit their aces to raise public morale, and the Germans made Immelmann and von Richthofen fly exhibitions to attract new recruits, "The British were more reserved. Nobody counted the number of kills, or made a commotion about it.

"The British had rules for everything: Never eat where enlisted men eat; never walk more than three together; always walk fast, as if you're in a hurry to get somewhere; dress better than enlisted men. All of these rules cost money, which I didn't have. You were supposed to stay in the best hotels, but when I got to London on leave I found you didn't need money because people would take you to dinner."

After his leave in August, Vaughn was transferred to the American 17th Aero Squadron, flying a Sopwith Camel with a dumbbell painted on the side.

"Our symbol was a white owl, but the artist couldn't draw a white owl, so he drew a dumbbell," Vaughn recalls.

Vaughn had three airplanes shot out from under him, he says, but he alway limped back to safety. Each new plane got his personal insignia— N—on the side for identification. Vaughn was flight commander of the 17th, but he still found time to account for seven more kills up until Armistice Day.

The Americans liked to cultivate heroes more than the British, and when the war was over, they gave him the U.S. Distinguished Service Cross: "Lt. Vaughn, while leading an offensive flight patrol, sighted eighteen enemy Fokkers about to attack a group of five Allied planes flying at low level. Although outnumbered nearly five to one, he attacked the enemy group, personally shot down two enemy planes, the remaining three planes of his group shooting down two more.

"His courage and daring enabled the group of Allied planes to escape. Again, on September 28, 1918, he alone attacked an enemy advance plane which was supported by seven Fokkers and shot the advance plane down in flames."

When he got back to Brooklyn, he was given a homecoming parade. The *Brooklyn Eagle* wrote: "Vaughn was at times almost panic-stricken at the idea that he would have to participate in a celebration in his own honor."

In another ceremony he officially received the British Distinguished Flying Cross from the Prince of Wales, in New York Harbor. "It could only be awarded on British territory, so they invited me onto the battleship *Reknown* and gave it to me there."

A different kind of honor came a few years later when the makers of

Heinz Rice Flakes and Heinz Breakfast Wheat put his picture on a series of "Famous Aviator" coupons in their packages. The back of the card described how "Bob" Vaughn had won thirteen victories "in the World War"—there having been only one world war at that point.

Nobody was thinking of future wars when Vaughn went back to Princeton for the February 1919 semester.

There was no problem adjusting for me. Maybe there was for men who served in the trenches with all the disease and the gas and the bullets. But for me, war was impersonal, distant. I just went right back to being a student. Of course, we were a little older. I guess you'd say we were a little more serious than when we went away."

For some of the wartime pilots, like James McMillen in the previous chapter, aviation ended when the guns stopped shooting. But for others, like George Vaughn, the military became a lifetime occupation. Vaughn tells how he organized the first National Guard Air Squadron in New York in 1921, staged aerial meets and mock air raids with surplus World War I planes in the 1920's, then formed a distributorship, selling Ryan Broughams and other popular models in the early 1930s.

"Flying was natural to our whole family," Marian Vaughn says. "We'd fly every day. Living on Staten Island, we'd put the children in a plane and go to a beach, have a picnic, and come home.

"We flew up and down the coast. I remember one time flying with my husband and Casey Jones, down in South Carolina, the plane started sputtering down, and the two of them trying to find the problem before we hit the lake. All of a sudden Casey remembered the mechanics had just fixed the flowmeter. He started playing with it and just as we skimmed over the trees, right toward the water, the engine started up again, and he just took it right up."

Vaughn and Jones organized the Casey Jones School of Aviation, which trained thirty thousand mechanics before and during World War II, and they then started the Academy of Aeronautics at La Guardia Airport.

He says he does not fly anymore, although he does enjoy taking the controls if a good pilot is with him. Since Rickenbacker, the greatest living American ace of World War I died, he's a frequent guest at aviation ceremonies. Some of his equipment is in the air museum in Dayton, Ohio.

"They built a Sopwith Camel at the museum," he says. "It was a duplicate, not an original. I had brought home the gunsight from my Sopwith—purely by accident. It just happened to be in my blanket roll when I got home. I thought I was going to put it on an American plane, but when the war ended, I forgot about it until I got home, you see. When I heard what they were doing with this Camel at Dayton, I gave them the gunsight, and they put my serial numbers, F 6304, on the plane."

He tries to see most World War I movies, and he tries to be tolerant.

"*The Blue Max* was reasonably accurate, but a lot of Hollywood there, too. A thing called *The Dawn Patrol*. Such a glorified view of aerial fighting.

"Bob" Vaughn No. 8

Collector card issued by a breakfast cereal company. As America's second-leading ace during World War I, Vaughn was also featured in cigarette collector cards. (George A. Vaughn, Jr.)

No. 8   **GEORGE A. VAUGHN, Jr.**   No.

Flight Commander of the 17th Aero Squadron in the World War American Ace credited with thirteen victories.

Prominently identified with the aviation industry for many years, he h been with the Casey Jones School of Aeronautics, as Vice-Presiden since 1932. Lt. Col. and Air Officer 27th Div. Staff N. Y. Nation Guard

Save These Famous Aviator Pictures in a Big Free Album

Save these pictures. There are two separate series in full colors—2 modern planes and 25 famous pilots—and a card from one or the oth eries will be found in each package of Heinz Rice Flakes and Hein Breakfast Wheat. H. J. Heinz Company will send you upon request beautiful sixteen page album in which you may collect either series pictures. Both albums contain many bits of interesting information regard ng aviation and a big world airway map. Merely address H. J. Hein Company, Department 136, Pittsburgh, Pa., stating which album is desire —Plane or Pilot—and it will be sent you promptly. 22738 LITHO IN U. S.

"I don't know why there should be such glamour in World War One pilots, but there was. It was much more glamorous than being an artilleryman or something, an infantryman, or a naval officer. I suppose that's because there was more individuality. An airman is in a plane by himself. Nobody but himself to boss him.

"Of course you were bombed at night. One of my tentmates was killed in a bombing raid, in a hangar, watching a movie. Bombing was worse than actual combat. In bombing you were just sitting there, a sitting duck, nothing you could do about it, whereas in combat there was something you could do.

"The spirit was very high in aviation. You never heard any grumbling. When you got back, you realized the danger you'd been in, more than when you were in it. The excitement of the moment. You never thought the bullets going through the wings might go through you next time. It didn't occur to you."

9

Forrest E. Wysong

Anaheim, California

One day he was a boy concocting a flying machine in the North Carolina countryside; before long he was learning from Beachey and Curtiss, little knowing that his lessons would qualify him as a slow-moving target in somebody else's shooting gallery.

This is the way Forrest Wysong recalls his career in the air. It happened so long ago, he could make up his stories out of thin air, and nobody would be around to contradict him. But he tells the truth: he never did expect to fly in combat.

We meet as Wysong is serving as convention chairman for the Early Birds, the dwindling flock of early pilots. Decades in California have not destroyed his sunny North Carolina drawl, though it is maybe only one-third as pungent as that of Senator Sam Ervin.

"My first attempt to fly was with a glider in 1911 on a hill in Greensboro," he says. "I didn't know what I was doing, and I just stalled the thing. Fractured my skull and dislocated my left shoulder. That was in 1911, November eleventh, the date of the crack-up."

Wysong pauses and then recalls the first time he ever heard about flying. He was walking home from school with another boy, who showed him a copy of the magazine *Aero*, which inspired a whole generation of young aviators. Using his own subscription, Wysong had built the twenty-foot biplane glider, and after the crash of the glider he dreamed of building a Curtiss biplane.

"What really got me intersted was seeing Lincoln Beachey when he was barnstorming in Greensboro."

Lincoln Beachey was the hero of an entire generation—a beefy, prosperous-looking stunt man, who also dabbled in prophecy—one prophecy anyway. He predicted the crowds would not be satisfied until he killed himself in a crash.

It turned out Beachey was right, even though he "retired" at least once to forestall his vision. In 1915 he returned to flying, only to plunge into Oakland Bay when the wings of his plane sheared off. By that time, however, his calling had been taken up by hundreds of young pilots, including Forrest Wysong.

Beachey was due to make some exhibition flights at the Fairgrounds in Greensboro, and Wysong sought him out at the hotel. Beachey took a piece of hotel stationery and wrote out a pass to the fairgrounds for the young man, and later spent hours sketching planes for Wysong and his brother, Paul.

"He also gave me a broken wing section when he came through Greensboro, so I could see what wing construction was like. Later he sent me drawings of his airplane that was doing all this looping stuff back in 1913–1914.

"I was collecting parts and my father allowed me to do it because he figured it improved my mechanical ability. I gradually accumulated the parts and got 'em built up by the time I was a senior in college. That was a copy of the Curtiss biplane, with a tricycle landing gear but without a front elevator. The elevator was in the back, the way Lincoln Beachey had modified it.

"One of the first graduates of North Carolina State agreed to buy a secondhand Roberts seventy-five horsepower, six-cylinder, two-cycle engine plus propeller, gasoline tanks, radiator tanks, for four hundred fifty dollars because I had to save something to pay express and incidentals. So we mounted the engine on my plane and we took it out to a farm near Method, but now it's just a part of Raleigh.

"There was a field with a big hay barn on it and the guy agreed to let us put the plane in the barn. We had to take the wings off to put it in the barn, and take them off again to put it outside. I ran it down the field a few times and jumped it off the ground a few times and finally decided, 'This is it, I'm going to fly it.' So I took off and went out over the trees.

"I knew I was supposed to bank it but I was a-scared to, so I made it very easy. I made a great long sweeping turn over the field, just a few hundred feet high, and swung around and I looked back for the field I had got out of. It looked questionable whether I could get back into it again. It looked so small, just like a postage stamp. But I kept easing it down, over the barn, making a series of roller-coaster descents until I got down over the field. I was very happy about that, due to the fact that I wasn't too good at landing.

"I made four more flights and the thing got in the newspaper and my father saw it and he rushed up to Raleigh, and before I knew he was there, I got a summons to come to the president's office, and when I walked in my father was sitting there.

"The two of them ganged up on me and told me I couldn't fly anymore. If I flew I was going to be expelled, and couldn't graduate. So I was very careful when I flew it next time—to get away from the college and keep quiet about it.

"As a result, I did graduate in 1915, but my father insisted that I mustn't fly an airplane anymore. The fellow that put up the five hundred dollars for the engine got upset because we had drawn up a little contract, where I was going to go barnstorming with the plane and we were going to make money on it, but my father wouldn't go for that.

"As a result, I got arrested for obtaining money under false pretenses. But they settled that by putting up the whole plane and engine over to the guy who put up the money. A friend of mine got me a job with Glenn Curtiss up in Buffalo."

By this time, Curtiss had gone beyond being a pioneer aviator, he was now an entrepreneur, with interests upstate and on Long Island.

"He was a friendly man, but a shy man," Wysong recalls, "and did not seem quite as heroic as I had pictured him. The first time I met him was after I worked in the engineering shop a few days, Mr. Curtiss called for me and said, 'I understand you've been doing some flying down in North Carolina,' and I said, 'Oh, yes.'

"I had flown eight times, in all. But he said, 'Well, I'll tell you, For-

Left: Lincoln Beachey, one of the most famous early pilots, took time to give pointers to young aviators before plunging to his death in 1915. (Nassau County Air and Space Museum) Right: Using plans given him by Lincoln Beachey, Forrest E. Wysong designed his own plane in 1915 and flew it, wearing a football helmet. (Forrest E. Wysong)

rest . . .' It was a funny thing. Everybody was calling everybody by their first name, but I wasn't used to that. In college, why, the professors called everybody 'Mister.'

"He said, 'Well, Forrest, we're probably going to have some use for you later on. You go out to the flying boat school at the foot of Porter Street on Lake Erie, and you learn to fly the Model F flying boat,' which I did.

"I also used to see him in the shop. He was a superb mechanic with a remarkable ability to think out problems. One time I was told to design a spring to hold the wing pins in place. We worked on several springs but when Mr. Curtiss saw them, he said, 'What do you want a spring for? It will add weight and vibrate until it falls. Throw it away, and put a cotter pin in each of the wing pins.'

"He was talking to a graduate engineer and a good mechanic and me. Neither of them had the judgment to realize such a spring was an absurdity. Being a twenty-one-year-old kid just out of college, I was too much in awe of all of them to second-guess.

"While I was working at Curtiss, Charlie Willard, who was the fourth man in the history of the U.S. to fly, came to work for them. He'd been my hero when I was a kid—taking lessons from Glenn Curtiss the way he did. Naturally, I polished the apple with him and was made his assistant.

"Charlie Willard was a spunky little guy, fight with anybody at the drop of a hat. He died in January of 1977, but was a grand fellow, smart right up to the end. Anyway, when the flying boat was finished and ready to be shipped, Charlie Willard quit and went to New York City, and I followed in January of 1916.

"In February of that month, I went to the motorboat show, and somebody invited me to visit the U.S.S. Granite State, anchored at the Hudson River. I had lunch and they offered me a commission if I would teach the navy boys how to fly.

"For them, I was a weekend flight instructor, meeting people like Commander John Towers and Lieutenant Commander Read. I was the only one who was not an Annapolis graduate, but I was also about the only one who could teach 'em how to fly.

"When the war came closer, Willard tried his damnedest to get me exempted, but I was already in the reserve, and I wanted to see what it was all about. I was young and patriotic, which I have since recovered from. When we declared war, I was automatically in."

Still under the illusion he was to be only a teacher of aviation, Wysong gave lessons at a naval base at Bay Shore, Long Island, and then was shifted to Washington, D.C., for six months of "groveling with paper work."

"I'd say things Towers didn't approve of, and he'd get me out in the hall and bawl the hell out of me. I was an ensign and he was a commander, so I didn't say anything. I had this training, aye-aye, sir, no back talk.

"One day the commander calls me in and said, 'I've heard you were fraternizing with enlisted men!' That's the kind of stuff that went on."

When he was sent to France, early in 1918, Wysong still thought he was going to teach other people how to fly.

"It slips up on you," Wysong recalls. "You go one step at a time. I helped ferry some flying boats down to southern France and was ordered to report to Pauillac, on the Gironde River, near Bordeaux. There was a naval air station where they were setting up airplanes. I reported to Lieutenant Commander Briscoe—the man who invented the Briscoe automobile, if you remember that.

"To me, it was a big adventure, going over there. Pauillac was away from the trenches, but the Germans broke through the line and we were rushing the Marine Corps up to help. They put me on a train with eighty-one guys that were being trained as airplane mechanics and when they told me I was going up to the trenches, I almost had a hemorrhage.

"They said, 'Well, you people have all been transferred to the Marine Corps, and we're going to put you in the front lines.' I said, 'No, sir, I'll go anywhere you tell me. I'll do anything you tell me. But I understand as a pilot I've got the privilege not to transfer to the Marines.'

"They said, 'All right, we'll send you back to Admiral Plunkett,' who was in a little town called Manonville behind the lines. He had this fourteen-inch naval gun mounted on a railroad battery. He had just gotten it set up. He had two DH-4 airplanes there, but no pilots. So when I reported with navy wings up there, he put me on duty right away, spotting for the gun at the battle of St. Mihiel. I'd send them a message by Morse code from the plane, using a trailing antenna.

"This was the first time I'd ever met combat. One guy was shooting at me, I thought he'd hit me because I felt some blood trickling down my leg. I put my hand down there and looked at it like that—and it wasn't red. That's how scared you get.

"I wasn't brave. I was scared all the time, to be perfectly frank with you, and on several occasions I ran.

"I got a German plane on my tail and nobody to protect me, I pretended I was hit and let the thing drop until the guy figured he got me and let me go, and then I'd go zooming back. I wasn't going to stay out there. I remember when they said, 'He who fights and runs away may live to fight another day.'

"And after that battle, they straightened out the line, the Germans just scattered like hell, they were just running, they could have gone on for forty miles but we had orders. We moved the gun down the railroad tracks to Metz, and we knocked that damn hill just to hell."

Wysong's next taste of battle came over the cold, churning waters of the North Sea.

"These two army officers showed up, and we were sent back to Pauillac, where I was setting up a production line. I took all that I'd learned from Glenn Curtiss and Charlie Willard and I organized those eighty-one men to put out more planes than a thousand men used to. We were flying them all over France, and I'd go up on delivery flights.

"They had two planes going up to Dunkerque, and I wanted to go up there to see what the hell was going on. When I got there, they said, 'You fellows can't go back. The Germans are trying to clear the harbor at Ostend and Zeebrugge, and we've got to bomb the hell out of them.'

"So I began flying missions over Zeebrugge. I wasn't prepared for combat. No, no, I was scared. I met a fellow that had been my roommate, name of Bob Grover, exactly my age to the day. Twenty-ninth of March 1894. We were roommates on the ship, so when I met him at Dunkerque, we agreed to protect each other the best we could.

"We'd fly over Zeebrugge and two or three times he came around and protected me when I was being shot at. But one day I saw him shot down. We were separated and there was nothing I could do. His plane was in flames, and he jumped to keep from being burned to death. Of course you know we didn't have any parachutes in that war.

"Another time I was flying an HS2L Flying Boat with a gunner out front with a Lewis machine gun. We had already dropped the bombs at Zeebrugge and we'd swing around on the North Sea, to avoid the antiaircraft from the land. It was as uncomfortable as hell to go back over land.

"This time a Pfalz plane got after us, just as we were swinging over the North Sea. He hit our Liberty engine, and as he went by, our gunner got him. I think he hit the pilot, because he just went down into the sea. We made an emergency landing down on the North Sea.

"I was terribly seasick, throwing up everything I could. We stayed there on the North Sea, two or three hours, firing our flare pistol until they spied us and sent a patrol boat. They tied a line on the nose and started towing through the rough waves. You go up on top of a wave and you wonder, "What happened to the ocean?' Then you get down in a trough and you can hardly see the sky.

"Well, they took us in tow, but it was so damn rough, the damn ring pulled out of the nose of the flying boat, so they attached the line to the scarf ring where the Lewis machine gun was mounted on the nose.

"Because it was coming on dark, and I was seasick, they invited us on board the patrol boat. The assistant gave me a bunk to sleep in. When I woke up the next morning the plane was gone and we were towing the scarf ring with the machine gun on it."

The war ended, and Wysong figured he'd made it: Now he had a chance to live to a ripe old age. But his aviation thrills were not ended yet. He was ordered to meet the U.S.S. *George Washington*, which was taking Woodrow Wilson to Europe for the peace talks. About fifty miles out of France, he had to ditch into the cold seas. Everybody else was too busy escorting Wilson to worry about Wysong.

"A screw was loose from the carburetor and had fallen into a screen below. After recovering from acute seasickness, I found the screw, fixed the carburetor, and got the engine going, but getting the plane off the sea—that was another question. All these torpedo boats were making too many waves; but finally, I managed to get the darn thing off by making an angle across the troughs."

After that, Wysong hoped for a safe assignment, but he should have known better. His experience with Curtiss and Willard, and ditching in the North Sea, had made him an expert in ocean maneuvers. Wysong was ordered to Killingborne, England, for some unexplained mission.

"They wanted to fly this little Sopwith plane off the gun turret of the battleship *Texas*. They were experimenting on how to use airplanes for the navy. Sure, Eugene Ely had landed on a battleship back around 1910, that's all in the record books. But this little Sopwith Scout biplane had wheels on it, and a couple of boards like skis or barrel staves. With those, you were supposed to be able to skim along the water.

"I took a look at the battleship. The platform was twenty-two feet long, and the ship was supposed to be steaming twenty-one knots into the wind, and I was supposed to get this damn thing airborne before I hit the rail of the ship. Heh-heh-heh.

"See, I was small. I was light in weight. They used to use me for all that monkey business. This was the flagship of the U.S. fleet in European waters, and it was a big deal to them.

"I got in the plane, and they had this tail skid backed into a contraption they called a sister hook in the navy. It would hold you back, you know? They snapped a lanyard, and this thing opens up. When the engine was wide open—everything you could churn up—I'd raise my hand, and they'd snap this lanyard, and I'd grab the stick immediately, before the plane crashed off the platform.

"It happened fast. I wasn't sure I cleared it until I saw the railing behind me. This was on the top gun turret, remember. There was another gun turret below me. One mounted above the other. I got over the railing all right, but the plane still wasn't at full flying speed, and it started mushing. I was afraid I would hit the wall down below. It cleared—but not by much.

"I landed on the water, and they were steaming at twenty-one knots, don't forget, so they pulled up alongside me, and I cut the engine and drifted alongside of them. They had this hook, and they hoisted me on board, and that was the end of it.

"I went back into Dundee, Scotland, and I went into this pub and I got roaring, stinking drunk. Then I went back to Brest and I told the admiral all about it. He seemed pretty pleased, you know.

"The admiral told me, 'I want you to be on a commission to make reports on German airplanes.' I said, 'Admiral, I'm married. My wife is expecting a child. I want to get back as soon as possible.' He said, 'You mean, you'd pass up the chance to get on this commission?' And I said, 'Damn right, Admiral, I sure would.' And he said, 'Well, if you're gonna be a big crybaby about it, I'm going to let you go.' That baby was my son, Neil, and he's now fifty-eight years old.

"I got back to the States and tried to work with Curtiss, but they were laying people off in 1919 because the government was so chintzy about aviation. I worked in New Jersey for a short time converting airplanes to carry the mail, but then I was offered a job in a clay company in Georgia and I couldn't get back into aviation again until 1934."

After the clay company went bankrupt during the Depression, however, he moved out to California, where he first worked for Lockheed in Burbank and then moved to the Douglas Aircraft Company in Santa Monica as a design engineer, testing most of the Douglas planes including the DC-8.

The only stipulation was that he wouldn't have to fly any of their craft off the gun turret of a battleship. Once was more than enough for that.

10

Carl Heinz von Pier

West Hempstead, New York

On the living-room table is an Easter basket, a gift from the young girl who delivers the newspaper. The neighbors are very nice to him, says Carl Heinz von Pier. He guesses most of them know he was a pilot for Germany during World War I, but he doesn't bring it up unless they do first.

"I was in that war, and we lost that war," he says. "It quieted me down. If we had won the war, it would be more comfortable for me to talk. I have no sad feelings, but I don't like to think back because of that."

But there are times when the memories draw him to aviation, as in 1977, when Lindbergh's first plane was being displayed in the arcade of the Roosevelt Field shopping center. Hundreds of people stood around the old plane, gawking at its small size, recalling the first time they saw a plane or the first time they flew one.

The members of the Long Island Early Fliers sat at the reception desk and smiled at stories they knew were untrue. (One person told a vivid story of seeing Lindbergh fly over the Bronx on his way to Paris.) Sometimes the visitors had a history that was even more ancient than the airplane on display.

One day von Pier drove over to the Roosevelt Field shopping center to see the old Jenny. By coincidence, the club member on duty that day was Erwin Hoenes, himself a native of Germany, and a former mechanic for several American aircraft companies. Hoenes and von Pier conversed in English and in German, but the old pilot was modest about his experiences during the war.

"I was a poor flier. I had no victories," he kept saying.

He says the same thing during my visit to his house, even as he produces his license—number 3228—which was issued by the Federation Aeronautique Internationale Deutschland, with instructions in six languages. His birthdate is given as February 12, 1892.

"I was living in Aachen in 1914, when the war broke out," he says. "When something like that happens, everybody volunteers. My job was to help show the armies the route to Belgium. I was using my own car, a Benz. I got them to Brussels and then I was a real soldier. I worked for the chief doctor in that sector, he went in the car with me. I had private quarters. I had a swell time."

Life as a driver could have been a safe way to survive the war, but its appeal diminished one Sunday afternoon near Brussels, when the Germans staged an air show for their men. The chief attractions were Baron Manfred von Richthofen and Max Immelmann, the two most glamorous pilots the Germans produced—one a hunter, the other an acrobat who perfected the extradimensional evasive loop known as the "Immelmann Turn."

The Germans kept Immelmann busy in other ways besides fighting duels at the front. He would be dispatched to Paris late in the afternoon, to buzz the rush-hour traffic and drop letters urging the French to surrender. Or he would perform stunts at exhibitions behind the lines, to recruit more pilots.

"I saw these two brilliant flyers, chasing each other like goldfish in a bowl," von Pier recalls. "I had seen airplanes before, but I was never in one. I said to my friend: 'That's for me.'"

He says he talked his way into aviation because "at that age you are a daredevil. You don't know what's going on. I'd been taking chances all my life."

Going into aviation in 1917 meant taking a chance. Technological evolution had speeded up, and generations of pilots were dying off every week doomed by new techniques of warfare as well as bad luck, bad judgment, sometimes even bad instruction.

"They sent us to Grossenheim, Germany, where we were assembled. There, they shoot us out to the flying school, with private quarters, servants taking care of our shoes. We were considered an elite group.

"The first time up in a plane, I had a teacher about five feet high. He taught me how to fly in the school machine with dual controls. He was behind me and he tells me, 'Keep your feet on the rudders, the pedals, and your hands on the stick,' so I can feel what he's doing. You absorb that.

"The bad thing was that little fellow was afraid to fly—and I adopted the way he flew. When you go into a curve, you are supposed to bank your wings. He went flat. That's dangerous. When the chief pilot tested my ability, he said I should bank. He told me the centrifugal force will hold you up."

When von Pier had completed just twenty-three tours of the field, the chief pilot had a question for him: "Do you feel like going off alone now?" It was not the kind of challenge that a German soldier would ignore.

Carl Heinz von Pier posed with his family before going off to serve his country.
Later he qualified as a combat pilot in the final year of the war. (Photos property of
Carl Heinz von Pier, copied by William E. C. Haussler)

"I rolled to a start, then he gave me the signal to start off. I was in the air faster than I thought. All of a sudden I saw only the blue skies. I took the stick and pushed it down—too hard—the ground came too fast. I pushed it up and all I could see was sky. I pushed the stick down and unfortunately the plane went down toward the ground. I did that several times, just like a crazy guy. I didn't know what I was doing.

"I was going to *schmear* off, go down. There was the pilot shed down on the ground, with a soldier on guard. When I saw him, I went for him. I don't know what I had in mind. I pulled back on the stick and went up in the air again.

"At this point I gave up. I said, 'Well, Carl, this is it.' I took my hands off the stick and put them around my forehead and closed my eyes and said, 'I'm going to wait for the crash.' But the crash never came. Would you know it, that machine flew without me. It was flying so nicely, I opened my eyes, and tipped the stick with my finger. My foot was on the rudder, very gentle. It responded for me. And that was how I learned to fly.

"I tell you, my whole short life, up to that time, came before my eyes.

"When I landed, the ambulance was cruising around in case of necessity. All the pupils did not look at me. They gave me up for lost.

"My instructor, he gave me a bawling out. The commander of the field, big shot, he came racing across the field on horseback with a monocle in his eye. Bawled me out. He said, 'We're going to send you back to the infantry—get out.' But the chief pilot said, 'Do you feel like making another try?' I said, 'Yeah, I feel like it.' See, my instructor *schmeared* the machine around the corner, so I learned wrong. The chief pilot said, 'Go have it gassed up and stay as long as you have gas, if you want.'

"I gassed up and went off, with no trouble. I did a perfect eight, which was one of the conditions we had to fly. They tried to get me down. They were shooting off flares but I said, 'Well, here I am enjoying myself, let them shoot.' But finally I came down.

"Then I got more conditioning. Special landing, more training. The last condition was, you had to crawl up to five thousand meters, turn the motor off, and come down gradually and land in a circle. Glide in. I must have been pretty good because I never came home with a bent axle."

When they felt he was ready, they shipped him to the front, near Strasbourg, to fly observation missions over the enemy trenches. Each pilot would have an officer on board to give commands, even if the officer knew nothing about flying, which was usually the case, von Pier says.

"One day the commander said, 'Fly around.' I flew above that beautiful cathedral with the clock. The plane had no machine gun. I saw all the soldiers running to a certain point. They were having an air raid, but I didn't know it. Then I saw a bunch of French airplanes coming. I was defenseless. They must have smelled me. Fortunately, they had a job to do, and they did it without attacking me. When I got back my chief said to me, 'You were lucky. You could have been a dead mouse.' The officers never saw those planes coming."

In the final summer, when the German forces were waning, the young pilot would go up every day.

"Right near the end, they put an officer into the cockpit to release the bombs. He had the orders where to go. I flew to the front, saw a lot of black spots, didn't know what they were. I was hot in the pants when I realized they were planes, and I was one single plane. I went down as quick as I could, over the treetops to our airfield.

"They were shooting at us, I knew that, because this stuff was hitting the plane. That machine was like a sieve. As we landed, I said over my shoulder, 'Willie, aren't you glad we're back?' But he didn't answer. Then I said, 'Well, Willie, we made it.' But when I looked around, Willie was dead.

"That same day was armistice. It was the last flight for me."

Von Pier says he was told he could fly an airplane back to Germany, but later the Allies became vindictive.

"I got in a train, a boxcar," he recalls. "The Belgians were shooting at us. I can't understand why I am still alive. I must have had an angel guarding me all along, including now. The train came to Aachen, and I marched home searching for my mother. The house was intact. Later it was destroyed in World War Two."

At first, von Pier had hopes of being a civilian pilot in Germany, but there was no work in the field. He got a factory job, but the German mark "lost value while I walked home from work.

"The French had occupied the Rhineland and the Ruhr," he recalls. "Industry was giving passive resistance. I was working as assistant to the works engineer at Talbot Wagon Factory. I told him, 'Since you are closing down this industry, this would be a good time for me to go visit the U.S.' My mother, who had been over there, told me all about the U.S. My boss said, 'Don't forget to come back.'

"I came on the steamship *Resolute*. Second-class ticket, Pier Forty-six. They dumped me on the street with two valises. A year later I met my wife, who had been stuck in Germany during the first war. I didn't go back to Germany, not once."

He wanted to fly, he says, but aviation "was kaput over there." So he worked for an elevator company, preparing machines that went straight up and down in a rigid framework, instead of the free-soaring machines he had once handled. His next flight was in 1949, when he took an airplane to the West Coast, to visit a relative.

"I was all enclosed in that big plane. It wasn't the same thing," he says. "After that, when I just stood on top of a stepladder I was afraid, so I didn't go on any more airplanes.

"It's too bad my flying career came to such a bad end. The times I loved best were the times I was alone. I was safe there. No girl could chase me there. I would pretend the clouds were mountains. I would fly under bridges. I did loop-the-loops. Now I read about this guy who climbed up the World Trade Center—one hundred ten stories, a human fly. This guy, he had guts. Now I'm not a fanatic. I haven't done anything in the aviation field. But when I was that age, I was like that guy. When you are young, you have guts."

III

Growing Pains

When the war ended, the world knew twice as much about building aircraft as it had four years earlier. But as soon as the emergency ended, the efforts of inventors, builders, and pilots returned to a piecemeal, personal basis.

The result was a time of fitful growth, of frustration, of private ventures without financial backing. One estimate is that $100 million in government airplane contracts was canceled within three days of the Armistice; the glut of surplus planes discouraged private industry from pursuing immediate mass production.

Certainly, one did not have to be a visionary in 1918 to reason that airplanes could carry passengers on schedule, move freight, perform crop-dusting and other specialized tasks, and span greater distances than before 1914. But as the world tried to return to "normalcy," some people wanted anything but to be reminded of the carnage of wartime air duels.

On both sides of the ocean, pilots were stunned to find few outlets for the machines and skills of wartime. In the United States, the surplus Curtiss Jennies and Standards, some selling for as little as one hundred dollars apiece, created a new class of impoverished ex-war pilots known as "barnstormers."

These men hustled to make a living performing stunts, scouting up passengers, teaching others to fly, altering their war craft so drastically that the pilot and writer, Ernest K. Gann, has called it an age of "aeronautical bastardy."

However, progress inevitably continued in many areas. Within a year of Armistice Day, rudimentary private airlines had been organized in Germany, England, France, the United States, and the Netherlands, with the French government subsidizing salaries of pilots on a commercial line.

One of the classically marginal operations in the United States was run by Claude Ryan, who has described Cal Rodgers' historic flight over Kansas earlier in chapter 3. Finding himself with a surplus plane and a piano crate for an office in San Diego, Ryan established a daily passenger service to Los Angeles in 1925. As he describes in chapter 11, this enterprise paved the way for more successful lines, and his remodeling experience also prepared him to later create a plane for a young barnstormer named Lindbergh.

While still debating the airplane's role in defense, the U.S. government was quick to explore its use in delivering mail around the huge nation. On May 15, 1918, the U.S. Postal Service initiated airmail service from New York to Philadelphia to Washington, using army pilots. Soon pilots were flying the brutal night route over the Allegheny Mountains, but the early loss of pilots and the continuing high costs soon prompted the government to turn over the airmail business to private carriers. In chapter 12, Russell Holderman describes his stint in the short-lived U.S. Air Mail Service.

The improved wartime planes also allowed pilots to explore the rugged countryside that had been untamed in the early years. In chapter 13, Walter Ballard recalls the joy of flying into canyons and deserts in the early 1920s.

To support his habit, Ballard and many others had to fly stunts for weekend crowds. In chapter 14, Harlan (Bud) Gurney, later a leading airplane captain, tells how he barnstormed with his friend, Charles ("Slim") Lindbergh.

Many people still think of Lindbergh as the first person to fly the Atlantic, but his feat in 1927 was only the most captivating in a series of transatlantic flights.

The push began right after the war, when the U.S. Navy deployed three Curtiss "flying boats"—lumbering biplanes which could land only on water on their large hulls—against the North Atlantic. On May 16, 1919, the three craft left Newfoundland, two of them floundering in mid-ocean. But the third, the NC-4, under the command of Lieutenant Commander Albert C. Read, reached the Azores, then Portugal, then England, for the first crossing by an air-bound craft.

Another World War I craft, a twin-engine Vickers-Vimy bomber, performed the first nonstop flight between the New and the Old worlds, on June 14, 1919, when British officers John Alcock and Arthur Whitten Brown linked Newfoundland and Ireland in sixteen hours and twenty-seven minutes.

Within ten years of Blériot, who flew forty kilometers across the English Channel, these two Englishmen had flown three thousand kilometers without stopping. There would be many other long-distance successes all over the globe in the next few years, many of them performed over land routes. The engines of the early 1920s were still too unpredictable to encourage pilots to take long flights over open water. By this time, of course, private companies were investing great effort into building better engines.

The U.S. armed forces continued to spearhead long-distance efforts. In 1923, two army officers, John Macready and Oakley Kelly, flew a Fokker T-2 monoplane from Roosevelt Field to San Diego in twenty-six hours and fifty minutes. (Remember that twelve years earlier, it had taken Cal Rodgers forty-nine days to cross the continent.)

On June 23, 1924, Lt. Russell A. Maughan, piloting an Army Curtis PW-8, flew from Mitchel Field to San Francisco in twenty-one hours and forty-four minutes.

As the technology improved, the demand for better service increased. The airfields had once been open farmlands, but now—even though still unpaved for the most part—they were being flanked by hangars, shops, factories, and offices to provide help to the increasingly sophisticated profession. Even restaurants and hotels began to cluster around the airfields, as visiting aviators and tourists needed places in which to relax.

The most active air base in the world in the 1920s was the adjoining complex of Roosevelt and Curtiss fields on Long Island, twenty miles east of Manhattan. Every famous aviator, from Glenn Curtiss to Jimmy Doolittle to Amelia Earhart to Lindbergh, used this field in that decade.

Living in a hangar on Curtiss Field, a young boy named George Dade hung out with the pilots, performed odd jobs, and learned as much as he could. Dade, who later became a youthful pilot and started his own airplane-shipping business, recalls in chapter 15 the bustle of life on an airfield during the emergence of a huge industry.

11

T. Claude Ryan—II

San Diego, California

In chapter 3, Claude Ryan recalled how his first solo in 1917 ended with the commandeered airplane splattered over the runway. Fortunately, the nineteen-year-old did not take this as a divine signal to look for another line of work.

If Ryan had gone looking for a safer occupation, he would not have become a leading example of the 1920s aviator who made good—first a pilot who would go anywhere for a few dollars, then the operator of the first year-round scheduled airline in the United States, then a builder of aircraft whose company would create Charles Lindbergh's airplane.

Imagine if Ryan had been scared off by crashing during his first solo. Today, instead of remembering "Lucky Lindy," we might all be celebrating "Dauntless Dick" Byrd or "Courageous Clarence" Chamberlin. It was Ryan's reputation that drew Lindbergh to the plant in San Diego, but Ryan no longer chats about that period in his life, for reasons that will become clear.

Ryan, who had been inspired by the historic cross-country flight by Cal Rodgers in 1911, was determined to fly. In 1917 he kept trying to enlist in the navy but, as he recalls, "They kept telling me the same thing: I was too young."

Sitting in his office—now the property of the massive Teledyne Corporation—Ryan remembers how he pursued any government pilot program until in 1919 the army accepted him. He was one of three students who received their pursuit-pilot licenses, out of seventy-five who entered the program.

One of the few government flying careers was with the U.S. Aerial Forest Patrol, in which he served until 1922, gaining experience in the rugged Northwest woods. Then he came back to California and tried selling automobiles and running a laundry, but inevitably he gravitated to Rockwell Field in San Diego.

While hanging around Rockwell (now part of the naval air base), Ryan heard that a tiny field, at the foot of Broadway, had "become available," as he puts it, because the operator had been caught ferrying Chinese aliens across the Mexican border.

Ryan was able to lease the field from the Harbor Department for no money down, but he quickly realized why the strip was such a bargain—it was bounded by high-tension wires, telephone poles, and the masts of ships bobbing up and down in the sea.

Nevertheless, he sold his car to purchase a government-surplus Curtiss Jenny for four hundred dollars. He set up a shop in a discarded piano box, just big enough for him to call it an office and to display a sign that "Ryan the Aviator" would take people anywhere they wanted to go. He had to bank the plane at steep angles to get in and out of the tiny field, but he always made it.

"The main idea was, I was flying," he says. "I'd get the money any way I could. Once I chartered a passenger for seventy-five dollars from here to L.A., so you know it must have been an emergency. But most of the time I took people up for five dollars."

Ryan's adventures were typical of the pilot in the early twenties. He barnstormed down to Tijuana, Mexico, attracting customers to a traveling carnival. He crashed a few times on both sides of the border, borrowed money to keep going, and learned to upgrade his aircraft through continual tinkering.

Ryan does not volunteer many of these details as we chat in his office, but his biography, *Ryan the Aviator,* written by his colleague Bill Wagner, discloses how Ryan struggled to build his own scheduled airline.

First, Ryan accumulated a couple of Standard J-1 biplanes, formerly wartime training planes, with an open cockpit. He and his old friend Hawley Bowlus felt the size of the Standard's fuselage would support a four-passenger enclosed cabin, which they built. Then they offered excursion rides along the coast, five dollars for fifteen minutes.

In the giddy days of 1924, many tourists to California were willing to take an introductory flight. Excursion buses began flocking to Ryan's new location on Dutch Flats. One day a flamboyant sportsman, Benjamin Franklin Mahoney, roared up in his convertible and introduced himself to Ryan. After some flying lessons, the two became friends, and Mahoney proposed they open a scheduled air service between Los Angeles and San Diego.

There had been many attempts to create regular service in the United States, starting with an air-boat line between Tampa and St. Petersburg, Florida, before the war. A dozen small companies sprung up after the war, including Aero Limited, which flew summer passengers between New York City and Atlantic City, and later shuttled people to the Caribbean Islands during Prohibition. Another outfit was Aeromarine Sightseeing and Navigation Company, which flew between Miami and Havana.

Dependent on creating new customers, Ryan and Mahoney hired a publicity man, Thomas P. Mathews, who recalled his efforts in Bill Wagner's entertaining book about Ryan:

"I tried everything," Mathews said. "Spot radio commercials, pretty girls, half-fares for children traveling with adults, convention flights, thirty-day round trips, travel bureaus, and everything. By the end of summer of 1926, I added it all up and told Ryan and Mahoney they should discontinue scheduled flights. But Claude was adamant."

To try to save the airline, Ryan and Mahoney decided to buy a bigger, flashier plane. They settled on the Cloudster, built by Donald Douglas—a huge, seven-passenger biplane, thirty–seven feet long with a wingspan of fifty–six feet and a 660-gallon fuel tank. They had to borrow money to meet the six thousand dollars sale price.

In the fall of 1926, Ryan's crew enlarged the cabin area of the Cloudster into a ten-passenger cabin with five single seats on each side of an aisle. The Cloudster gained them considerable attention, but not enough passengers to save the regular service, which was discontinued late in 1926. The Cloudster finished its career making beer runs down in Mexico.

By this time, however, Ryan had another pursuit. Seeing the U.S. government failing at its airmail service with 1918-vintage De Havillands, Ryan believed that private carriers would soon be carrying the mail—and would need better planes. He had designed a sleek monoplane that combined speed and economy, and he persuaded Mahoney to build the M-1 (M for "Monoplane," 1 because it was the first in a projected series).

But these brief or seasonal attempts faltered because flying was still a novelty in the early 1920s—all right for a one-shot taxi service, all right for a thrill. But if people were planning a vacation, they built it around an automobile or passenger train, not around a fledgling airplane line.

Mahoney and Ryan, however, decided there were enough people who would patronize a ninety-minute service between San Diego and Los Angeles. Ryan estimated the cost of flying a Standard between the two cities and back was $22.50, so he felt he could break even with one passenger, and made that the round-trip fare. The one-way ticket was $14.50.

He would start in Los Angeles at 10:00 A.M., arrive in San Diego at 11:30 A.M., depart San Diego at 4:00 P.M. and arrive in L.A. at 5:30.

On March 1, 1925, the Los Angeles–San Diego Air Line made its first flight, with movie director Robert Vignola and actress Vera Reynolds helping to attract publicity. Dozens of curious people, lured by the movie celebrities and the festivities, stayed to take the five-dollar sight-seeing special in another Standard.

For the first few months, the scheduled service broke even, passing out five-dollar rebates if the plane was delayed by an occasional forced

Claude Ryan in the cockpit of one of his first planes, as he tried to establish a flying service in San Diego. Small World Department: The young woman, who had brought several passengers to the field, is Doris Richardson. Many years later she would work for the Ryan Aviation Corporation, and still later would marry Martin Jensen, a former associate of Ryan's. (Ryan Aeronautical Library)

landing. It flew between Ryan's new headquarters on Dutch Flats, adjoining the Point Loma Golf Links, and the Los Angeles terminal at Ninety-ninth and Western, a few miles inland from the current L.A. International Airport.

They hung out a sign that said "Builders of Air Craft" and went to work on the first M-1, with a crew that included a young engineer named John K. Northrop, who was moonlighting with permission from the Douglas company. With a powerful Hispano-Suiza engine installed, the M-1 made its first flight on February 14, 1926. Around that time Ryan moved into an old fish cannery on the bay, the current site of the Teledyne offices, where we are meeting.

Before long, the M-1 planes were used to fly airmail, and Ryan also flew his own creations to help Pacific Air Transport lay out its coastal routes. These routes were later incorporated into an airline that survived—United Airlines.

But the many ventures ate into the capital and produced a strain between Ryan and Mahoney. Late in 1926, Mahoney bought out Ryan for $25,000 and one M-1 plane, but kept Ryan on as general manager for $200 a month. Mahoney had complete control of the company by that time, but Ryan's name remained on the M-1 and M-2 models that followed—a beacon for anybody seeking a well-designed craft. However, Ryan's loss of financial control seems to have dampened his sense of involvement with Lindbergh.

As we sit in his office, I keep waiting for Ryan to volunteer some reference to the Lindbergh era. But Bill Wagner has already told me that in 1977, before the fiftieth anniversary of the Lindbergh flight, Ryan told Wagner to pass out printed answers to the inevitable questions from the press, since Wagner knew them by heart.

"It just doesn't mean anything to Claude to have attention," Wagner has told me. "He's too busy in the present."

Ryan was general manager in February of 1927 when his secretary handed him a telegram that read: "Can you construct Whirlwind engine plane capable flying nonstop between New York and Paris. Stop. If so please state cost and delivery date."

The telegram was signed by the Robertson Aircraft Company of St. Louis, but had actually been sent by one of its employees, Charles Lindbergh. The twenty-five-year-old airmail pilot had never flown a Ryan plane, but he was familiar with their reliability on the overnight mail runs. Also, he had been turned down by several other manufacturers as he tried to buy an airplane that could be the first to fly between New York and Paris.

Lindbergh felt the basic J-5 Ryan monoplane with a Wright Whirlwind engine was ideal for a long flight over the ocean. (He had never flown over water before.) He was willing to sacrifice heavy cockpit equipment for added gas tanks, and he would not think of using a copilot.

Ryan consulted with his aeronautical engineer, Donald A. Hall, as to whether they could extend the wings and fuselage of an enclosed Ryan Brougham.

"Nobody's airplane has ever taken off with a load of fuel big enough to go that far," Ryan has recalled saying. "We sure could use the business, but they are talking about a three thousand mile range."

Lindbergh arrived on February 23, 1927, and immediately impressed the Ryan crew with his flying and engineering ability. He supervised every detail until the plane made its first flight on April 28, and a few days later he flew eastward to St. Louis—and, as it turned out, Paris.

Ever since that famous flight, the name of Claude Ryan has been identified with Lindbergh, but Ryan never received much praise or money for his contribution, since Mahoney owned the company by then.

Lindbergh once carefully described Ryan's role as: "Claude Ryan . . . built the company that built *The Spirit of St. Louis*." When Lindbergh returned to San Diego for a banquet in his honor, Ryan paid for his own ticket and sat quietly in the audience.

Without much nudging from the impending Depression, Mahoney went bankrupt on his own in 1929. Shortly afterward, Ryan started another company, using his own name, producing his own Ryan S-T monoplane in 1934.

The low-wing, open-cockpit S-T plane soon became the most popular training plane in the United States. Ryan expanded his building operation to include three training schools in Southern California, in which twenty thousand pilots, mostly military, were trained by the end of World War II.

"I used to bump into airline captains," he says in our interview. "They'd get me into the cockpit, most of those fellows are retiring now themselves. They'd say, 'Mr. Ryan, I took the course at your school.' The clock has gone around fast. I don't like to call myself a has-been, but I'm not one of the boys anymore."

Some of his old associates in San Diego wonder what Claude Ryan does with his time these days. Does he putter around in a boat or play golf five days a week or drive around the country in a motor home, as an old man is expected to do?

Not content with being a "has-been," Claude Ryan spends his time in a back hangar on the Teledyne lot, tinkering with his new powered glider. Instead of talking about 1927, Ryan wants to talk about today—the glider, not *The Spirit of St. Louis.*

He got the idea, he says, when he was a boy of seventy-three, and he and his son, Jerry, flew in a rented sailplane for two hours. Not content with gliding around in circles, bound by prevailing winds and the need to stay close to a landing field and towing facilities, Ryan wondered if he could combine gliding and powered flight.

"It's a true story, this longing in man's nature," Ryan says. "People lie down in a meadow and watch the birds. Something you can't describe. It's similar to longing for the sea."

After that, he and his son and a crew designed a metal glider-airplane with enough power to go 135 miles per hour, and enough sleekness to soar for hours without using the engine. They called it the Ryson (Ryan and Son) ST (Soaring and Touring) 100 Cloudster.

In August of 1977, Ryan's longtime chief pilot, Ray Cote, flew the Cloudster from California to Oshkosh, Wisconsin, squeezing fifty-nine miles per gallon out of the plane, soaring for eighteen hours of flight, using the engine only for thirteen. Now Ryan is awaiting the final Federal Aviation Administration tests.

"Ray Cote told me his greatest thrill was soaring in the Cloudster in a thermal, about eleven thousand feet above the ground, and seeing this huge bird, he guessed it was a buzzard.

"Ray told me, 'We soared in the same thermal, me and the buzzard, for a long time, and finally I had to go. I felt like I wanted to tell the buzzard good-bye.' I can understand how Ray feels. He's part bird, just like the rest of us."

"Part bird." This romantic notion doesn't fit the concrete offices, the heavy gates and security guards, the secret tests, impassive workers with badges and mechanical pencils in their shirt pockets at the Teledyne office. This is the aviation industry today—tied into military security, grim and efficient. The men who were part bird are supposed to have died off, like Cal Rodgers when he crashed in the surf. What is there left to dream about?

Claude Ryan says there used to be more "fraternalism" in the old days, then he looks at his watch, and the introspection is ended. We shake hands, and Bill Wagner escorts me across the hall, still talking with reverence about Ryan after forty years of working with him.

"He's a good talker when he wants to talk," Wagner says. "The thing is, he's just so doggone busy all the time."

Just before I leave, I offer my hope that the old man's last project will be a success.

"Oh, no," Wagner says quickly. "This isn't his last project. He's trying to get another company to build the Cloudster. He's anxious to get it started because, to tell you the truth, he's got another plane he wants to build after that."

12

Russell Holderman

Brighton, New York

The rain is pouring so hard that all the golfers are in the clubhouse of the Oak Hill Country Club, betting on next Sunday's football games. Only the ghosts of the Iroquois are out roaming the woods in early November. In another day or another week the rain will turn to snow, and the next time people in the Rochester area see the ground will probably be April.

All of this is drearily predictable, says Russell Holderman. He is telling me and the country-club bartender about the time he flew whiskey into Florida during Prohibition. Even the mention of that state seems to light up this rainy afternoon.

"Whaddaya say, Mr. Holderman," the bartender says. "Whaddaya say we just get in the plane and go to Florida."

Not a bad idea. The thought is written all over Holderman's face. Until he had the pacemaker installed in 1974, he had flown everything from a homemade glider to a U.S. Air Mail Service plane to a Blue Angels jet, in one of the longest, most varied careers of anybody I will meet.

Florida would be a nice place to visit this time of year—he and Dot flew there on their honeymoon, and Dot sold Florida real estate by plane, before she set her own glider records. But now Dot is confined to the house, a nurse helping her through each day.

"I really can't stay too long," Holderman says, still nursing his first drink. "I told Dot I'd bring her back a sandwich. She can't do much for herself. Damn shame. Damn shame."

He makes a mental note to order a sandwich for Dot, and then he starts telling me and the bartender about his sixty years of flying. There are enough adventures to entertain us for the length of a New York winter. I am waiting for his recollections of the ill-fated Air Mail Service, but how can I ignore his memories of the first decade?

"I was born in February of 1895, so I was already eight when the Wright brothers flew. I used to cut out clippings from the newspapers, sure. I was a nut on aviation right from the start.

"My father was building sidewalks in Buffalo, but it wasn't a good business because you could never see the sidewalks in the winter, so we moved to the Bronx around 1908 and that's where I met Schneider—Fred Schneider, he was building airplanes in a shop on One Hundred Eighty-seventh Street, a pretty well-known guy then.

"Schneider built a thirty-foot biplane out of aluminum, and he was going to fly it at Morris Park in the first airplane meet in this country. There were twenty thousand people there, and they all wanted to see a plane fly. I'd help Schneider get gas for the tank, so I was out there on the field. I don't remember what people said, but I know they were disappointed when the planes couldn't get off. They just weren't ready.

"There was this one guy who said he was game to try. He asked me, 'Hold the plane until I'm ready, then let go.' I did that, but when I released the plane, I could walk faster than his plane was moving. Anyway, he got up a little speed and finally hit the fence at the end of the field. He wasn't hurt."

This is the same 1908 meet the Newell brothers described for me earlier, in which the only craft to get off the ground was a double-wing glider that crashed, breaking the ankles of the pilot. Holderman recalls a peculiar invention by one Wilbur R. Kimball, that had dozens of little propellers and "didn't do anything."

"Nobody was really discouraged by that Morris Park meet. They were flying at Belmont Park in 1910. I used to take the elevated train at One Hundred Seventy-seventh Street—an old wood-burning locomotive—and get off at the Brooklyn Bridge. You'd take the trolley car to Jamaica, take another trolley out to Long Island. It took a long time, that's all I remember.

"When I got to Belmont Park, I didn't have much money, and this guard saw me and said, 'There's a hole at the end. I'm going to turn my back, and you run inside.' I did just that, and when I looked around I was near the planes. I could see the Wrights, Hamilton, Curtiss, Moisant, Graham-White. They were standing there, just like gods. They were busy and I didn't talk to them, but I was standing around them."

Standing so close to the heroes of the first decade inspired Holderman to make his first flight in 1910 with a homemade glider.

"At the corner of One Hundred Seventy-seventh Street and Third Avenue there was an embankment of twenty feet down to a baseball diamond. In those days I didn't know you needed a little wind. I just wanted to test it. I knew it would cause too much trouble during the day, so we waited until after midnight, me walking up One Hundred Seventy-seventh Street carrying the glider, and my father thinking I was a damn fool.

"We picked up some people walking down the street and we got to the embankment, and I explained to them I had a few ropes at the end. They were to run, pulling the ropes, and when they got to the end of the embankment, to let go. Well, they did all that, but I landed with my feet first, and then my whole body and broke my collarbone and two ribs. It was the only injury I ever had from flying.

"Then my club went down to Obert Heights in Staten Island to practice with the glider. I was the lightest one in the group and we did some short hops and got the glider up to fifty, sixty feet. I thought it was a thousand. A member of the club down there, Louis S. Ragot, explained why I cracked up the first time. My center of gravity was all wrong. But at Staten Island—that's when I got it right.

"Now I was really hooked. All I cared about was aviation. My father was putting up a new building at Forty-second Street and Madison—the Union Carbide Building. I had a job laying bricks and sometimes I'd take a construction elevator up to the top, but if there was a sound of a plane, I'd just stand there and wait for him to fly by. When you're determined, you'll do something, and I wanted to fly.

"My first flight in a powered plane was 1911. My father took me out to Nassau Boulevard and paid ten dollars to George Beatty. We stayed up for ten, fifteen minutes. My father knew how nutty I was. That's why he took me out there.

"After that I asked Schneider to teach me to fly. He had a flying school by then. He was German, and he had a Lieutenant Walb from Germany, who was sent over here to learn to fly. When the war started, Walb had to go back to fight. I even got a postcard from Walb during the war. He was flying a Zeppelin, but I don't know what happened to him after that.

"Anyway, Schneider wanted me to be the youngest pilot, and some other teacher had a guy he wanted first. So Schneider would take me out to the field and we'd go grass cutting. I'd take it off a little, go down the field, get out, turn it around.

"My first solo was May 7, 1913, in a modified Curtiss pusher built by Schneider. I had long trousers on. They were flapping in the breeze. I remember that. I got around twenty feet in the air and said, 'Geeeeez.' I can't remember how the world looked, but I felt like I had lead shoes on, and all of a sudden they got light.

"Coming home in the subway train, I remember thinking to myself that of all the people sitting there, I'm the only one that had the experience of flying a plane.

"Right away somebody asked me to make a flight over to Newark, but my father wouldn't give me permission because he said he wasn't going to sign my life away. Maybe he was right. The pilot who replaced me on that trip to Newark overshot the runway and broke two legs. My father pacified me with a new motorcycle and pretty soon I was doing ninety-two miles per hour on that. People would stay out of my way because they knew I was nuts.

"But my main love was still flying. My brother was born eighteen years after me and I named him Wilbur after Wilbur Wright. Do you know for his whole life he called himself John W. Holderman? But I called him Wilbur. I always figured he'd come up here and take over my house and help out with things, but right after he finished teaching school he died of cancer this year. It's a damn shame, but what are you going to do?"

We move into the dining room of the country club, while Holderman tells how he taught flying to army recruits at Hazelhurst (later Roosevelt) Field on Long Island during the first war. But he wouldn't take a commission "because it would be like a cut in pay."

Holderman continues: "I met my wife during the war. She lived in a big old house in Jamaica, Queens, and her family used to invite soldiers home for dinner. She had a beautiful house with fireplaces, and we had a great dinner, but the only thing wrong was, she made me go to church with her."

With an Allied victory in sight, Holderman's next career was being developed by the U.S. Post Office, in the form of the world's first scheduled airmail service. This venture would prove to be one of the most challenging and dangerous periods in American aviation, and would greatly add to the skill of flying.

There had been earlier attempts at flying the mail by air. The French had lofted five hundred pounds of mail in balloons out of besieged Paris as early as September 23, 1870, and an American pilot, Earl Ovington, had flown a Blériot monoplane on a short hop on Long Island forty-one years later, to the day. That first airmail flight in the United States was followed by sporadic attempts before the United States got deeply involved in the war.

With the capacity of airplanes being upgraded during the war, Assistant Postmaster General Otto Praeger made plans for a regular New York–Philadelphia–Washington run, early in 1918. He even prodded Congress to allocate one hundred thousand dollars, and then informed the Army Service it had nine days to prepare for the inaugural flight on May 15, 1918.

The first official flight was a dud: Lieutenant George Boyle got lost twenty minutes after taking off from Washington and landed in Waldorf, Maryland, breaking a propeller. But the southbound flight was more successful, and regular service was soon in operation, cutting many hours off the usual time for delivering the mail by train.

At first, the government printed airmail stamps at twenty-four cents, then it eliminated all extra charges beyond the standard two-cents-per-ounce surface rate. Later, when service extended westward, it charged eight cents for each of three zones (New York–Chicago, Chicago–Cheyenne, and Cheyenne–San Francisco). Still later, it charged a flat ten-cents-per-half-ounce rate.

The post office used the army planes for several months, before purchasing seventeen planes and hiring flying instructors from army bases. One of them was Russell Holderman.

"We started with nothing," Holderman recalls. "I flew a few runs in 1918–1919, but basically I was a mechanic. They were taking De Havilland planes left over from the war and putting different engines in them, but they were lousy engines, unbalanced and everything else."

The Air Mail Service killed thirty-one of the first forty pilots it hired, mostly on the "graveyard run" from New Jersey to Chicago, over the foggy, murderous Allegheny Mountains. Those early pilots had no radio beams, no weather stations, no blind-flying instruments, no lighted beacons. Even on the East Coast, the conditions were brutal.

"At first I was at Hazelhurst Field on Long Island," Holderman says, "but then they moved the operation to Heller Field in New Jersey. I didn't like that at all. They took all the woods away, but it was right next to the Tiffany factory. If you overshot the field, you went into a canal. This guy Smith hit a tree and was mad because he tore his leather coat. He was lucky he didn't get burned up. This fellow Santa Maria hit the middle chimney of the factory, went over on his back, but he wasn't killed.

"That field was dangerous. I would delay a flight because of the fog and they would wire back, 'Why was it delayed?' The mail must go through, they said. Otto Praeger (the assistant postmastmaster general) was sitting behind a desk somewhere. He never flew. He said, 'Fly by compass.' I wrote a letter about that field, but they didn't move it back until some pilots got killed."

Even in the first full year, 1919, the performance record was remarkably high—96.54 percent completions of all flights, although 30 percent were flown in poor visibility. However, in flights over the Alleghenies, the penalty for miscalculation was sudden death, usually splashed on the front pages of the newspapers.

A typical disaster was the disappearance of Charles Ames, a hardy veteran who insisted on flying with an open wound in one leg. Ames left Hadley Field, New Jersey, on October 1, 1925, scheduled for a stop at the infamous Bellefonte Field in Pennsylvania. When his De Havilland plane never appeared out of the clouds that night, hundreds of people began "the biggest rescue attempt since explorer Floyd Collins was trapped by a falling boulder in a Kentucky cave eight months earlier," wrote Jessie Davidson in the anthology, *Saga of the U.S. Air Mail Service.*

Ten days later, Ames' body was found in the broken plane, two hundred feet below the summit of Nittany Mountain. He had been flying directly on course, apparently at high speed, relaxed and with no anticipation of a crash.

The government kept sinking money into better equipment, as soon as it was produced, and accidents like Charles Ames' became rare. From February 2, 1926, until April 22, 1927, Air Mail Service pilots logged over three million miles without a fatality.

Above: The first airmail flight was made on September 23, 1911, by Earl Ovington between Garden City and Mineola, Long Island. (Air and Space Collection, Nassau County Museum) Right: After World War I, regular airmail routes were established around the United States. A young pilot named Charles Lindbergh had to parachute for safety over Maywood, Illinois, one foggy night in 1924. Lindbergh is wearing boots and jodphurs. (Paul W. Trier)

But the government had never intended to maintain the airmail service, and in 1927 it began parceling out the routes to private carriers. The New York–Chicago–Cheyenne–San Francisco run, which had cut days off the travel of mail between the coasts, was divided between two carriers. The Chicago–San Francisco end was assigned to Boeing Air Transport, while the Chicago–New York portion went to National Air Transport. Within a few years these lines would be blended into today's giant United Airlines, and many of the same airmail pilots would become United's pioneer passenger pilots.

The U.S. Post Office Air Mail Service would last less than ten years, with a loss of forty-three lives in ground and air accidents. Some famous pilots would be included among the 2,713 employees: Paul Garber, later the curator of the Smithsonian Institution; G. H. Bellanca, the builder; E. Hamilton Lee, one of United's pioneers; and Russ Holderman.

But Holderman was long gone from the Air Mail Service when it went out of business in 1927. He lasted three years with the outfit, shuttling between Long Island and New Jersey fields, but his eye was on starting his own flying school. In 1921, he married Dot—Dorothy Currier Harris—and they took a honeymoon in his rebuilt airplane, and when they returned, he opened a flying service on Long Island.

"My wife ran a candy stand at the field in Queens Village and I gave lessons," he says. "We worked hard, but at night it was a thrill to come home and toss the money on the bed and count it and take it to the bank the next morning.

"That was the incentive to do something. If you inherited something, you wouldn't get as much of a kick as we did in working hard. By the end

of the year I bought a new Packard car and had ten thousand dollars in the bank.

"I used to put on shows to attract people, so we could do some business. I broke the world's record by looping fifty loops in seven thousand two hundred feet. I used to do one-wheel landings. I built up a reputation as a pretty good instructor. The heir to the Borden Milk money would pay me sixty dollars an hour to instruct him. Some days I'd work up to six hours a day."

They must have been good times. Holderman shows me a picture of four young dandies of the 1920s—he and Dot and George Halderman and Ruth Elder, two other famous pilots. The four of them are leaning casually against a dark sedan, looking properly dapper for the Roaring Twenties.

The only thing wrong with teaching on Long Island were the hard winters, so the Holdermans moved to Florida, where they gave aerial tours of property to prospective clients in the Sarasota keys. ("We were ten years ahead of ourselves," he says.)

He had another mission in Florida—flying bootleg whiskey from the Bahamas for one hundred to one hundred twenty-five dollars an hour, plus 25 percent of the take.

"This was the time they were giving out pilot licenses," Holderman recalls. "I had license number two twenty-seven, but I could have been down in the one hundreds except that when I landed to take my examination, they came over to inspect my cargo and I didn't want them to see those big bags of whiskey, so I kept going. Now the pilot licenses are up in the millions, but I could have been in the hundreds."

While working in Florida, Holderman met Donald Woodward, from the Jello family, who wanted him to build "the country's finest private airport" at Leroy, near Rochester, New York. Holderman constructed Woodward's airport over the next several years, and he taught Dot how to fly. She became so proficient at gliding that she set an endurance record of five hours and seventeen minutes in 1935—"and they even put her picture in the Camel ads for a while."

In 1934, Holderman became one of the country's early corporation pilots, flying Frank Gannett and his newspaper executives on trips around the country. Gannett let him use the company plane in major races like the New York–Miami MacFadden Trophy race. He also flew Gannett's guests and played golf with them—politicians such as Richard Nixon, who came to court the publisher.

"In 1959, when I was sixty-four years old, I was invited to fly with the Blue Angels, you know, the famous drill team. I went up with this pilot and we got twenty thousand feet over Long Island and I told him, 'You know, we're right over where I first soloed, where I did fifty miles an hour, and now we're doing two hundred sixty-five miles an hour.'

"Recently I was in a Grumman Gulfstream II and the pilot was showing me, 'You want to go to Denver, you just push a button.' I said, 'Let me

Top: Russell Holderman at the controls of the Curtiss biplane in which he made his first solo flight in 1913. (Russell Holderman collection, copied by Gerry Patt.) Bottom: By a margin of only thirty-eight seconds, Russell Holderman, left, lost the McFadden Trophy Race from New York to Miami to Max Constant, right, on January 7, 1939. Dorothy Holderman, center, a noted pilot herself, accompanied her husband as a last-minute addition. (Associated Press Photo.)

see the ends of your fingers', and they were all calloused from pushing buttons. That's flying today. You just push a button.

"It's funny, with all that flying, I logged twenty-six thousand hours and never got hurt since that glider at One Hundred Seventy-seventh Street. Then last winter I broke my leg paying my taxes at town hall. I stepped on a marble floor and slipped. The next day they put a rubber mat down on it. I'm just not going to pay my taxes anymore. That's the only answer."

As we walk back to the bar, Holderman tells me how he retired from Gannett in 1961, but still flew for recreation until his heart operation in 1974. Also in 1974, he received an honorary degree from Embry-Riddle Aeronautical University in Daytona Beach, Florida, which also named a building after him.

"Florida," the bartender says. "I'm telling ya, Mr. Holderman, we oughta fly to Florida today."

Russ Holderman looks at his watch.

"Look at this. I promised Dot I'd bring her a sandwich and it's way past lunchtime. No, I don't do any flying anymore."

13

Walter Ballard

San Diego, California

In the back room of the San Diego Aero-Space Museum, where a few old-timers are renovating a Jenny, Walter Ballard is having trouble keeping his mind on the project: Hunting season opens tomorrow.

"I'm going out with a bow and arrow," he says. "Going back in the mountains, just to be alone."

He will use a four-wheel-drive Jeep tomorrow, he says, but he can recall the days when you could hunt by airplane. Those were different times, when the Southwest was a dangerous playground in the air or on the ground.

As the eighty-one-year-old Ballard talks, his string tie bobs up and down. His voice is a little scratchy, like a desert sandstorm. Like most of the old-time aviators, this native of Arizona has gravitated to the edge of the ocean, but his memories are of the badlands he used to traverse, when he and aviation were young.

"All my life I thought I'd be a locomotive engineer," he says, "but when I told the navy I'd like machine work or blacksmithing, they said, 'How about flying?' I learned to fly at the end of the war, and when I got out I went down to the San Diego waterfront and bought a Jenny that used to belong to Martin Jensen (see chapter 22) for three hundred dollars.

"There were a lot of Jennies around after the war. It was a Curtiss JN4-D pretty much like the one we're fixing up here.

"If I could go back to this Jenny, I'd like to fly again. You didn't have the high regulations you have today, tying you down. You could chase a deer or a coyote, or wave at an engineer on the railroad. Land on the desert, anywhere you wanted.

"If I wanted to take a leak, I'd land. One time I landed out on the desert near Yuma because I had to take a leak. A couple of cars drove right over. They thought I had a forced landing, so I had to hold it in.

"Back in 1922, back up here on the mountain, I chased a deer with an airplane, chased him until he got tired and lay down in the shade. Then I landed my plane and took my gun and got right up the hill, but the guy wouldn't let me go through his ranch. Probably got it himself.

"If I was going to buy a plane today, I'd buy an amphibian. Got more versatility. Land at a lake and go fishing. There ain't nothing today like what we did. Out by Yuma, there's strips of volcanic rock that are perfect for landing. Just like they were built for it. Nobody lands there now. Nobody has a plane that slow.

"These things, these Jennies, landed at thirty-five miles per hour. The planes today, there ain't anything that lands at less than seventy. You couldn't do it, even if you didn't have the restrictions. There was more room in those days.

"If I wanted to go from here to Tucson, I'd put those five-gallon cans

in the plane with me. When I needed gas, I'd land, put ten gallons in the tank and fly on. There was no airports in those days, but you didn't need 'em. Remember those gas stations with those old tanks with the glass at the top? I'd taxi right up to them and gas up.

"Of course, barnstorming was the highlight of aviation, far as I'm concerned. I was taking passengers around for five dollars a ride. This parachute jumper joined me, Harold Tibbetts—he's still around here. I wanted to attract crowds, so I'd land in a school yard or parking lot. People would see us do stunts, then pay five dollars a ride. Do tailspins. He'd jump and I'd come down to land.

"I used to do spins. It feels like the whole world is spinning around, if you're not used to it. We'd tell somebody to put a hat on the ground and my parachutist would hang from a ladder on the bottom of the plane. We'd come by and he'd pick up the hat. We flew all over—New Mexico, Arizona, Nevada, California.

"One time I turned the plane over in Casa Grande, forgot I had a bag of tools in the plane, tools fell right in the main street of town, we landed

Walter Ballard standing in front of his Curtiss JN4-D "Jenny" in which he barnstormed in the twenties. On the top wing is the stunt man, Harold Tibbetts, who scampered around on the wings 1,500 feet above the ground. Sometimes Tibbetts would hang by his knees from a rope and ladder and scoop a hat from the ground when Ballard executed a low pass. All for a few dollars from the crowd. (American Hall of Aviation History, Northrop University)

and I got 'em back. Landed in a school yard. Do that today, they'd throw you in jail.

"You couldn't see the passengers' faces. They wouldn't get sick unless you spun 'em a lot. None of 'em terrified. I didn't make any money stunting. I'd work as a garage mechanic and I'd fly on weekends."

As the airlines began regular service, jobs opened up for some of the stunt pilots. Ballard says he got a job flying the airmail in a Northrop Gamma for the early TWA, before they expanded into passenger routes.

"They'd give you a thirty-minute reserve of gas and expect you to land at Indianapolis," he says. "You'd get there and see the boundary lights of the airport, but it was so foggy, I couldn't land. I had to land by my watch. Knew I had thirty seconds from when I saw the boundary lights. Then I'd cut my engine, put it down through the fog. So thick you couldn't see the depot.

"I wasn't too happy with this arrangement, so I quit TWA and got a job with American, from San Diego to Phoenix in a Fokker F10-A trimotor. Lasted eighteen months and they canceled the run and laid me off in 1933.

"I still had to make a living, so I opened a charter and ambulance service from San Diego to where they were building a dam at Parker Lake. One weekend, these two guys came home with me. On the way back, I went to open up the center tank of gas, and the engine quit.

"We were just mushing in, heading for some level ground, when the wind switched. If it hadn't of switched, we wouldn't have gotten hurt. But we came down in the thickest jungle you ever saw, on an Indian reservation near the Colorado River.

"When I came to, I was standing near the plane. I always carried an extra canteen of water, so I put it in their laps, so they'd have water while I went for help. Only thing was, my arms wouldn't work. Both broke.

"I knew there was a road on the other side of the river. This was about four-thirty in the evening. Front end of a thunderstorm. I couldn't crawl through the jungle because my arms were broken. Just had to crash through the woods. Apparently the crash smacked my goggles into my head, mashed 'em all up, so as I was walking my head started hemorrhaging. I knew I had to stop this, so I found this fine silt ground, like mud, put my wounds right down in the dirt, salty soil. Naturally it stuck all over my face.

"I tried all night long to wade that river, but it was in flood stream, and here my arms are floating downstream. I waded all night trying to find a place more shallow. I could see coyotes peering out at me. If I fell down, I knew they'd come at me. Or particularly wild pigs, they would have been worse.

"When it got light, I saw a place where the water was a little ripply. I could see pebbles at the bottom. I don't remember walking out of the river. Must have blanked out, I guess. Next thing I knew, I was near the road. I saw the milk-ice truck driver. He'd seen me dozens of times, but he didn't recognize me at first. Then he stopped and backed up and I said,

'Hey, don't you know me?' He took me to the hospital, then I helped find those two fellers. One of them was unconscious and the other was dead, the engine right in their laps."

Giving up his own charter business, Ballard began flying for Grand Canyon Airlines in 1935, then moved to Central American Airlines (T.A.C.A), one of the largest cargo airlines in the world, in 1938, flying heavy mining material into mountain and jungle runways.

"I can recall one load in particular," he says. "Four loads of diesel fuel, dynamite caps and fuse, four passengers—and just enough fuel to reach our destination. These mind-boggling experiences, plus a malaria spell, finally resulted in my resignation in 1939."

He later helped train pilots for the Royal Canadian Air Force before being activated by the U.S. Navy in 1941. After the war, he became a real-estate broker, finding a prize lot for his own: a three-story hillside home with a nine-passenger elevator. After his retirement, his friends at the museum talked him into supervising the renovation of the old Jenny, which he describes as "a labor of love."

One day a few retired American Airlines pilots visited the museum and heard about his eighteen months of service on the San Diego–Phoenix line. They were in San Diego for a convention of the Grey Eagles, an association of veteran American Airlines pilots. They grabbed Ballard by both arms and hustled him over to the Hotel del Coronado and installed him as the newest member of the organization—and the second oldest, too. Instant seniority.

Ballard says he appreciated the gesture, but he doesn't stay involved with old-time aviators the way some people do. When he feels hemmed in, he goes off into the hills for some hunting or fishing.

"There isn't anything today that I'm interested in," he says, patting the refurbished sides of the Jenny.

"Oh, I'd just love to get in one of these and have the freedom I used to have."

14

Harlan (Bud) Gurney

Woodland Hills, California

The hummingbirds are pausing for lunch outside Bud Gurney's window, hovering in midair like minute helicopters painted by Chagall. The old pilot stares at the tiniest aeronauts, admiring their freedom; hovering in midair is one trick he has never mastered—not as a teen-age wing-walker in the 1920s, not as jet pilot for United, nor even today, when he flies his tiny De Havilland Moth.

He has been flying for most of his seventy-two years, but when a writer drives out to the San Fernando Valley to see him, Bud Gurney assumes the writer wants to talk not about him so much as about "Slim."

They met in Nebraska in the fall of 1921 and stunted together for several years. Their friendship was tested a generation later, when Slim began making public statements about the impending war. Then one Sunday morning just after Pearl Harbor, Slim himself drove out to "the valley" to explain his actions to his old friend. This is where Bud Gurney begins an interview that was supposed to be about himself.

"The tape recorder isn't on yet, is it?" he asks. "Let's just talk for a few minutes. See, I can't tell you too much about Lindbergh because I made a vow to Slim that I would never give away the details of what he did, and I'm not about to break that vow. Let's just say it killed me to hear people question his patriotism."

Gurney is a trim, middle-sized man with midwestern plainness to him. His years are just starting to show in his face. He looks like Bill Boyd, the actor who used to portray Hopalong Cassidy, but he speaks in the American monotone that made Gary Cooper a star—gulping off the end of sentences rather than enunciating too many syllables.

But Gary Cooper characters cannot even talk about their horses without blushing; Bud Gurney, on the other hand, surprises me with his sentiment for his late friend Slim.

"Let's just say Slim did more for his country than anybody knew. When the president called him a liar, he had to resign his commission. Slim would never lie, and neither would I. The only time I lie is for courtesy, like if my wife comes home with a new hat and says, 'Isn't that beautiful?' I'll say, 'yes,' of course. But I never lie for myself, and neither did Slim."

This defense made for his friend, Bud Gurney nods at the tape recorder. He isn't at all sure that his story is important, he says. But people have been telling me to look up Bud Gurney out in the valley because his career spanned the generations from the early barnstormers to the big jets. He isn't comfortable, at first, talking about himself. Western heroes never are. He stares out the window, at the San Fernando Valley overrun by houses, and he warms up for his takeoff.

The first pilot he ever saw, he says, was Lincoln Beachey, when he raced Barney Oldfield around dirt tracks to prove that a plane could outrace a car. Gurney was born in 1905, so the year must have been either 1909 or 1910.

"We lived right near the state fairgrounds in Lincoln, Nebraska, and children under twelve were admitted free. I went every day. When I saw Beachey loop-the-loop, I knew that man's ancient dream was in my blood. Later on I performed in that same fair as a parachute jumper and wing-walker, when I was fifteen or sixteen.

"Of course, I never met Beachey at the fairgrounds. I was just one little boy in the big crowd."

A year or two later, Beachey retired from flying, telling the crowds bitterly that he meant to cheat them of his public death. But apparently Beachey missed the thrill of risking his life with the crowds gaping up at him. In 1915 he went back to stunting, and his wings sheared off over Oakland Bay, and the public exacted the penalty he had tried to avoid.

The memory of Lincoln Beachey lived in the little boy from Nebraska, who after seeing the famous pilot, went home and started building wooden model planes in his father's carpentry shop.

"I had some idea what it took to make an airplane stable." Gurney recalls, "because, after all, a model had no internal control. It had to fly by itself. Kids of that time were ahead of our own designers, who had no such concepts of trying to make them fly. The planes of World War One were terribly unstable. The faster you'd go, the faster the tails would lift, and the more you would dive. The early airplanes wouldn't come out of tailspins, either. There was a complete lack of understanding of some of the principles of stability."

Gurney tells how he studied the Standard airplane in the showroom of the Nebraska Aircraft Corporation on North Twelfth Street in Lincoln, and in 1922 built a faithful model.

"It had about a twenty-four-inch span, using pins and piano wire, strands of the finest wire, moving parts, and all painted up just like the bigger one. I set it down deliberately in the showroom just next to the main one, and I timed it so the boss and his staff came in. He took a look at it and said, 'I'd like to have that. How much would you take for that?' And I said, 'A job.'"

In a short time Bud Gurney proved his value to Nebraska Aircraft, which sold and repaired airplanes, and gave flying lessons. He thought he was an expert on Hispano engines—until the day a new aviation student came in, a college dropout from Minnesota.

"I was told to instruct the new student," Gurney recalls. "We sat down and he started asking questions, and I started telling him all I knew, and the next thing I knew, I was asking him. I wasn't a very good teacher, was I?"

The student, Charles Lindbergh, still had ninety dollars worth of lessons due him, but the manager had to sell the instructional plane to raise some money. To compensate Lindbergh, the manager offered him a parachute, allegedly worth ninety dollars, made out of cotton cloth and a car steering wheel. Gurney told Lindbergh the parachute wasn't worth the money or his life.

"I told him, 'Slim, you know how dangerous a parachute jump is. I'd be as likely to make a parachute jump as you.'"

But Lindbergh accepted the offer, and when he made his first jump he landed in a field, Gurney recalls.

"I raced out to see if he was all right and Slim handed me the parachute and said, 'Buddy, it's your turn.' I tried to back out by saying I was a minor and my parents wouldn't let me and the boss wouldn't let me, but Slim said 'Why don't you ask him?' To my amazement, the boss said OK.

"I'd only been in an airplane once in my life. To make it worse, the boss, Ray Page, sold a passenger a ride for ten dollars while I was making this jump. In those days, the parachute was tied out on the wing. We had to walk out on the wing almost halfway, sit down, fasten the parachute on, then swing down, hang below the parachute, and pull the laces—and then you fell free. That's how it was done. The parachute was made out of muslin, same as you use for shirts, just a big sheet, and fish cord, with an automobile steering wheel at the bottom, and harness snaps, with a belt around your waist.

"Well, I was scared to death, shaking in my boots, but I wasn't going to show it. I climbed in the cockpit, the passenger climbed in after me, I walked out on the wing when we reached fifteen hundred feet or two thousand.

"I had never been out of the cockpit before. It sure felt awful empty out there. I sat down, fastened on the parachute, did as I was told, sat down, hung below the bag, and waited until I heard the whistle, he had a particularly shrill whistle. He put two fingers to his mouth, and you know what kind of whistle that is. Pretty soon I heard the whistle and I pulled the rip cord.

"Scared—oh boy. Figured I'd never live another day. This is the end. The parachute blossomed. I could hear the airplane circling around, I could hear the church bells ringing in the distance, it was a Sunday morning. Trains puffing over the hump where they were switching freight cars over in West Lincoln.

"I could hear the voice of the crowd below, voices, it was beautiful. I enjoyed every moment of it, Slim chasing across the field in his motorcycle the way the wind blew me.

"I made a normal landing. That was my first jump, but it wasn't my last. I made so many, I lost track."

Living on his own, not eating properly, Gurney was both slight for his age and hungry—perfect attributes for a wing-walker. A former circus acrobat named Dick Hazelrig took him down to the YMCA and taught him tricks on the trapeze. Then it was just a simple matter of transferring those tricks to an airplane flying thirty, forty feet above the ground.

"I'd have a cable tucked into my coveralls and attached to the plane," Gurney said, "but of course from the ground you couldn't see that too well. I'd have this iron bar hanging down, and I'd hang by my feet, or by my teeth, and people would say, here is this crazy guy going fifty, sixty miles per hour hanging by his teeth. But if you look carefully, my feet are in a straight line and sticking up over the trapeze, but you can't see the cable because it was too thin. It looked dangerous, but you couldn't have pulled me off with a truck.

"That was showmanship. Aviation was not for transportation then. The airplane couldn't go as fast as a train for any distance."

The aviators were out to give the crowd a thrill, not to transport them. Lincoln Beachey had known the secret of the crowd in 1910 and both Lindbergh and Gurney knew it in 1922.

One time Lindbergh came back laughing and told Gurney he had nearly got arrested up in Wyoming for making a dummy out of coveralls, a helmet, boots, and gloves and chucking it over the fairgrounds from one hundred feet. The crowd got so excited over the falling body that the sheriff would have arrested Lindbergh if he could have figured out what statute he had broken.

Lindbergh now had his first airplane: that cantankerous World War I surplus, the Jenny—it "was always on the ragged edge of not flying," Gurney says.

One day Slim and Gurney placed a sandbag on the wing of the Jenny to test it for parachuting, but the plane refused to lift more than ten feet above the ground, skimming over cattle, horses, cars, houses, and people, until it ditched in a wheatfield and they cut the sandbag free. Then the Jenny flew like a dream back to the airfield.

"The Jenny was just too sensitive for that excess weight," Gurney says.

Gurney recalls how Lindbergh left Nebraska in 1923 to barnstorm, but they agreed to meet at the air races in St. Louis later that year. Gurney was nearly broke, so he shipped his parachute to St. Louis and jumped a freight train across the Midwest, until he spotted Lambert Field from his perch in a banana car. He rolled off the train, down an embankment, washed his face in the clear stream, and walked to the airfield. He couldn't afford the two-dollar admission, so he waited outside until somebody identified him as a competitor.

The first event was a race to the ground by parachute.

"We would all leave airplanes at the same time," Gurney recalls. "The first one to hit the ground won—if he was still alive."

The other competitors were slick army paratroopers, with silk parachutes and shoulder harnesses and the chutes strapped on their backs, who could open their chutes as they plummeted. (By this time, the army had adopted parachutes, too late for all the pilots who died during the war for lack of one.)

Gurney's homemade parachute had to be opened as he dropped from the wing, but his stunting days had taught him a few tricks, and besides: "I needed the money. I wasn't going to eat unless I won.

"The military men went right past me," he recalls. "But I knew how to slip a chute. I grabbed a quarter of the shroud lines, and went up hand over hand, till I had hold of the canopy, and it waved like a flag."

The effect of his maneuver, which he describes with his hands, is to tauten the chute, reducing the drag of the canopy and making it fall faster. But it has a few inherent dangers, Gurney says.

"You have to make sure the lines don't get tangled. I started above the military boys, but by now they had opened their parachutes and mine was folded, so I went right by. When I was around fifty feet from the ground, I opened it up and stopped on the ground, right in front of the grandstand."

Gurney looks out the window into the San Fernando Valley and starts to laugh. "It was spectacular," he says. "The head of the committee said, 'You had everybody scared to death.' He was raving. I guess they were saying over the loudspeaker that the parachute had failed."

He won fifty dollars for that jump on the first day, and when Lindbergh arrived the next day, they teamed up in a spot-landing contest, and Gurney finished second. He won money on all three days, pitting his slender body against the laws of gravity, accumulating enough money to go back to high school. (For all his experiences, Gurney was still just a teenager.)

Charles (Slim) Lindbergh and Harlan (Bud) Gurney during their barnstorming friendship in Nebraska in 1922. (United Airlines)

On the last day, with his pocket bulging with money for another year of school, he was asked to make one more jump into the grandstand, a final thrill for the fans who had been so nice all week. He couldn't say no.

Gliding down from two thousand feet, slipping his chute for speed, Gurney saw another pilot coming in to land.

"He didn't see me—almost ran into my parachute. At the last second he saw it and poured on the coal, and pulled up. Well, the downwash from the wings and the flutterblast at the same time blew my canopy closed. The rest of my fall was headfirst. I landed on one arm, fell clear across the rest of my body, and broke my arm pretty badly."

The hospital bill ate up all his high school money and more, and the hospital wouldn't let him leave until he paid the balance. "I wouldn't ask for charity," he says. He stayed in his room until the next morning, when the nurse told him he was free to leave. A fellow named Lindbergh had paid the bill.

"He sold his Jenny to pay my hospital bills," Gurney says, his voice growing even more raspy. "He sold his only airplane, and then he enlisted in the air service in Texas."

Months later the two were reunited when Lindbergh became an air-mail pilot for the Robertson Company in St. Louis, and got his friend a job there repairing the De Havillands that had been sitting around in crates since the war.

"They were all rusted out and weren't very reliable," Gurney recalls. "We had plenty of engine failures. Slim bailed out of two that winter, but he learned to be a very good instrument pilot. We used a gyroscope, the only way you could know which way you were going."

"Slim found out by driving ducks up higher into the atmosphere that they couldn't fly without instruments either—they get disoriented. They didn't have gyroscopes. You had to have a gyroscope to maintain your position in the clouds, to know up from down, right from left, because your inner ear would give you false signals. You had to learn to disregard your own feelings and trust your instruments. And that's the way it is today. Emotions have no place in flying because they're false. Well, Slim conceived this idea. He knew he'd never have this air transportation he dreamed about until we had better instruments.

"I remember one time we were living in a rooming house in St. Louis. I had my license by then and had to make a forced landing in a charter flight. I had to use a flare at low altitude and was very lucky to get away with it. Still, I was sick about it. Because of the passenger delays, we had to hire a car and refund some of the money. I just felt terrible.

"But Slim said, 'Bud, don't be so discouraged. You just want everything to come at once. Hey, you'll see engines that will never fail. Some day we'll fly above the highest mountain as if they were never there. People will climb on airplanes just the way we hop on a Toonerville Trolley.' That's the kind of thing we talked about then.

"Somebody was doing a documentary on Slim one time and they

wanted to spice up the part about our younger days. They asked me: 'Were there any women involved?' I had to tell them no because it was the truth. We didn't have time for it. I don't think Slim ever dated a woman until he met his wife. But I know he used to talk about getting married. I asked him what would happen if he loved a girl and she didn't fall for him. 'I'd make her,' Slim said. He wasn't bragging. That's just the way he was."

In 1927, Lindbergh left Robertson and made his bid for the first mainland-to-mainland flight across the Atlantic. Bud Gurney stayed behind in St. Louis to tote the mail around the Midwest, and read about his friend's triumphs and tragedy from a distance.

Then in 1932, Gurney joined the move to the passenger airlines, which were inheriting and expanding the old government airmail routes. He wangled a job with United Airlines in the Bay area. He remembers shocking his superiors on his first day at work by ferrying a Ford Tri-Motor, with one engine out, across Oakland Bay.

"I told my boss, 'We do that all the time back East. It's old stuff,' " Gurney recalls. "I got off the ground with a third of the runway left."

For sheer terror, he recalls flying a 40-B biplane through the frozen Rockies in the winter of 1932, fighting pass after pass after most of his instruments had stopped functioning. He remembered Lindbergh teaching him that instincts didn't count in the dark, and he felt his plane slipping perilously below the barriers of the big Rocky passes.

"I sent a message that I was going to bail out," he recalls, "but even if I didn't get chopped up in the propellers, I figured I'd hit the side of a mountain going seventy miles per hour in the middle of the night. I might as well get killed in my plane.

"Just then I noticed a box on top of the instrument panel. It was sealed off. I opened the box and found they had installed an artificial horizon detector. There were no instructions, but I could read the instrument and could tell I was headed to my left. I kicked the right rudder and climbed right out of it, and crossed right through the Donner Pass without hitting anything.

"Now why did I have that particular plane that day? Why did they choose to put that new instrument in that plane? It goes back to Slim and me. One time he saw me loop-the-loop and he said, 'Buddy, the Good Lord takes care of children and fools—and you've got a double hitch.' "

The memory of Lindbergh diverts Gurney from his own story again. Old-time western heroes are not supposed to express how they feel—it's just not manly—but Gurney clears his throat and says:

"Too bad Slim's gone. I can't believe it. I still miss him. He's one man who put his own personal honor above all things. He was as compassionate as he could be—loved animals—and he was a tremendous patriot, more than anybody knows."

"I'll admit that when I read some of the things Slim was saying, I wrote him a letter saying I didn't like what I was hearing. Right after Pearl Harbor, one Sunday morning, I was getting ready to take the kids down the church where I teach Sunday school. The doorbell rang and there was this man. Hilda had never met him. We were just married. My first wife had died of pneumonia and Hilda was an angel. She raised the four kids as if they were her own. They *are* her own.

"He said, 'I'm Charles Lindbergh, may I come in?' She said sure. I was tying my tie. I said, 'Honey, take the kids down to church and tell them I won't be down today.' So Slim and I sat in the living room and he told me the story. He said he knew exactly what he was doing. He didn't want to see a whole generation of Americans getting slaughtered because we had no tanks or airplanes. He said he couldn't stand by and see that. That's all I'm going to say on the subject, but let's just put it that Slim knew what he had to do—even if he sacrificed himself in the process.

"He told me in my living room that he never even knew that Goering was going to slip that medal around his neck. It was already done. And Slim never lied.

"Nobody knows how much Slim did in World War Two. He flew fifty missions when the limit was twenty-five.* He was getting forty percent more out of that plane than the regular pilots were—and he was coming back with gas in the tank. They couldn't believe it."

Gurney never did fly in combat. He says he was sent to train pilots after a number had been lost in Alaska ("You never read about it, but it was a fact") and later helped ferry wounded soldiers out of the South Pacific. He says he always wondered why the government never allowed him to take a commission as a military pilot.

"I found out later that United wrote a letter to the government saying I was too valuable flying passengers to go on active duty."

By the time the war was over, Gurney was one of United's leading pilots, breaking in the new machines and the postwar routes. He spent his last five and a half years flying DC-8's between Los Angeles and Honolulu, until a "federal ee-dict" said he must retire on his sixtieth birthday. The way the schedule broke, his last flight was to Hawaii.

"All the time I flew jets, I never had an engine failure," he says. "But on my last flight, the fuel line broke. It wasn't any big thing. See, I never could sleep in the cockpit, not even on those jets, because I figured you're paid to scan the instruments, not to sleep. Nothing had ever gone wrong in a jet, but something could, and you're supposed to see it right away.

"On this flight, I saw this indicator that my number one engine had trouble and I sent my copilot to the back of the plane to see what it looked like. He called me a few seconds later and said, 'Number one engine.' So we shut off the fuel right away. Just a few seconds had elapsed. When it happened, we were at midpoint. We didn't even tell the passengers. Heck, that plane could fly with two engines and you'd never even know.

"The Coast Guard was supposed to meet us and escort us back. That

---

* Without a commission to fly in combat, Lindbergh did take part in combat missions in the Pacific as an "observer."

jet moved so fast, we were off the coast of Hawaii before they even reached us. We landed before he did. And that was the only problem I ever had in a jet."

That "federal ee-dict" was supposed to mean Bud Gurney was too old to keep a plane in the sky. But since giving up his DC-8, he has been flying his De Havilland Moth, a sliver of an aircraft, at a private airport at Santa Paula. In this long, safe valley, pilots can do a little stunting without too much FAA supervision.

"My little Moth feels every little feather of a breeze," he says. "I love to get alongside some new boy in a modern plane. All of a sudden I'll pull away from him. They can't believe that my little Moth can do it. It really tests your reflexes, though. That airplane will tell me in nothing flat if my reflexes are still fast. When I test behind, I'm going to quit flying."

At seventy-two he is still flying, but there are signs that time is passing. He and Hilda started their ranch in 1940. He laid the concrete blocks out himself and built the house room by room; soon they added horses and orange groves, a swimming pool and dogs, in the rural San Fernando Valley. They could look out the windows and watch the valley undulate in the summer heat. But Los Angeles sprawled over the spinal ridge into the valley, pushing a killer tide of suburban tract houses.

A few years ago, for financial reasons, Gurney felt compelled to sell most of the lower part of the ranch. The orange groves and barrier space have now been converted into a stereotypical, newly-built upper-middle class suburb. Perched on the hill, the Gurney ranch has the feeling of a vestigial armadillo, hunkering above the ants. Still, because of his investments in land, Gurney says he is not pinched by inflation the way some of his colleagues are.

"Many of my fellow pilots have had to sell their houses," he says gravely. "Inflation is so bad, and even with the good pension plan United started, some of them don't have cars. Some of them are living in these mobile homes—or worse. But they won't go on relief because they've got pride. It's got to be a sad commentary on this country when our local governments can undo everything the federal government has set up."

Gurney sounds perplexed, like an old cowboy forced to live in a frontier town, hemmed in by a civilization he had never anticipated. I ask him a few questions about ranching as he escorts me out to the driveway, but as usual he steers the conversation back to Slim.

"You know," he says, "I'd like to tell you more about what Slim told me. I could tell you what Slim was really doing over there in Europe, and you'd have a different idea of him. I'd like to break that confidence, but Slim held me to my promise, and I'm not about to break it now."

15

George C. Dade—I

Glen Head, New York

George Dade is surrounded by aviation. He has turned the basement of his home into a mini-museum, cabinets containing models of old planes, pictures of Lindbergh and all the other heroes of his youth, when he was also surrounded by aviation.

Few youngsters had a better view of the airfields of the 1920s than George Dade. From the time he was nine years old, in 1921, he lived right in the middle of Curtiss Field. Later he became one of the youngest pilots at the field, and still later he developed a major airplane-transporting company from his modest beginnings on Curtiss Field. He is a strapping man with a deep voice, yet he retains the excitement of a youngster when he talks about the heroes of his boyhood.

"The 1920s were probably the most exciting period in American aviation because so much was happening at one time. I always say I was privileged to have a keyboard seat for those performances. I was a teen-aged kid living in a hangar on the busiest airfield in the country.

"I'm not pretending I was a major figure in aviation, but if I have anything to contribute here, it is the things I saw—right outside my window.

"My family lived on Curtiss Field on Long Island, right next door to Roosevelt Field, named after Teddy Roosevelt's son, who was killed in France. The two fields were side by side, and the most famous pilots in the world—Charles Lindbergh, Jimmy Doolittle, Al Williams, Amelia Earhart, Elinor Smith—were performing some new feat every day.

"When you're young, you look around and expect people will always remember what life was like at this moment. You don't realize how fast history changes. Now I drive around Long Island and I feel a thousand years old. A fascinating period in American history has vanished from the earth. There was one road marker where Lindbergh took off—but some souvenir hunter stole it during the fiftieth anniversary, in 1977.

"Where I used to live, there were thirty hangars bustling with life. Now there is a shopping center but that doesn't tell you anything about the human courage or inventiveness present at the airfields in the twenties.

"Even with all the deaths, it was a wonderful era, like a frontier town, with something happening every day.

"My first glimpse of an airfield came on Halloween Eve of 1921. We got off the Toonerville Trolley and walked toward our new home, smack in the middle of Curtiss Field. I remember the kids were already out trick or treating, wearing costumes like devils and skeletons, but nothing they wore could have stunned us more than the first airplane we saw.

"We were walking along this grassy field where Macy's department store stands today, and here came this flying machine. It seemed to be bearing down upon us, tail high, propeller spinning, roaring like a thousand buzz saws. I was sure it was going to slash right through my whole family, but it rose triumphantly from the ground like an awkward bird and passed over our heads, belching huge clouds of black smoke.

"Later I found out it was Bert Acosta, the bad boy of aviation, an Errol Flynn type, fond of liquor and women. Acosta was hanging around a bar and nobody knew what time it was. He jumped in his plane, flew a circle around the Metropolitan Life Lock Tower in Manhattan, and flew back to the bar to give the report. A few years later I was bringing him cigarettes at the county jail where he was cooling off for a few days.

"I was still gaping at that sputtering airplane of his, but my mother was more intent on finding our new house. Finally she spotted a barrel that held our belongings, on the porch of a wooden building. A sign said 'Hospital,' and that was our new home.

"In our own way, we were joining the brigade of pioneers—the inventors, mechanics, kids off the farm, veterans from World War One, people willing to risk their lives to be pilots. They were flocking to an airfield Glenn Curtiss had developed on the Hempstead plains. He came down to New York City, looking for a flat place, and when he came to Long Island he must have felt like Brigham Young when he crossed the last mountain and said, 'This is the place.'

"The field had been called Hazelhurst. But during World War One, they renamed part of it after Quentin Roosevelt, Teddy's son, who took his training there before he was killed in France. After the war, the other part of the field was named Curtiss Field.

"When the war ended, Curtiss was developing new airplanes despite the government's slim financial support. He was starting to hire specialists, which is how we got to Curtiss Field in the first place. My dad was a homesteader from Minnesota, the postmaster of a little town called Black-

When Curtiss Field was officially opened on May 15, 1921, a large crowd motored out to Long Island to view the stunts by pilots in their surplus Jennies. (Air and Space Collection, Nassau County Museum)

duck at the time I was born in 1912. He also operated a lumber mill and was an expert in sitka spruce. When he heard Curtiss was building planes out of sitka spruce, he got a job for himself and was given this apartment in the old base hospital.

"I was just a kid, and of course I fell in love with my new home the first time Bert Acosta came roaring down the field. I couldn't wait to pitch in around the field. Our next-door neighbor in the hospital was Mr. Jack Whitbeck, division manager of the U.S. Air Mail Service, started in 1918.

"The airmail came in once a day around five or six in the afternoon. In the summertime that was obviously daylight, but in winter it frequently arrived after dark. There were no paved fields, no lights. I'm not even sure there was a beacon in those days. When the plane would arrive over the field, it would dive over Mr. Whitbeck's house—that was our house, too —and we kids would go racing out of doors.

"Mr. Whitbeck kept around thirty pots of kerosene in an old Model T truck. We'd jump on the truck, he'd turn the crank, drive out to the air-mail hangar, look at the wind sock and point the truck into the wind. Then

we'd grab these pots, light them and set them out, so eventually we'd have a series of them pointing into the wind.

"We were so proud to help. Curtiss had a school where for eight hundred dollars you could learn to assemble planes and fly them. There were probably twenty-five men learning to build planes. There would be wings in one building, tails in another, engines in a third. I can remember one building where there must have been one thousand OX-5 engines. These fellows were always looking for someone to help them steady a wing or go locate an eighth strut. If a man had a ripped wing, he'd let me sew it up or paint some dope on it. It was a love. You couldn't have a finer, more exciting childhood than I had.

"Then came the day they'd take it out to test the engine. I was too young to turn the propeller for them, but sometimes I'd hold the throttle. Then they'd take it up. So many times you'd hear they were killed later.

"Even when they learned to fly properly, what could they do with it? There were not many steady jobs. They had to go barnstorming—create excitement, attract crowds. They practiced these feats at Curtiss Field and

sometimes they'd get killed. Seven men within seven days once. Nice fellows, following a dream.

"All that time, with crashes so frequent, I was absolutely forbidden to take a ride. If it hadn't have been for that, I'm sure I would have learned to fly even younger than I did. It was an unwritten law that I'd be disowned or beaten.

"By the time I was fourteen, in 1926, I was walking around the hangars looking for a job. Harry Rogers, a former World War One pilot, had purchased amphibians made out of plywood. If the wood was not varnished regularly, moisture would get in. The outside was easy to varnish, but a full-sized man could not get within ten, twelve feet of the narrow tail. I'm six feet four now, but I was just a little fellow at the time, and Rogers said, 'Maybe we could give you a job. Start at the tip of the tail and work your way out.' Using that varnish in the narrow tail, I was almost asphyxiated twice, but they pulled me out just in time. That was my first job. As in

The bad boy of aviation, Bert Acosta, could fly anything with an engine and a propeller, but sometimes the boys had to bring him cigarettes down at the county jail. (Left: Gerard H. Hughes. Right: The Garden City Archives)

Intense Glenn Curtiss, who brought aviation to Long Island, at the wheel of one of his early Pusher biplanes. (Air and Space Collection, Nassau County Museum)

so many of my stories about early aviation, the punch line is this—Harry Rogers was later killed in an airplane.

"I used to spend a lot of time at Hangar Seventeen when Igor Sikorsky was taking the biplane wings off the Jenny and turning it into a monoplane. Or on Saturday I'd take my father's lunch pail to the Curtis shop where

An early visitor to Curtiss Field was Captain Charles Nungesser, left, France's leading war ace. The hero appeared in aviation films and barnstormed around the United States before returning home. In 1927 he tried to make the difficult east-west crossing of the Atlantic but disappeared over the English Channel. He is shown chatting with a Major Hensley and J. E. Whitbeck, manager of the eastern division of the U.S. Air Mail (Edwin B. Emerson)

(Overleaf) The Curtiss plant on Stewart Avenue in Garden City, 1917. At the left is the first Curtiss Eagle and on the right is a Curtiss F pusher flying boat, predecessor to the NC4, the first plane to cross the Atlantic, in 1919. (Air and Space Collection, Nassau County Museum)

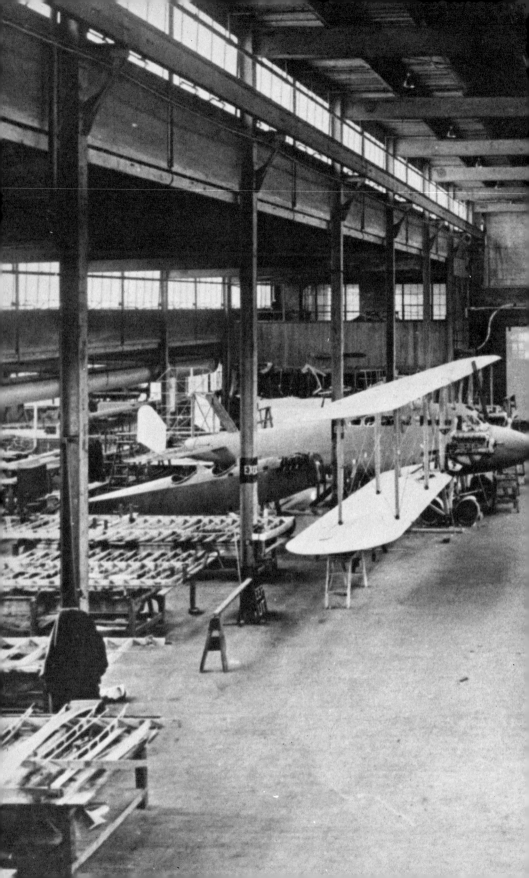

they were making planes for Al Williams and Jimmy Doolittle. The smell of the dope—banana-oil glue—was just so pungent, I loved it. I still love it.

"There came a time when Curtiss was laying off workers. There was no money because Congress had not adequately supported the industry after the war. My father could see there was no future for him at Curtiss, so he got the idea of building prefab garages and small bungalows. He laid out a factory in Hangar Sixty, the oldest hangar on the field, built all the way back in 1909 by John Moisant. It even had Moisant's name on it. My father built a demonstration bungalow right inside the hangar. In 1924 we moved from the base hospital to Hangar Sixty. One day a plane hit a telephone pole in front of the house and for two days we were without electricity.

"I don't think my mother minded so much being at the edge of the field. I think she was just afraid I would be part of the next tragedy. Flying was still a no-no for me.

"But I'd haunt the hangars, particularly in 1927, when so many pilots were competing for the twenty-five thousand dollar Orteig Prize. I knew Bert Acosta pretty well by this time, and for a while it looked like he was going to fly Charles Levine's plane, but the two of them were both too eccentric to get along, so Levine got together with Clarence Chamberlin.

"I got to know some of the mechanics on the field, and even in my immature judgment, if I were to put a bet on who would be the first to cross the Atlantic, I would have put the money on Admiral Byrd. He had unlimited finances.

"Then, here came this fellow just in from the West Coast. Although there was a certain aura to him, his airplane just didn't look as sturdy as the others.

"I remember the false alarm early in May when Nungesser and Coli, the two Frenchmen, were supposed to land in New York. I went out and turned on the beacon so they could see the field, but they disappeared over the English Channel. The French were so disappointed, but that gave the Americans at our field a second chance.

"I was only fifteen that year, so I can't say I really met Lindbergh. Oh, but I used to see his airplane. One morning just before his epic flight I saw him sitting in the cockpit, his ear cocked out the window, listening to the engine. My only contribution to that flight was finding a chamois strainer for making sure the gasoline was clean.

"I can't say I really rooted for Lindbergh over the others. On the morning of May twentieth, I was sleeping at the other end of the airport, a mile and a half away. So many mornings, I used to wake up before dawn and walk over to the field, to see who was flying, before I went to school. Because of the rain the night before, I slept late on the twentieth, until it was time for school.

"I felt sick when I found he had taken off, but then again, people were trying new flights all the time. When he landed in Paris, that made it a worldwide event, and I felt double sick about missing it. When he returned to Roosevelt Field, I helped lay out a big circle of cars to welcome him. By that time, he was a hero to everybody—particularly to me. In later years his image would inspire me toward a career in aviation.

"I'd have to admit, I've been tempted to tell people I was there. But a couple of guys know I wasn't, and once they knew, it was hard to change my story."

IV
The Age of Heroes

By the middle of the 1920s, stunts and homemade airplanes were going out of style. Commercial aviation was being born, with a new emphasis on endurance, consistency, high technical skill—and teamwork.

No longer could somebody putter around in an old garage, build some hybrid airplane with no help from anybody, and fly it off some isolated flatland, hoping to surpass the factory-built planes and engines already in the sky. The level of knowledge was too high, too sophisticated, and too widely dispersed to encourage solitary geniuses. Ironically, it was just this triumph of the team over the individual that produced the greatest number of individual heroes and heroines in the history of aviation—men and women who in company-built craft captured the hearts and suspended the breathing of the multitudes. These aviators could push an airplane for the first time to its ultimate capacity, and their reward was to be featured in newsreels and front-page headlines. It was they who took the risk, but they were relying on machines built by dozens or hundreds of others.

Just a few of these celebrity-pilots were: Lindbergh, Byrd, Chamberlin, Doolittle, Elinor Smith, Hawks, Earhart, Post, Maitland and Hegenberger, Goebel, Jensen, Gentry, Costes, LeBrix, Bellonte, Assollant, Lotti.

Many forces combined to produce this golden age of aviation: the giddy, positive mood of the twenties; the fact that one success engendered another success; the courage of the pilots; the quest for scientific advance. And money. Big companies were starting to make large amounts of money producing airplanes, engines, stabilizing devices, radios, and field equip-

ment. Profit bolstered courage in dozens of different ways. Hopes for bo-
nuses and salaries lured new pilots. Newspapers, magazines, and newsreels
offered big fees for "how-I-did-it" features. Commercial endorsements
were available. Big spenders put up prizes for the first run between two
points.

Probably the most important prize was offered in 1919 by Raymond
Orteig, a Frenchman who owned two hotels in New York City: twenty-five
thousand dollars for the first nonstop link between New York and Paris. By
the time the Orteig Prize was finally collected—eight years later—at least
seventy-five persons had crossed the North Atlantic by air, one way or the
other, but never on a mainland-to-mainland nonstop flight.

The barrier was both physical and psychological, and cost more than a
few lives. Flying over water was far more dangerous than flying over land,
where any flat space was a suitable landing field for a 1920s craft. The
Atlantic had its stepping-stones like the Canadian coast, Bermuda, the
Azores, England, and Ireland, but for the big jump the pilots poised at the
edge of the water, like small children waiting for somebody else to stick a
toe in first.

Because the Atlantic winds blew eastward consistently, it seemed logical to fly from New York to Paris. In 1926, the French war ace, René
Fonck, prepared a Sikorsky plane at Roosevelt Field, Long Island. But the
overloaded craft flopped into a gully that separated the higher Roosevelt
Field (on the east) from the lower Curtiss Field (on the west), and crashed,
killing two of the crew.

In April of 1927, two U.S. Navy officers, Stanton H. Wooster and Noel
Davis, crashed and died in a preparation flight in Virginia. Tony Fokker
damaged the plane he had prepared for Richard Byrd, when he hit a
muddy spot in a routine landing at Teterboro, New Jersey. Early in May of
1927, another French war hero, Charles Nungesser, made a grim and
gallant effort to buck the headwinds from Paris to New York. But he and
his colleague, François Coli, disappeared over the English Channel.

After this tragic process of elimination in the spring of 1927, nobody
on the French side was quite ready to follow Nungesser, but three planes
gathered at the best field in America, the Roosevelt–Curtiss complex on
Long Island. Byrd, in his repaired Fokker, made last-minute adjustments
in the early days of May. Charles Levine's powerful Bellanca proved it
could endure the time barrier of an ocean flight when Clarence Chamberlin and Bert Acosta kept it aloft for fifty-one hours over Roosevelt Field.
But the ocean may have seemed a more formidable barrier than the clock,
and Levine was still puttering with the plane and arguing with his pilots
when Charles Lindbergh arrived on May 12.

The young airmail pilot, who had arranged his financing in St. Louis
and supervised the preparation of the plane at Claude Ryan's company in
San Diego, was in a hurry. He worked almost around the clock in Hangar
16 at Curtiss Field, where the Wright Whirlwind engine people put him.
He wanted to be first across the Atlantic. There was no logical timetable,

but a three-way race—or maybe even a dare—to see who would try it first.

Among the men most closely involved in the Lindbergh operation were John Frogge and Harry Bruno. Frogge was a young reporter for *The New York Times*, assigned to trail Lindbergh twenty-four hours a day, as he describes in chapter 16. Bruno, once a pioneer pilot, was one of the publicity agents assigned by Wright to protect the introverted young pilot. In chapter 17, Bruno describes those hectic days leading up to Lindbergh's flight, eight days after his arrival on Long Island.

The breakthrough by Lindbergh was a breakthrough for a dozen other pilots. Both Chamberlin and Byrd reached Europe nonstop within weeks after Lindbergh had proved it could be done. The manufacturers began spending money for a variety of testing and promotional flights that produced new stars overnight.

Elinor Smith, a teen-ager who attracted headlines by flying under the New York City bridges to help win a bet, was soon subsidized by manufacturers. The teen-ager with the broad grin soon broke most endurance records and became the most celebrated female pilot in America (chapter 18)—ahead of her friend, Amelia Earhart.

While most builders tried to improve upon established design, a few dreamers still tried radical new approaches. In chapter 19, George Smith, who was a mechanic in a shop on Long Island recalls how a wealthy pilot named Len Bonney believed an airplane could be shaped like a gull, and Smith also recalls Len Bonney's last flight.

The success by Lindbergh and the loss of Nungesser in 1927 was a blow to French pride, and several other French pilots died trying to compensate in 1927 and 1928. Because of public pressure over the deaths, the French government banned long-distance "raids." But one dashing Parisian, Armand Lotti, smuggled his airplane from Le Bourget, France, to a sandy beach in Maine, to restore French aviation honor. In chapter 20, Arthur Schreiber provides a bird's-eye view of one of France's most unusual celebrities. And in chapter 21, Armand Lotti tells his own story of the first nonstop crossing by a French crew.

The other ocean—the Pacific—was an even more formidable barrier to long-distance flights, because of its spaciousness. Yet in June of 1927, only a month after Lindbergh crossed the Atlantic, Lester J. Maitland and Albert F. Hegenberger, with only a two-degree margin for miscalculation over twenty-four hundred miles, linked Oakland with Honolulu in the first nonstop flight. This remarkable feat produced the enthusiasm for one of the most gory events of that decade, the Dole Race of August 1927, which Martin Jensen (chapter 22) was happy to survive.

Jensen also excelled at endurance flights, first on one tankload of fuel, later with primitive refueling methods. One of his friends and competitors was Viola Gentry, a poor girl from North Carolina who worked as a cashier to support her love of flying. In 1929, Gentry proved that not even a massive hickory tree could keep her out of the skies (chapter 23).

In a very few years, aviators proved they could overcome not only spans of ocean but barriers of darkness and fog. Advances were made by test pilots like Jimmy Doolittle, who made the first "blind" instrument-only flight over Roosevelt Field in 1929, with a hood over his cockpit.

But there was still one obstacle left as the twenties ended: The brutal headwinds blowing from North America toward Europe had precluded the first France–New York nonstop flight. In 1930, Dieudonné Costes and Maurice Bellonte became Lindberghs-in-reverse when they flew from Paris to Long Island. Their machine and their skills had become so sophisticated that they arrived—as Bellonte notes in chapter 24—"two minutes late." It was a modest flaw. The fact was, aviation was right on time.

16

John Frogge

Westbury, New York

On the morning of May 20, 1927, when Charles Lindbergh was about to head east toward Paris, seventeen people were allowed inside the police ropes at Roosevelt Field. One of them was John Frogge, a young reporter for *The New York Times.*

John Frogge has outlived the man he covered. At an age when most men are happy to be pushing a shuffleboard stick, Frogge works almost exactly on the spot where Lindbergh lifted above the telephone wires and disappeared to glory.

The area has totally changed now. Huge department stores and grotesque Chinese restaurants have gobbled up the flatlands. On the eastern fringe of Roosevelt Field there is now a harness-racing track—Roosevelt Raceway, which employs John Frogge as a public speaker. Most of the time Frogge delivers speeches to community groups on the glamour of horses pulling buggies around an oval track, but in his seventy-seventh year—the fiftieth anniversary of Lindbergh's flight—he found more people asking him: "What was Lindbergh really like? What was it like that morning of May twentieth?"

Well, he says, it was exciting. Aviation was a front-page international sport in the 1920s, bigger than any pastime in America today. Reporters gave Admiral Byrd as much "ink" as they gave Babe Ruth or Calvin Coolidge, who was president of the United States. The readers wanted to know what Clarence Chamberlin ate for breakfast, and how his engine was tuning up.

149

"The *Times* told me to follow Lindbergh," Frogge recalls. "In those days, that meant staying with him twenty-four hours a day."

He laughs about it now: the front-page anxiety for scoops, the speculation over who was going to take off first. But in 1927 it was a big deal.

We talk about the rainy days of May 1927 on a rainy afternoon in 1977, while we enjoy lunch in a French restaurant called Ty Coz, near Roosevelt Raceway. John Frogge (the name rhymes with "vogue") is a huge man, closer to three hundred than two hundred pounds. He speaks with the high-pitched twang of Mud River Valley in western Kentucky. As courses come and go, John Frogge relishes the telling his story even more than the meal.

"I worked in Louisville for a while, then I came to New York in 1922. I tried getting a job at the *Times*, but there were ten, twenty, fifty reporters applying every day. I went to the YMCA employment office, just looking for any kind of work, and they told me they had a job as a clerk at *The New York Times*. I couldn't believe it. I filed things in the morgue for eighteen dollars a week, right next to the newsroom. I'd go in there every chance I got and try to write something. After a while I got transferred in there."

He had no background in aviation. The *Times* already had two reporters on that beat—Lauren (Deke) Lyman and Russell Owens, both of whom would later win Pulitzer Prizes for their work at the *Times*—but there was more than enough work for Frogge, too. The fields of Long Island were bustling with stunt pilots and barnstormers, and the new breed of serious, long-distance, navigators, the endurance pilots, the builders, and the dreamers.

"Everybody was nuts, but some were nuttier than others," Frogge says. "There were young guys arriving every day. They'd sleep in barn lofts and trade their bicycles in for flying lessons.

"These guys were characters. They were originals. Casey Jones—they told him his eyes were bad. He took out a Hawk, did every stunt in the book, then buzzed over the field and touched his wheels on the roof of the hangar without killing himself. When he landed he said, 'I couldn't fly, huh?'

"Byrd was a real gentleman, but he was a little too stiff. One time Bert Acosta was taking us up for a flight. Byrd made the mistake of not putting a quart of booze on board for Acosta. Wouldn't you know it, Acosta landed in a gully flooded with water. He got out in his hip boots, but the rest of us had to wade knee-deep in water with Acosta just laughing at us."

By 1927, Frogge was busy at Roosevelt and Curtiss fields covering the competition among many of the greatest pilots in the world for the Orteig Prize—the twenty-five-thousand-dollar purse put up by a French-born hotel owner in New York City, for the first nonstop flight between New York and Paris.

That pile of money had become flecked with the blood of the pilots who had gambled for it. René Fonck, a French war ace, had tried taking off from Roosevelt Field in 1926, but his overladen ship hurtled over an embankment, killing two crew members. In early May 1927, Nungesser and Coli left Le Bourget, outside Paris, and were never seen again.

These deaths heightened the public's interest in the race for Paris: The pilots out on Long Island were not just aviators anymore, they were an endangered species. See them while they last! Read all about them in the morning paper! Byrd tightens some bolts! Chamberlin fills his fuel tank! Extra! Extra!

"I didn't know anything about aviation, but they sent me out to help out the other two guys. They had a pressroom out there, Dick Byrd put it in. You could sit around, there was a telephone. Lyman picked Levine and Chamberlin. Russell Owens picked Byrd. I picked the screwball who wasn't going to make it."

Frogge describes Byrd as "a perfect gentleman, a hell of a nice guy," intelligent with excellent financial backing, and a head start on the others. But a training accident in the mud early in May put off his attempt for a while.

That left the door open for Clarence Chamberlin, a highly respected flyer, sponsored by Charles A. Levine, who had a history of bickering with his pilots.

"Levine's father was a junk man. Charlie was in all kinds of deals, very excitable. He got arrested for smuggling in the 1930s, always in some kind of trouble, but great copy, of course.

"See, the thing is, you could not know Lindbergh as an individual. Those other guys, yes. Byrd was a swell feller, Levine was crazy. Bert Acosta was a ladies' man. But with Lindbergh, there was no discussion of a personal nature."

Nevertheless, the world wanted to know about this slim, handsome pilot who had raced from San Diego to St. Louis to New York in early May, in a Ryan Brougham outfitted for an ocean flight.

"He was supposed to be the great American boy, all that crap," says John Frogge. "But I remember he met his mother at the airport, not a word, no kiss, no feelings. I don't know if you should use this in your article, but what the hell. He just kind of looked at her and went back to work. She went to the hotel or whatever. You know, I never had that much respect for him."

Some people claim Lindbergh's poker-faced reaction to his mother was just to foil the press, who wanted to see a sentimental reunion in time for the next edition. Others insist the mother-son relationship would be worth a separate Freudian interpretation. Frogge's feelings are simplified by his journalist's instincts: Lindbergh could not open up, could not reveal himself as a human being. He was, as reporters put it, bad copy.

"I've heard so much about him being a practical joker. I never saw anything of this," Frogge says.

Assigned to stick to Lindbergh every moment, the young reporter discovered that the young pilot *would* occasionally talk about his plane—how he filtered the gasoline through a chamois, to make sure not even one speck of dirt would get inside. Lindbergh showed Frogge how he put pieces of aluminum in the corners of the gas tank, to keep the fuel from sloshing around.

While Byrd repaired his plane, and Chamberlin and Levine bickered, Frogge began getting the feeling that this callow new pilot actually knew what he was doing.

"There was this doctor in Garden City we used to see when we wanted to get pills to stay awake," Frogge recalls. "He was the only doctor who would prescribe them. About two days before some deputy sheriff told me Lindbergh had gone to see this doctor. Lindbergh always claimed he never took any pills, but how are you going to stay awake that long without something?"

On May 19, Frogge was on serious stakeout for a takeoff, despite rainy weather. Lindbergh had gone into the city to see a show, but when he received a report the weather was going to let up, he raced back to the Garden City Hotel, which was overrun by reporters.

"I knew he was upstairs in his room," Frogge recalls, "so I was trying to sleep on a plush sofa in the lobby, in front of the fireplace where the brides always had their pictures taken. Before dawn, the rattling of the elevator woke me up. I knew he was going to get out. He was wearing the only clothes he had—riding britches, military boots, shirt. He was carrying a little packet, obviously two sandwiches.

"There was a hard shower outside. Real hard. It was between five and five-thirty. We stopped at the bottom of the stairs. By now, we knew each other pretty well. John and Slim. I called out to him, 'Captain?' He looked down at me. I said, 'Are you going, Captain?' He held out his hand and said, 'In this?' But I knew better than to believe what he said.

"He had borrowed a car from a mechanic, a real disreputable-looking thing. I looked at the clock, called a photographer friend of mine in Queens that I had promised to call. I called my wife. Then I got over to the hangar, but there was no plane. They had already towed it out to the field. They towed it up the hill, turned the plane around. The rain had stopped but the ground was cold, there were weeds all over the field, so you were cold up to your knees.

"I spoke to two, three people I knew. I recognized all the cops, of course. I knew I was either standing on the threshold of history or wasting my time. Then I got the bright idea of putting names down. I was scribbling on a bunch of copy paper—we didn't have notebooks like you young fellows do now. But I wrote the names down on an envelope. I remember there were seventeen people inside the ropes. Most of them are dead now, but I can't remember exactly who they were, because we had a fire at our house a few years back and my papers were destroyed.

"While his plane was being gassed up, I asked him a few questions. Had the plane been load-tested for weight? I mean, had it been taken up with all that weight in it? He said no, that wasn't necessary, because he had engineered the plane for that.

"He really didn't say much. You know, for years everybody quoted one of the cops at the field as saying Lindbergh told him he would feel as if he were in an electric chair from Long Island to Paris. But there was no truth to it. If you were going to make up a quote, Lindbergh was the last guy you'd choose.

"Like I said, there were just seventeen people inside those ropes, and if anybody wasn't standing on their toes and holding their breath, they weren't human. The way I saw it, it was a toss-up for that feller. Instant fame or flaming gasoline.

"I remember he smiled as the motor turned over.

"At takeoff, it was the most breathless thing I've ever seen. At the circus, I can't watch the aerial acts anymore. Going down the runway—well, it really wasn't much of a runway, just weeds and a dirt field, no cement. He got off lazy. He had a bar sticking down from the tail, no wheel, just this little knob at the end of the bar. This would catch the weeds, and they'd hold him back. A bunch would fall off, and more of them would catch on. He must have known something was holding him back.

"But he got off the ground, up-sank, up-sank. You could see the telephone wires at the end of the field. You knew the plane would not break through those wires, and he would go down. Finally he pulled over them. I know from the pictures that he cleared those wires by two, three feet, but from that distance it looked like an inch. The plane was a silver color. It was getting quite light. You could see the left wing dip, the right wing rise, he was banking for the great circle. There was no cheer. Everybody was just getting their breath. We knew he was over the first hump, but it was still three thousand miles. No motor had ever gone that far, pulling an airplane."

It was slightly after 7:52 in the morning, and John Frogge had no story to write because the *Times'* last editions had gone to bed hours earlier. But

The Spirit of St. Louis minutes before Charles Lindbergh took off for Paris. John Frogge, the young *New York Times* reporter, counted seventeen people inside the police lines, but later he lost that valuable record in a fire. (The Garden City Archives)

journalists are creatures of habit, so he rushed to the telephone in Admiral Byrd's hangar, just to inform his office that Lindbergh was off the ground. Then he received a call from Lindbergh's competitor.

"The phone rang, and it was Dick Byrd on the phone. He had heard about it on the radio, down in Virginia, and he asked me what had happened. I was so astonished I just described the takeoff, told of the trouble getting down the runway. But I never even thought of asking how Dick felt about it.

"Byrd didn't say anything remarkable.. He wasn't the type to show emotion. If he had expressed an opinion to me, it would have been in the *Times* the next day."

With Lindbergh gone, Frogge was left with nothing to do. The story now was whether Lindbergh made it on the other side of the ocean. The main story would be written by senior reporters. Frogge fed information about the long night and the takeoff, but when the newspaper of May twenty-first came out, Frogge had no by-line, no story. In today's journalism, there would have been a "color" sidebar about the takeoff, but the *Times* didn't indulge in such frills in those days.

"I wish I could have talked with him more," Frogge recalls. "I could have learned so much. I still saw him when he came to Long Island, but never to say much. The last time I saw him was in a lunch wagon on Long Island, early in the morning, twenty or thirty years ago. He was coming back from somewhere. We talked about the old days, but all details, like who flew what kind of plane, you know, nuts and bolts. He was still hard to talk to. I always liked Anne. She had some sense. . . ."

Even after Lindbergh crossed the ocean, there were still plenty of record-breaking attempts to be covered by the papers. Emboldened by Lindbergh's success, Charles Levine rushed Chamberlin toward a flight to Europe.

"Charlie kept telling the press they were going to have a crew of two, but nobody knew who the second person was going to be," Frogge says. "Just before they closed the doors, the press asked him, 'Charlie, who's the mystery crew member?' and Charlie shouted 'me' and he jumped into the plane. His wife was standing there. She didn't know his plans. She screamed because Charlie never had a lesson in his life—didn't know the first thing about planes. But they flew all the way to Germany before they ran out of gas."

In recent years Frogge has searched the New York area for Charles Levine, convinced the old "Flying Junk Man" is still alive, but he has been unable to locate him. Not all of his subjects survived, however.

"Frances Grayson was hiring a pilot to fly to Denmark. She offered me a seat on the plane. I knew the *Times* wouldn't go for it, but I kept thinking about being the first journalist to cross the ocean.

"I kept telling myself, 'Get on it—go ahead—nobody will know until later.' But at the last minute, I thought about my wife. I was sure there was

John Frogge, left, recalls the Lindbergh flight during the fiftieth anniversary celebration, May 20, 1977. Listening to his tales are Kenneth and Mary Churchill Van de Water, Jr., and George Vecsey. As a seven-year-old boy, Van de Water had watched the Lindbergh flight. (Photo by William E. C. Haussler)

no life insurance for flying on that plane. If anything happened to me, I'd be disgraced. My wife would have nothing.

"Besides, I had no admiration for Oskar Omdahl's reputation as a pilot. At the last minute, I backed out. They hit a storm and never came back.

"But they put my name on a passenger list, and some of the newspapers wrote that I was killed. Later, the *Brooklyn Eagle* did a big story about all those who had sacrificed their lives for aviation. They made a big mat of this story, and for years, every time somebody was killed, they'd run it. I had the pleasure of reading my obituary in the papers."

The Grayson tragedy was one of the last escapades Frogge covered for the *Times*. On assignment in Old Orchard, Maine, he rented a car, but the managing editor didn't want to cover the expense. Frogge says he threatened to toss the managing editor out the window, which was why he found himself working for the *Herald Tribune* later that day.

Frogge worked as a stringer for the *Tribune*, filing articles on the "air circus" over Long Island, but despite all his exposure to aviation he never touched the controls of an airplane.

"The freedom of a bird. That's a lot of crap. When I flew I was just happy to get back on the ground again."

As the years went on, Frogge became known as one of the few who saw Lindbergh off. After the *Herald Tribune* went down in 1966, he got a job with Roosevelt Raceway. He still makes speeches about trotting, at the age of seventy-seven, and people continue to ask him about Lindbergh.

"I've probably met fifty-thousand people who say they were there that day. I've met people who say they saw him pass over the South Seas or the North Bronx on his way to Paris, but that's all a lot of bull.

"People forget that Lindbergh was the two hundred eighty-third person to cross the Atlantic," Frogge says. [The Smithsonian Institution says approximately seventy-five aviators had crossed the ocean, one way or another, before Lindbergh's first nonstop, mainland-to-mainland flight.]

"I don't know if it was the greatest feat in the history of the world," Frogge continues. "Just think of all the science, all the military, all the history. But maybe it was the greatest stunt of all time.

"I just wish I could have talked with him some more, so I could have known more about him.

"It's actually my big claim to fame. Now that the fiftieth anniversary is over, I've got something else to talk about next year. Remember in the Bible, when God took a rib from Adam and created Eve? Well, I was there, too."

17

Harry Bruno

New York City

The picture is frozen in Harry Bruno's memory: Lindbergh has bounced for the third and last time, and now he is squeezing his airplane toward the treetops and the telephone wires. Who at this moment in history is the closest person in the world to Lindbergh? Who is gunning his yellow Chrysler Roadster down the muddy field, gripping the steering wheel and shouting prayers he did not know he remembered?

It is Lindbergh's press agent, Harry Bruno, doing what a press agent is supposed to do, following his client down the runway of life to put out any incendiary incidents that might occur. Harry Bruno was aviation's most prominent public relations man, serving Tony Fokker and Admiral Byrd and some of the airlines, too. He was standing on the ground in Lakehurst, New Jersey, when the *Hindenburg* blew up, and says he helped pull the *Hindenburg*'s captain out of the wreckage. It is what he would have done for any of his clients.

But Harry Bruno was himself a pioneer aviator. Now that he has outlived most of his clients, he feels it is all right to talk about himself—how he flew a glider in 1910, before Lindbergh knew east from west.

These are the personal memories Harry Bruno can enjoy now—not just the glories of others—as he sips fruit juice in his apartment on the East Side of Manhattan, waiting for another spring. The last heart attack cut down that sheer vitality that made him one of the great press agents, but the doctors have allowed him to chat for a while.

Bruno is still the perfect press agent, and he just happens to have a copy of an important press clipping in the December 24, 1910, issue of the magazine *Aero*—a two-page spread on the "Bruman Midget Monoplane."

"This was the smallest plane ever built in America," he says. "Seven feet long and four feet wide. My friend, Bernie Mahon, designed it in 1909 and '10 in Montclair, New Jersey. We wanted to learn about flying from Glenn Curtiss, but on the day he was supposed to demonstrate his own plane, he refused to take off because of the winds. So we went back to Montclair and finished the plane ourselves."

Late in 1910, Bernie Mahon pushed the glider off a platform and sailed—430 feet before plummeting to the ground. In the snows of December a few weeks later, after some repairs, Harry Bruno slid down an iced pathway, soared over a cliff, and glided 265 yards to a perfect landing.

"I was in a daze," he recalls.

They never got around to motorized flight on that plane, because other events took precedence in their lives. Bruno touches briefly on how his parents perished aboard the *Lusitania,* the great ocean liner that was destroyed in 1915. He even makes a joke about being the only person connected to both great disasters, the *Lusitania* and the *Hindenburg*—not an auspicious record for a press agent.

He mentions how he learned to fly a motorized plane in the Royal Flying Corps of Canada during World War I, under the famous dancer and pilot, Vernon Castle.

"He insisted on flying up front in the training plane to prepare the student for a solo," Bruno said. "He didn't want to endanger a student up front, but he was killed in 1918 when he crashed sitting up front."

After the war, Bruno helped establish Aeromarine Airways, Inc., one of the earliest airlines to attempt scheduled flight—operating flying boats in the Great Lakes and along the Atlantic coast. In 1921, he received a trophy for the first circumnavigation of the Great Lakes in a flying boat, but he prefers to tell how he designed the first airline luggage stickers for the line, after he moved into the management-promotion end of aviation.

"It's a helluva situation," Bruno says, sticking up for a client he hasn't represented since 1923. "We had the first flights from Miami to Havana, double daily, starting in 1919. But now Pan Am, which was another of my clients, is saying they are celebrating the fiftieth anniversary of the first international flights. I'm caught right in the middle of it."

One of the legends of aviation is that Harry Bruno was a master of every public relations trick, and maybe even invented a few. He flips open his book *Wings Over America,* and shows how he promoted the flights to Havana during Prohibition: He hired a handsome copilot, a war aviator, to romance the women travel writers in the rear cabin of the plane.

But Aeromarine went out of business in 1923 and Bruno began his career in public relations. His first project was making Anthony H. G. Fokker palatable to the American public, which remembered Fokker's wartime success in Germany. Fokker was now manufacturing airplanes in New Jersey. At the same time, Bruno formed a public relations partnership with Dick Blythe, another former Canadian pilot. One of their first cients was the Wright Aeronautical Corporation, whose powerful Whirlwind engine

Harry Bruno, left center, and Dick Blythe, right center, were both Canadian-trained pilots who later formed the first aviation public relations firm. The partners are shown at the National Air Races in Cleveland in 1923. (The Garden City Archives)

was being installed on all the planes preparing for the Atlantic crossing. In 1927, the Whirlwind was also placed in a Ryan Brougham, to be flown by one Charles Augustus Lindbergh.

"He got to New York with fifty dollars in his pocket," Bruno recalls. "Wright told us our job was to protect him. That's all they ever said. I remember riding in a car one day, Lindbergh turned to this guy from Wright and said, 'Who is this man Blythe? And who is this Bruno?' We were right in the back seat. This fellow said, 'They're both pilots. They're OK.' "

Apparently, Lindbergh never did make up his mind whether Bruno was "OK."

"He told me he couldn't afford our services, but he didn't want anyone else paying the bills, either," Bruno recalls. "So he offered us ten percent of anything he made if the flight was successful. As far as I was concerned, he was a straight-on-the-line guy, trying to show his brother pilots he wasn't a bad pilot. Geez, he had jumped ship three or four times on the St. Louis–Chicago run."

For reasons of human dynamics, Lindbergh seemed more comfortable with Blythe than with Bruno. Blythe was the classic midtown twenties type, sporting a polished moustache and slicked-down hair. He was a bachelor, a ladies' man, easygoing. Bruno seems to have put Lindbergh on edge with his more direct ways. The partners agreed it would be better to have Blythe stick with Lindbergh, while Bruno stuck to business. Lindbergh, who had arrived from San Diego and St. Louis on May 12, was coordinating the race to tune up *The Spirit of St. Louis.* He rested when he could.

"They took a double room in the Garden City Hotel," Bruno recalls. "Dick always described them bedding down 'like two wildcats, each in his own hole.' You've got to understand that Lindbergh was very quiet, very intense. But on the third morning, Dick was awakened by Lindbergh throwing ice water all over him and laughing, 'That'll teach you to wear pajamas.' " They became friends after that. A few mornings later, Lindbergh shaved off half of Dick's moustache."

Since Lindbergh liked practical jokes, Bruno decided to play one on him:

"One time I put forty women in a room, all waiting for the chance to kiss and touch Lindbergh. I told him, 'There's somebody who wants to see you in the next room.' Boy, when he saw that, did he take off. This was three days before the flight. I was just trying to take his mind off it."

People who worked around Roosevelt Field in 1927 suggest Harry Bruno may have offered to provide female companionship to relax his new client. The second part of the rumor is that Lindbergh was so incensed at the offer, he told people he wanted nothing to do with Bruno.

"I never tried to fix him up," Bruno says. "Nothing like that. But it is true he had absolutely no interest in women. None whatever. I remember, for a prank at a dinner, we brought in a chorus girl from Earl Carroll's *Vanities* to sit next to him. We were taking pictures for a series in *The New York Times,* and we got a picture of Lindbergh next to this beautiful girl.

"We made her promise to never discuss it. That picture would have made a fortune for her when he came back from Paris, but she kept her word. I've often wondered who she was. Never heard from her again."

One afternoon when Lindbergh was not tinkering with his machine, the press agents took him to Coney Island. He was having fun on the rides until some woman recognized him and shouted, "There's Lindbergh" and then he panicked to get away.

Bruno and Blythe thought they had a public relations coup when Lindbergh's mother showed up unexpectedly. A picture of him kissing his mother would have hit every front page in the country. But instead, Bruno recalls, mother and son stared at each other like strangers in a brief meeting at the airport.

"She was snappy, not even courteous," Bruno says. "I couldn't even get her to smile until I found a kitten and handed it to him. She said, 'Good-bye, Charles, and good luck.' After the flight, we brought her back to New York and she told me, 'I don't understand your interest in my son unless you're making a lot of money.' I told Lindbergh his mother was a little upset and he just kind of shrugged and said something like, 'Aw, don't let it bother you."

The press agents tried to entertain Lindbergh until the rain stopped. They drove him into New York, arranged dinner at the Newspaper Club and a Broadway show, *Rio Rita*. But first Dick Blythe placed a call to Dr. James H. Kimball, head of the U.S. Weather Bureau, whose predictions were used by all the pilots in New York. Dr. Kimball reported that the weather over the East Coast would clear up the next morning—May 20, 1927.

"I was in a phone booth at Forty-second Street and in the next booth was a cartoonist from the *Daily Mirror* named Ed Randall. He must have heard me say, 'All right, Dick, I'll pick up Russ Owen (of *The New York Times*) and leave around midnight.' That was around six-thirty. The *Mirror* came out with the first edition around nine P.M. saying 'Lindy Flies' or something like that. The press started calling my office, and I had put in twenty extra phones, but they were all ringing. There was so much traffic, we didn't get to the field until two-thirty."

Some people say the crowd at the field that morning was no more than a few hundred. Harry Bruno says there were ten thousand cars on the highways. Either way, he got his client to the field in time to tune the engine as dawn broke. Then Bruno grabbed his fire extinguisher and collared two Nassau County policemen into his yellow roadster and barreled down the field alongside his client, as Lindbergh tried to get the Brougham off the ground.

"Slim had put a gas tank up front, so he couldn't even see," Bruno recalls. "With all that gas, I was afraid the undercarriage would catch fire and spread to the tank. He took off at sixty miles per hour and bounced three times and I thought, 'Oh my God, he isn't going to make it.' He just missed a steamroller that somebody had left at the end of the field and I shouted, 'Thank God, he made it,' and then I remembered I was still going sixty miles per hour, and I slammed on the brakes, and just missed the fence."

"You know, I almost forgot to put on the brakes. The policeman told me: 'Harry, I have never heard anyone pray so fervently, and so loudly, driving a car at sixty miles an hour.' "

Bruno did not see his cient again for several weeks, by which time he was a world celebrity. When he returned on the U.S.S. *Memphis* to be honored at home, somebody in the Army, remembering Lindbergh's army service, sent a colonel's uniform to the ship for Lindberg to wear to the ceremonies.

" 'You can't wear it,' we told him," Bruno recalls telling him.

"He didn't understand why not. We told him people identified him as a private citizen, wearing an old blue serge suit. People could identify with that image. But if he wore all that brass, he would start getting labels. He wouldn't just be a typical American. He would be an army colonel. It was bad for his image. It took awhile but we convinced him. Later he knew we were right, when the papers all stressed he was just a regular citizen."

The two partners soon discovered their job was harder now that Lind-

bergh was a hero. Everybody wanted to make him offers, to get into the act, for tangled reasons of patriotism, hero worship, altruism, and greed.

"We had four big businessmen offer to pay him a million dollars, so he wouldn't have to take any offers for advertising," Bruno recalls. "Dick told them Lindbergh would never take money for nothing. They didn't believe it and asked us to relay the offer, but Lindbergh turned them down. He was very upset that people would offer him something for nothing.

"People wanted his name on everything. Automobile ads. Cigarette ads. He wouldn't go for it. Everybody always said he made millions of dollars from that flight, but he didn't. He made a quarter of what he was supposed to make—and one tenth of what he could have made.

"I always put the figure at half a million—it was two hundred thousand for writing *We*, two prizes of twenty-five thousand dollars each, writing his story in *The New York Times* for one hundred twenty-five thousand dollars, and Harry F. Guggenheim twenty-five thousand dollars. Later, of course, he got stock from TWA and Pan American. But while we represented him, we protected him from social climbers, people who wanted to throw dinners in his honor so that they'd make the profit, people who wanted publicity.

"I remember Marion Davies, the actress, had it all planned, how she was going to slip up to Lindbergh just as the photographers started snapping, and put her arm around him. I knew she also liked Dick Blythe, so I arranged for Dick to accompany Lindbergh. At the last moment, Dick slid over and she put her arm around him, thinking it was Lindbergh. You had to be careful about that. You never saw Lindbergh photographed with women, did you? He was everybody's idol. You had to keep up that image."

The partners felt they did their job excellently, but after three months Lindbergh switched to Ivy Lee to handle his publicity, apparently on the advice of Guggenheim.

"He was still close to Dick Blythe even after that," Bruno recalls. "Just before his trip to South America with Anne Morrow Lindbergh, he heard that Dick had pneumonia, and offered to postpone his trip to give blood. Dick got better, and it wasn't necessary, but Lindbergh wouldn't leave until I assured him Dick was OK.

"Dick always said Lindbergh would have given his blood, but not his heart. Dick said he thought he wanted to, but he had built up a wall around him. I couldn't say. I don't really think I ever knew him that well."

Bruno and Blythe protected Charles Lindbergh before and after his historic flight. In this photo, Blythe, at left, and Bruno, at right, are escorting Lindbergh to welcome Richard Byrd back from his own flight to France, later in 1927. (The Garden City Archives)

Many years later the time came when Bruno publicly criticized his former client for overemphasizing German military strength.

"The Germans respected him, made a big fuss over him, and he ate it up," Bruno says. "When he went to Russia, they were so informal, just like the Americans, that he couldn't enjoy being treated like one of the boys. When he moved to England, he said he wanted to be alone, but I'm not so sure about that. I'm English myself, you know, and the English give you a lot of room.

"I talked to a psychologist once about why Lindbergh liked the Germans and didn't think the English could stand up to them. The psychologist said Lindbergh subconsciously resented the English for giving him his solitude. He wanted all the attention the English wouldn't give him."

In his 1942 book, *Wings Over America,* Bruno chastized Lindbergh's "admiration for a state that professed to make machines out of men." The two men, who had never been close friends, kept their distance after that.

The Blythe-Bruno team broke up before World War II, for reasons Bruno does not explain. Blythe returned to military duty and was killed in a training-flight crash. Today, sitting in his Manhattan apartment, Bruno says "I lost a good friend there."

As he talks, the losses seem to string together: Blythe, his parents on the *Lusitania,* then several people on the *Hindenburg,* which he had agreed to represent in 1936. He had taken a flight from the United States to Frankfurt in October of 1936 and visited a hidden observation post on the dirigible, realizing it was used to make aerial maps of the Atlantic coastlines.

He returned to the United States by other transportation and went to New Jersey to greet the *Hindenburg* upon its return. "They had dropped the ground ropes and the crew was leading the ship to its mooring masts," he recalls. "I was looking up and talking to the captains in their cabin when I heard a pop like a paper bag bursting. I looked around at the tail. There was a tremendous yellow ball of flame and the *Hindenburg* broke in half. We ran for cover, but I did help Captain Lehmann out of the wreckage. Afterward, they tell me I drank half a bottle of whiskey as if it were water."

Bruno says he thinks "certain groups" in Germany put bombs on the ship "because they didn't want to see such close ties developing with the U.S."

He touches briefly on his work during the war, which consisted of setting up special trains to tour the country for morale purposes, liaison and volunteer work—enough to gain him awards and medals when the war was over. He remained the leading publicist for many airlines, races, expositions—almost anything concerning aviation—until his retirement in the late 1960s.

His first wife, Nydia, an entertainer descended from Polish royalty, died in 1970, and in 1972 he married Evelyn Denny Witten, a longtime friend. She has nursed him through the heart attacks of the past year, telling visitors, "He's doing so wonderfully. Mr. B. is so brave."

Harry Bruno gestures around the apartment, which has many mementos of his career.

"You should see my home at Montauk," he says. "I've got Dresden china coffee cups from the *Hindenburg,* a flag that was flown on the moon. It's a regular museum. As soon as I'm well, I'm going to have you out there. The doctor says it will be a few more months before I'm strong again. Then I'm going to start writing my next book. I'm going to make some predictions in that book about aviation. We'll be flying to London in a minute. There won't be airplanes as we know them. We're on the brink of something fantastic in aviation.

"A lot of the old aviators are on their way out. I get letters from my old pilots, half of them are sick and the other half have lost their wives. A lot of sad stories. All I can tell you is enjoy yourself while you're young, because I know that's what I did."

18

Elinor Smith Sullivan

Manhasset, New York

In 1930 Jimmy Doolittle was voted the outstanding male pilot in America, beating out Charles Lindbergh. That same year, Elinor Smith was voted the top female pilot for breaking most of the women's endurance and altitude records. Amelia Earhart had not won that award yet.

Today Elinor Smith Sullivan is a free-lance writer from suburban Long Island. She works in her living room beneath pictures of her grandchildren, who are scattered from Santa Cruz, California, to Alice Springs, Australia. Elinor Smith (most people know her by her maiden name) talks of her grandchildren as one of the rewards for her stepping out of endurance flying, in contrast to her friend, Amelia, who let herself get pushed by ambition into an endless ocean.

"I always wanted to have children," she says. "Amelia never did."

But before she hung up her goggles from serious flying, Elinor Smith was the star, one of the last of the twenties celebrities, a teen-ager with a wide, mischievous smile, who once flew under the bridges of the East River for a prank. Her smile is exactly the same almost fifty years later. A few wrinkles surround it, but it has yet to be dimmed since the era when a headline writer tagged her "The Flying Flapper of Freeport."

"Oh, how I hated that name," she moans.

Elinor earned that nickname as one of the celebrities of that boisterous decade, just as Babe Ruth became "The Sultan of Swat" and Jack Dempsey became "The Manassas Mauler." She came by excitement naturally as the daughter of the vaudevillian Tom Smith, one of the stars of the Keith Orpheum Circuit. Today the daughter recalls how her father loved to recite

Dickens at home—"his Micawber kept us all in stitches"—and how he was a regular at the baseball games, when they were played at the proper hour of three o'clock.

"Still the best sport of all," says Elinor Smith. "Individual excellence. Babe Ruth. Lou Gehrig. You get out there and do it yourself."

There was another pastime that required individual excellence, if you did not want to suffer the big strike-out. Tom Smith had learned to fly around 1916 or 1917 in California. He was "trying to cut down on the time between towns," his daughter says. He was "the first major entertainer to get into flying."

They lived in Freeport, Long Island, so her father always kept his biplane at Roosevelt Field. He was a good pilot who didn't believe that two people were needed to turn over a propeller. After all, he reasoned, you don't always have two people when you get stuck out in the countryside. One day he turned over his own propeller at the field, leaped into the cockpit, stumbled over the wrong lever, and sent the plane scurrying in circles along the ground until a friend grabbed the wing struts and slowed it down.

"You'd have to say he was impulsive," Elinor says with a chuckle.

One of Tom Smith's favorite friends at the field was none other than Bert Acosta, the romantic, hard-drinking hero, who enjoyed stunts like touching his airplane wheels on the roof of a car on the Vanderbilt Parkway.

When she was eight years old, Elinor Smith was taken for her first airplane ride by Bert Acosta.

"The first time I took the wheel, I loved it," she says. "I couldn't wait to do it myself."

Nobody could have had a better set of parents and mentors for a career in flying. Acosta was "a fascinating man, a great pilot," she says, in the midst of writing her own memories of him.

Her father, of course, encouraged Elinor, and so did her mother, whom she remembers as "a beautiful woman with a beautiful singing voice, who had been held back by her own mother. My mother kept telling me: 'There are times in your life when you've got to do it.' "

Which Elinor Smith did, as soon as she could. If personal courage and initiative are any criteria of "liberation," then Elinor Smith was certainly a liberated young woman in the 1920s.

"My general feeling was to be a pilot—not a woman pilot," she says. "Just like women reporters don't like being called sob sisters. They want to be accepted for their ability. Well, I think I was."

Her father provided her with the best of teachers—Russell Holderman, who was then giving lessons from a private field on Long Island, after quitting the U.S. Air Mail Service.

"Russell realized I had learned a great deal from other pilots," Smith recalls, "and he let me solo very quickly. But the way he was a great teacher was in observing me from the ground after I soloed. He'd be able to pick up on my mistakes better from the ground—and he'd tell me, no holds barred."

In early May of 1927, the fifteen-year-old made her first solo flight, just days before Charles Lindbergh arrived at the Curtiss-Roosevelt area for his attempt to cross the ocean.

"He was already a celebrity before he made that flight across the Atlantic," Smith says. "He asked to see the fifteen-year-old who had so-loed. He didn't know I was a girl. They just said, 'the Smith kid.' He was taken aback when he saw me, but he realized I could tell a strut from a wing curve. Later we became good friends, of course, but that week he was terribly busy."

Lindbergh's success stimulated a thousand other pilots to do what they wanted. Elinor Smith received license number 3178 on about her sixteenth birthday in August of 1927, and at first she was content just to fly friends over Long Island. But that impish smile did not arrive on her face the day before yesterday. In the fall of 1928 the young pilot received a challenge she could not turn down.

"By 1928, flying under bridges was passé," she recalls. "New York was a sophisticated area, but this character from Iowa came to New York and decided to fly under the Hell's Gate Bridge. This was fifteen months after Lindbergh, but he felt this would help him somehow.

"He was stupid. He got caught in a downdraft and busted up his Jenny and got picked up, I'm glad to say, by a garbage scow. He was making life miserable around the field, and Herb McCrory, the photographer for the *Daily News*, told him: 'Even Ellie here could do it.' Like I was the lowest branch on the tree."

What could Ellie say? Exactly what she did say: "I could do it."

McCrory was not content with prodding the teen-ager into challenging the bridges. He promoted a little wagering between the manufacturers of the Jenny and the manufacturers of her plane.

"So here's the Curtiss people betting against me, and here's the Waco people betting on me," Smith recalls. "There was five thousand dollars riding on it. I decided to do it on a Sunday. Mack called my father and said he was sorry he got me into it, but if I didn't want to do it. . . .

"It put me in a position where if I backed out, I was yellow. Father put it up to me: 'If you feel it's important enough.' I didn't, but others had put up the money. I told Mack, 'If you're just going under the Hell's Gate Bridge, that won't do it. Let's do the four East River bridges. Once could be a lucky break, but four have different clearances.'

"I was still nervous. I had just got my license at sixteen, and I didn't want to get in trouble. All that week I hung by my heels from all those bridges, checking every angle out. But there was one thing I didn't notice: workmen on the first bridge.

"On Sunday morning they left the ropes and blocks hanging down. That narrowed my clearance. As I headed downriver toward the Queens-borough Bridge, my heart leaped. I was heading for the narrow span between Welfare Island and Long Island City, and I had to remember that going too fast would be a problem, but if I went slow I could ride out any problem.

"Then I saw a white scarf on the bridge. I knew it was Dave Oliver of Paramount News, cranking out the film. Right away, I knew this was going to get me in trouble. All the newsreel crews were there. Fox. Pathe. Trans-Lux. Everybody had heard about it.

"I got under the first bridge and kept heading downriver, under the Williamsburg Bridge, under the Manhattan Bridge. Then at the Brooklyn Bridge, there was a navy destroyer, right across my path. I had to go sideways, make a vertical bank, over the destroyer. Then I went by the Statue of Liberty. Boats were blowing their whistles at me. Everybody knew about it.

"I got back to the field, Mack yanked me out of the plane. He was in seventh heaven. I said to Mack, 'I want to see you. I'll lose my license.' Then he told me what happened. That barnstormer from Iowa kept saying my father had Red Devereaux in the cockpit flying for me. That's why Mack had all the newsreel boys out. That night it was in every newsreel theater in Manhattan. 'Teen-ager Flies the East River Bridges.' It made the Chicago fire look like a Boy Scout picnic, believe me.

"Three days later I got a summons from New York City. Jimmy Walker was the mayor then. My father went with me. I got all dressed up in a skirt, looking like any other teen-age girl. We met Major William Deegan, Walker's assistant, a typical Irish politician, very personable. He

Elinor Smith, sixteen years old, flew under four New York City bridges in 1928 to settle a bet between a photographer and another pilot. (Air and Space Collection, Nassau County Museum)

admitted there weren't many complaints, just from the shipping companies. Then he took us in to see the mayor.

"Naturally, Jimmy Walker knew my father from show business. I don't think he had connected the name until that moment. Walker looked at me and said, 'You mean, this is the girl who flew under the bridges? This is the aviator we have to chastise publicly?' I can still hear the mayor saying it, to this day. There were just the four of us in the room.

"Walker said, 'It's funny for a while.' I told him I was worried. I didn't want to lose my license. This was ten days afterward, when we finally got to see him. Anyway, he announced he was suspending me—grounding me—for ten days. And he made it retroactive.

"The Department of Commerce sent me a letter from Washington, to censure me. I was only a sixteen-year-old. To be censured was not so bad. I could understand their feelings. But the letter from the Department of Commerce included a hand-written note from the man's secretary. A separate note. She said she was glad to see a woman flying, and asked if I would sign my autograph and return it."

The exploit under the bridges made Elinor Smith a celebrity, and it also proved she could fly a plane. Manufacturers began asking her to fly their equipment in races or endurance efforts. On January 13, 1929, she flew thirteen and a half hours above Roosevelt Field, enough to get an offer from Giuseppe M. Bellanca, who was building one of the best long-distance aircraft of the time.

"That was a big honor," Smith says. "It was the first time a female had been permitted to fly that five-passenger monoplane. It was heavy and solid, and a breeze to operate after that other plane. I was holding it with both arms to keep the nose up, but it was a breeze."

The Bellanca company wanted her to break Lindbergh's thirty-three-and-a-half-hour record for a nonstop flight. With Bellanca flying near her in the *Daily News* airplane, sending her messages by chalk and blackboard, she flew a triangular course above Long Island, with enough gasoline, food, cocoa, and chewing gum to stay up nearly two days. But a stabilizing cable came loose and she had to come down after twenty-six hours, twenty-one minutes, and thirty-two seconds—enough for a world's record for women, but a distinct disappointment to her.

Later she set women's altitude and women's speed records, and, at the end of 1929, in a poll by the American Society for the Promotion of Aviation, she was voted the best woman pilot in the United States.

"I hope I don't sound arrogant," she says today. "But I knew I was the best around."

This includes—and Elinor Smith makes no exception in her statement—the woman who is now accepted as America's most famous female pilot. Amelia Earhart had been a licensed pilot in 1923, four years before Elinor Smith, but her efforts to fly had been frustrated by lack of money and little encouragement to women. It was not until 1928, when she was contacted by a promoter named George Palmer Putnam, that Earhart

After her triumph, the teen-ager was hired by manufacturers to test their planes in endurance flights. She quickly became America's most famous woman pilot, featured in newsreels and magazines for her altitude and endurance records. She gave it up to marry and have a family. (Air and Space Collection, Nassau County Museum)

dared to dream of flying again. With Palmer acting as her promoter, Earhart was placed upon a plane that crossed from Newfoundland to Wales in 1928, making her the first female to cross the Atlantic. She was only a passenger on that flight, but her new celebrity gained her access to airplanes, particularly with the aggressive George Palmer Putnam finding sponsors and publicity for her.

Elinor Smith recalls her first meeting with Earhart in 1929. This is a painful part of the interview for Smith, because of her feelings for her friend who disappeared over the Pacific in 1936.

"I don't want to injure her," Smith says. "She was a nice person."

Nevertheless, she recalls how the former social worker asked for a ride in Smith's powerful but heavy Bellanca plane in 1929.

"Amelia asked to take the controls," Smith recalls. "She knew the basics, I guess, but she didn't have that much practice. I don't think she had flown that much for months. As sure as God is my judge, she could not keep her nose on the horizon."

Earhart's reflexes and desire soon made her a superior pilot, and nobody could ever say that George Palmer Putnam did not have *his* nose on the horizon. He married his client on February 7, 1931, and set about to make her a star.

"Everybody knows what Putnam did," Smith says. "He promoted her. He hired other pilots to fly the planes. He called me in and offered me a contract for seventy-five dollars a week for two years, but said I could not give interviews for four years. I couldn't even be in the pictures unless it was unavoidable."

This proposal was being made to the daughter of Tom Smith, to the girl with the big grin who had flown under the New York City bridges for all the newsreels.

"I told him where to go, and a few worse things, and stormed out of his office. He told me he would ruin my career. He said I was finished. He said with all his contacts, he could ruin me. But I talked to Mr. Bellanca and some of the reporters, and they told me I had people on my side."

With Putnam planning her career, Earhart soon emerged as the leading female pilot. She became the first woman to fly an autogiro in 1930, first to fly across the United States in 1932, first to fly solo across the Atlantic in 1932, and first to fly from Hawaii to California in 1935.

Despite Smith's problems with Putnam, she says she remained friendly with Earhart through the association of women pilots called the 99's. They competed in some of the air meets of the early 1930s, but Smith eventually dropped out of the group when, she says, Earhart and a few others wanted to compete for the same prizes as the men.

"She was like Billie Jean King because she felt women should make the same as the men," Smith says. "I agreed with her, but there weren't many of us who could compete with men, and I didn't want to see some second-caliber woman pilot getting killed because of it."

By the time she reached the age of twenty, in 1932, Elinor Smith began to realize the risks she was taking in the sky. She had reached the top at such a young age that she hadn't thought about it. This is why armies like to have nineteen-year-olds on the front lines; they will take risks that twenty-year-olds won't take.

She had acquired a sense of her own mortality the year before, while pushing the Bellanca toward an altitude mark, twenty-six thousand feet above New York City. When the engine suddenly died, she fumbled with the controls, but in her confusion she let the oxygen tube slip out of her mouth and slumped unconscious in her seat. The plane glided eastward, and she did not revive until the plane was two thousand feet from earth. She made a hard landing between two trees on a vacant lot, but she had a sudden insight into why there were not many old test pilots around. Ten days later she broke the altitude record.

Also in 1931 a company had proposed a flight over the Alps at night, into Rome.

"I didn't think I could make it without a sophisticated earth-inductor compass," she says, "and the compass would have cost them fifteen thousand dollars. It was my biggest opportunity. They said I'd make it, but to me, it was a calculated risk. Sure, I'd make it—if everything went right. I walked around Long Island for many an hour thinking about it. I knew people would say, 'She's lost her nerve,' but I canceled it anyway.

"It was a very hard decision. My reactions at twenty-two, when I was married, were far different than at seventeen. What else were they going to give me—more medals? More dinners? I had it all before. I was never like Amelia—to prove I could do it, become a heroine."

As she questioned whether to try more endurance feats, Elinor made a brief appearance in a musical comedy, and she wrote and made broadcasts about aviation. She also watched Amelia Earhart's career take off—the nonstop flight across the Atlantic by a woman in 1932, exactly five years after

Lindbergh, with whom Earhart was being compared in the newsreel clips, the headlines.

"Amelia was a very private person," Smith recalls. "You had the feeling, even in the sister's book, even the sister didn't know her. What motivated her? Her father was an alcoholic, a brilliant man. You see, I had my father around when I was growing up. He was very supportive. But Putnam, he promoted his wife. This made up for the times her father let her down.

"Putnam put her in that Lockheed a few months later. She should have had the Congressional Medal for what she tried. In that last flight with Noonan [Earhart's attempt to cross the world with Fred Noonan, a navigator, in 1936], she was so far away from him, they were passing notes by conveyor belt. She was all alone out there."

In 1936, when Amelia Earhart disappeared in the Pacific, Elinor Smith was already married for three years to Patrick H. Sullivan, an attorney and state legislator from New York City.

"I depended on my living to be near the factory," she says. "You either lived near the factory or you cut it off. It was like cutting off my air hose. I'd been flying since I was seven or eight, but I wanted to have a family, so I quit."

Her husband died in 1955, leaving her with four children. Elinor Smith never returned to endurance flying, but she did keep up with the new equipment, including jet fighters at Mitchel Air Force Base until 1960, and she still flies occasionally, when somebody supplies the plane.

"I like going to the field and flying for a few hours, then doing something else," she says. "I guess I don't have too much in common with the Ninety-nines anymore. It's more social now."

Rather than gab with other old-timers, Elinor Smith prefers to write about aviation. Having written magazine articles over the years, she is now compiling memories of her career. Elinor Smith should be able to write a good book about herself; my visit to her house started out to be an hour, but lasted three times that, without my noticing.

"I enjoy talking to one person," she says, "but I've never been great at socializing. When the women pilots get together, all I can think about is how competitive it used to be, how you had to produce or else the company would find somebody else. To me, aviation was competition, not cocktails."

19

Len Bonney

AS RECOUNTED BY GEORGE SMITH

Farmingdale, New York

Not all the pioneers and the dreamers lived to tell their stories. Sometimes they ran out of time before they had the chance to become legends.

Suppose Lindbergh had hit the telephone wires at Roosevelt Field. If that had been the case, old-timers today would probably only vaguely recall him as a brilliant technician, who had a little bad luck at the end of a runway. If they remembered him at all.

Leonard Warden Bonney is one of those dreamers of the 1920s who is remembered only by a handful of people old enough to collect Social Security checks. In the history of aviation he is a footnote to a footnote. But when Len Bonney was about to test his strangely shaped airplane, with wings that fanned out and retracted like the wings of a sea gull, it was occasion enough for young George Dade to hawk the event on the loudspeakers, to pull in the crowds at Curtiss Field.

The crowds have long since dispersed, but there is another George who hasn't forgotten Len Bonney. He is George Smith, and he spent months in a machine shop putting together that bizarre plane. Smith can remember Bonney pacing around the shop holding a stuffed sea gull in his hands, lifting the wings to show their flexibility, as if an airplane shop on Long Island could construct wings that duplicated the suppleness of a bird.

Smith is a middle-sized man, thickening as he passes his seventieth birthday, his speech mixed with the concrete-and-chewing gum accent of New York. He and his wife live in a comfortable house on the Long Island flatlands, where he was raised.

"My family had a farm out here in Bethpage, across from Central Park

Airport, another of those airfields they used right after the war. I'd be working on the farm, and these planes from Central Park and Roosevelt and Curtiss and Mitchel fields used to fly overhead. Mostly Jennies. Every time a plane would go overhead, I'd watch it like a hawk.

"One day I was down near the Central Park Airport on my bike and I saw a plane actually land—I mean, touch down. When I saw that, they couldn't hold me back.

"You'd get so you knew the pilots and the planes, just from hanging around. There was this fellow, Blakeley, who was trying out a new plane with a guy named Higgins. This day in January, I can remember that, it was plenty cold and I was out chopping wood at the farm because we didn't use coal. Just chopping wood, but I'm watching these guys overhead. There was Blakeley, trying out the plane, doing loops at five thousand feet. Loop-loop-loop, then he'd roll out and go into a spin. I never saw anybody spin like him. As he came out of the spin, he'd land right on the field.

"This one afternoon, I'll never forget it. It was around two-thirty in the afternoon. He started doing his loops, but this time he didn't come out. He spun right into the ground on our farm, a couple of hundred yards away, maybe. There it was. The ground was frozen like cement, and this thing came right in on its nose. This guy Blakeley, he was maybe fifty, seventy-five feet from the airplane, still strapped to his seat. It was like he was swimming in blood. Higgins was still in his seat, but his whole body and face was like right on the engine. Just folded up like an accordian.

"Nobody was coming. I was just standing there, looking at this terrible thing. Then an old car pulls up with four guys in it, and this guy says, 'What are you doing here, kid? You'd better get away from here.' I was just around twelve years old, and it was so messy, he didn't want me to see it, but I'd seen enough."

George Smith had seen enough for that one cold afternoon, but he hadn't seen enough of aviation. After school, he took a job in a plant run by the Sperry gyroscope family.

"Lawrence Sperry was building a two-seater biplane and trying to sell them in England, but one day he was crossing the Channel and got into a bad storm and that was the end of it. His father wouldn't support the operation anymore, so we closed it down," Smith says.

But there were always airplane jobs for young men on the plains of Long Island. The next stop for Smith was Charlie Kirkham's shop in Garden City. Charlie Kirkham was an independent and creative engineer, who had helped develp the OX-5 engine for the Curtiss Company. Today, that engine is recognized as one of the best aircraft engines ever built, and it even has an active alumni association of satisfied pilots. Despite his contribution, Kirkham's name was kept out of the patents and profits on the OX-5. That was incentive enough to go out on his own.

"He developed the K-6 engine, then an eight-cylinder engine, then the Curtiss Conqueror," Smith says. "He had a machine shop, built planes, was a designer, not just an engineer. He was quite a man."

Kirkham's shop on Stewart Avenue became known for its new products. People sought him out with their inventions, and one of them, in 1927, was Leonard Warden Bonney.

Bonney was born in Ohio in 1886 and had learned to fly at the Wright School in Dayton, in the same class with Cal Rodgers and H. H. ("Hap") Arnold, the famed air leader of World War II, in 1911. Bonney had then moved around the country, flying dozens of planes for many companies, and was a civilian air instructor on Long Island during World War I.

There are rumors that Bonney had grown rich in the oil business in Texas, but others say his only source of income was from his wife, the daughter of the mayor of a Long Island town.

"The story was, he got involved with some very wealthy woman on the North Shore, married her, really had a lot of dough," George Smith says. "Those airmail pilots all had more women than they could manage. These wealthy women from the North Shore estates used to come around and just pester these guys. Take 'em back to their estates in their fancy roadsters.

"Bonney used to go down to the beach and study the sea gulls. He had the idea of a plane shaped just like a sea gull, with wings that would work the same way. Believe it or not, Bonney even had a gull mounted on a pedestal. He brought that in to Charlie Kirkham. He knew Kirkham had this outstanding reputation, and like I say, Bonney was loaded with dough."

Kirkham made some sketches, then made a scale model of a gull-plane. The basic idea was to have a curved breast, a tail sticking up in the back, with a steerable fin section. The wings were to come in two sections, made of pieces of metal connected by pulleys and cables. At the end of the wing was another tip, that could be moved up and down by about twenty degrees.

The wings could also be folded back, so the plane could be pulled or driven in traffic, just like an automobile. The cockpit was enclosed in plastic, had two seats abreast and upholstered interior, and was generally more comfortable, more modern, than its contemporaries.

While Kirkham and his men worked on the plane, Bonney used to visit the shop.

"He was always immaculate," Smith says. "I don't think I ever saw him wear the same suit more than three times. But he was small and sickly. I don't think he weighed more than one hundred ten pounds soaking wet. He was on a diet that you'd never believe. He lived on soup, graham crackers, and milk. He had ulcers real bad. We had an old fellow that did the sweeping, and cooked meals for us, and he always had to make up something special for Bonney, because that's all he would eat.

"Bonney was a nice fellow. He told us what he wanted. He'd point to the model of the gull, but he wasn't dramatic, he was low-key. He always had good control of himself.

"We didn't see much of his wife. She'd come around a few times. She wasn't a smart dresser, kind of mannish. I don't even remember her first name, or what family she was from. He didn't talk about her much. He'd come about three times a week, all dressed up, stay until two o'clock, then take off. Later we found he had a girl friend who was an actress and he was seeing her most of the time."

After testing the model in a wind tunnel and watching the prototype grow, Kirkham was not satisfied with it, Smith says. They went back in the shop, moved around a few pieces of metal, cranked up the pulleys and chains, and tried it on the ground again.

Not many pilots at the field had much heart for testing the Bonney Gull, except for Bert Acosta. Bert Acosta would fly anything.

"One time Acosta looked at an engine and said, 'If you put that much power on a barn door, I'll fly it,' " Smith recalls.

In 1927, Acosta had flown Richard Byrd on the third transatlantic flight, landing in the surf off the French coast when Byrd's inadequate communications failed in the dark.

"The man had a national reputation but you couldn't keep him sober," Smith says. "He'd come in around nine o'clock, and by ten-thirty he'd be just sitting there. Still, he could fly anything."

Acosta was working in the Kirkham atelier mostly as a concession to the pilot he could be when he was sober. And Acosta was willing to fly Bonney's concoction, if and when it was finished.

"Bonney was like a flyer with a dream," Smith says. "He was just like that movie, *Rocky*. See, he was a very good pilot, but when we put wings on it, Charlie didn't like the engineering. He told Bonney: 'Look, if you try to fly this thing, you're going to get killed. I want to tell you now, it's too dangerous. I'm not going to finish it. I've gone as far as I'm going. If you want to fly it, take it out of here.' "

At this point, Smith says, Kirkham was developing financial problems and could not afford to keep doing Bonney's work. One day Bonney folded the wings back, tied the plane to a car, and hauled it to the hangar of George Wies at Curtiss Field. The staff at Kirkham's watched the strange plane disappear down the tarmac, and they heard rumors that Bonney was taxiing it on the runway, maybe even hopping a few feet off the ground, preparing for its test flight.

George Smith left Kirham in the early spring of 1928, when he was still owed three months back pay. He was not around on the day Len Bonney decided to take his plane up for a test. But George Dade, who was a teen-aged spieler on the public-address system at Curtiss Field, remembers the event clearly.

"People used to come out for flying lessons or watching the barnstormers or go up for a ride," Dade recalls. "My job was to get on the microphone and tell them how safe it was. If some celebrity was around, I'd introduce them—Amelia Earhart, Frank Hawks, Jimmy Doolittle.

"That day somebody came running up all excited and said, 'Bonney's going to fly his gull.' We all knew about it. We'd seen it on the runway, but we'd never met the man. They stopped all the other planes because it was considered dangerous.

Len Bonney believed an airplane shaped like a sea gull would be a new step in aerodynamics. (A. J. McRae)

"Maybe it would work, and maybe it wouldn't," Dade recalls. "Well, the people crowded around, and the plane started from the northeast corner. You could see the whole thing because the whole field was wide open then. He got in the air very quickly, at a rather steep angle. Then, what happened, I don't know. We'll never know. Maybe he tried to pull a lever, but he lost lift and just nosed over, and went straight in.

"Naturally, the people started running across the field, to save the pilot if they could, but also for curiosity. I must say, the philosophy of people who came to the field was to see something like this."

They saw it that day. Len Bonney died almost instantly, his plane demolished from the fall of fifty feet onto an adjacent golf course. His actress girl friend, who was waiting nearby, became hysterical, and John Frogge, the correspondent for the New York *Herald Tribune,* bought her a few quick drinks to take away the shock. Frogge recalls her asking him to take money out of Bonney's savings account, so she would have something to live on, but he told her that was illegal. Frogge says she committed suicide a few weeks later, the second victim of Len Bonney's dream. His wife, who was also at the field, lived until 1967.

"I don't know what happened to the wreckage," George Smith says. "I heard they towed it away to his estate, but I don't know where that was.

"You ask me if aviation learned anything from the Bonney Gull. People felt it was a bad design, and maybe it was. But you look at some of the planes people have designed since then. Look at the Gruman Wildcat, with wings that fold back so you can put 'em on elevators on the aircraft carriers.

In its first test in 1928, the Bonney Gull went fifty feet up and fifty feet down, killing its inventor. (A. J. McRae)

Or, look how they're moving the wings farther back on the new planes, so they will be shaped more like a bird.

"They keep saying these are new things, but if you go back fifty years, that's what Bonney was trying to do. He was ahead of his time, that's all. He had to try flying it, just once.

"You know, it's funny. I worked on that plane so many months, I knew it as well as anybody. I just keep thinking it's too bad he had to fly it. If he hadn't, that plane would be in the Smithsonian today."

20

Arthur Schreiber

Pomona, California

"He's with me," Arthur Schreiber says, nodding to the guard at the club-house gate.

And with that, we pass majestically into the clubhouse section of the racetrack without benefit of tickets. I worry out loud that the guard is going to come to his senses, rush after us, and ship us off to the Los Angeles County Jail, but Arthur Schreiber just laughs and says, "They all know me."

Good enough. They all know Arthur Schreiber as the friendly busi-nessman who looks fifty years old but is actually seventy, who rents a booth every year at the county fair to sell jewelry cleaner, who strides imperially into the clubhouse section of the fairgrounds racetrack without displaying the tickets they assume he has.

But do they also know Arthur Schreiber as the world's first celebrated stowaway of the air? Do they remember how he nearly got his brains dashed against a stone jetty in Maine in 1929, but instead wound up in a joyous motorcade on the rue de Rivoli in Paris?

"Every so often somebody will introduce me as, 'He's the guy who stowed away across the Atlantic.' But that was just one adventure in my life. I've had so many."

None of his other adventures, however, got the attention of his 1929 escapade. It was the prank of the year—an unknown boy slipping into a French plane attempting to make the first French crossing of the North Atlantic. Some people insisted it was a publicity gimmick; others censured the young man for endangering three brave Frenchmen.

"You can't imagine what it was like unless you lived in that era," says Arthur Schreiber. "Prohibition had just come in, bootlegging was colorful, it was a glamour era, incomparable to anything else in the world—the age of flagpole sitting, human flies walking up the sides of buildings, guys standing on their heads in the lobby of the Metropolitan Opera, people in raccoon coats, bathtub gin, eating goldfish live.

"It wasn't any more licentious, if we're speaking of sexual freedom, than it is today. But there was a great manifestation of offbeat things, and they were all acceptable. And I guess I was a product of it."

After he figures out the first race, Schreiber begins telling me his story. He was a twenty-two-year-old high-school dropout, waiting for something exciting to come along, when three Frenchmen, products of the same era, came soaring out of the sky.

The plane was yellow, a stunningly bright yellow, and in the June sun it looked like a gaudy tropical bird. It had long, sturdy wings—a French Bernard with a Hispano engine, built for stable flights over great bodies of water—and it poised on the sands of Old Orchard, Maine, facing east.

The owner of the *Yellow Bird* was Armand Lotti, son of a well-known hotel operator in Paris, a young man of charm and influence who had lost an eye in a hunting accident and turned to aviation for his next challenge. Although he had taken lessons at the Blériot school, he was neither licensed nor qualified to pilot an ocean "raid." To overcome this obstacle he had formed an alliance with Jean Assollant, a former war pilot, and René Lefèvre, a skilled navigator.

They were three courageous fliers from a country tired of seeing its courageous pilots die. The nation of Montgolfier and Santos-Dumont and Blériot had met little success trying to cross the North Atlantic. When Fonck crashed on Long Island in 1926 and Nungesser disappeared over the Channel in 1927 and other French aviators died attempting "raids" (the French word for the long-distance flights), the government banned all long-distance flights.

Yet Lotti and his companions would not accept the government ban, and they spirited their airplane out of France, and took a steamship to America. Not liking conditions on Long Island, they flew to the beach at Old Orchard, which had a flat, hard surface and was one of the most eastward points in the United States. As the Frenchmen prepared their plane to leave as soon as possible, a few hundred quiet Maine people stood around and watched. Somewhere in the crowd was Arthur Schreiber, a hot-eyed youth spoiling for some fun.

His eyes are still hot today, nearly fifty years later, when he is in his fourth marriage and twelfth career. His voice has a youthful hunger to it, as simultaneously he explains his betting strategy for the first race, analyzes all four of his wives, and describes what drove him onto the *Yellow Bird*.

"I come by adventure from my father," Schreiber says. "He came to this country at the age of fifteen, selling matchboxes, a peddler on foot in Pennsylvania. He wound up making money in the fur business in Ontario,

The little beach town of Old Orchard, Maine, was buzzing in June of 1929, as three Frenchmen prepared to fly the Atlantic. From left to right, navigator René LeFèvre, owner Armand Lotti, and pilot Jean Assollant had been forbidden to fly in France because of the many deaths to earlier long-distance pilots. (Anthony Bitetti)

went back to Europe and met my mother. They had six children in four different countries. Tell me—was he a mad Hungarian or a wandering Jew or what? That's how I got the way I am. I dropped out of high school, tried song-and-dance numbers in the Jewish theater, tried a lot of things. Just waiting for the next adventure.

"When the Frenchmen arrived, I went out to the beach with just a casual interest in airplanes. There were two reasons to go out there—to cool off and see what girls we could see. When we saw the airplanes, that's where the challenge came in. I told my friends, 'Sure, I'll fly, if I could get on.' So I stayed up all night helping the crews of both airplanes that were going to leave. Any way I could, by carrying cans of water, I was trying to ingratiate myself. By morning, around six o'clock or so, came the people and the press, newsreel cameras. I was anxious to see the pilots.

Also poised on the sand was the *Green Flash*, which Roger Q. Williams and Harold Yancey were preparing to fly to Rome in a separate venture. Schreiber says he gave up on joining that crew because the Green Flash had an open cockpit with seats for just two pilots.

"But the *Yellow Bird* was a cabin plane and, in my ignorance, I figured as much room as there is, that's how many people you could get in. Just like my automobile. We'd pile six guys into a little Model T Ford Coupe. That's as much as I knew about aviation.

"When the crew from the French plane came, there was a great to-do from everybody, and I heard one fellow speaking English, and I addressed myself to him. "I said, 'Mr. Lotti, I've been up all night helping the crew because I wanted to meet you, and I'd love to go with you across the Atlantic.' He smiled and said, 'Thank you, old fellow, I appreciate your efforts, but if I took everybody I wanted, I'd have to have a dirigible.'

"So I was sloughed off, and I just about gave up hope, but I still stuck around. Then they called for volunteers to help push the plane up the beach so they could get a runway on a flat, hard beach at low tide. I, being right there, was the number-one volunteer.

"The ludicrous thing about the whole thing was that I had an older brother who was with the Army Air Corps, and he was an experimental parachute jumper who had an old aviation outfit that consisted of a leather jacket and butterfly trousers—leather puttees which I used when we went out to ride horses.

"The day before, when we were at the beach, I figured, 'Well, I'll go home and get into that outfit.' My mother said, 'What are you doing?'

"I didn't want to worry her, so I said, 'Oh, we're just going to ride some horses out at Old Orchard.'

"So I'm out at the beach dressed like an aviator, and the three Frenchmen are dressed in business suits. I look like a pilot, from all outward appearances, and when they called for volunteers, I put my hand on the door to help push, and as I put pressure on the handle, the door flew open."

Is Schreiber telling me he really didn't intend to stow away on the ship, that he merely dressed like an aviator on the outside chance somebody might ask him along?

"Well, yes, the first intention was to cross the ocean if they'd take me, but they wouldn't take me. When the door opened, that was my invitation. I wanted at least to see the inside of an airplane, so I got in and looked around and found this little section in the tail, and figured, 'Why don't I stay in there, and they won't find me.' I weighed one hundred and eighteen, one hundred and twenty pounds at the most, but who thought of weight or size?

"I secreted myself behind this door where there were three inner tubes partially inflated, three pairs of boots and a box with Thermos bottles and wrapped-up sandwiches and food. So I stayed there and felt the vibration when they started, and I felt the thing shake, and this was a big thrill to me. I was in an airplane.

"I waited. I lost all sense of time, the excitement was so great. Then I figured, 'Aw, I've had enough of this, it's uncomfortable in here.' I was contorted so I wouldn't hurt the control wires. I knew that much. I drove my own car and did my own repairs, and I knew enough not to foul up the mechanism. But it was uncomfortable, so I decided to come out.

"When I came out, I saw Lotti bent over a little map table about the size of a card table, and he's very much engrossed in this. The door is on the left side, so I figure, 'Oh, this is great, there is so much noise in here with the vibration, I can just step outside and nobody will be the wiser. I can go back and tell the fellows I was just in the plane.'"

When the large yellow Bernard monoplane was being moved into position on the firm sandy beach, a twenty-two-year-old named Arthur Schreiber found an open door to adventure. (*New York Times*)

Not exactly. While he was hiding in the back, Schreiber had become airborne—and only by a terrifyingly narrow margin.

A few weeks earlier, the *Yellow Bird* had made an easy take off from the hard sand at Old Orchard, though they soon returned when the crew noticed that the fuel was not mixing properly. With that problem solved, they were confident of a similar easy takeoff on the second attempt. But the plane kept lumbering toward the stone jetty, while Assollant squeezed every bit of power out of the engine, and the men shouted in anger and surprise. They had gone too far, defied too many French bureaucrats, asked too many favors, exhausted too much patience to cancel this takeoff. They were either going to clear the jetty or die trying.

Crouched in the back, Schreiber knew none of this—did not know that a radio broadcaster was telling his listeners that the plane was about to crash into the jetty. With yards to spare, the yellow plane lifted off the beach, missed the jetty, soared to the left over the ocean, and struggled bravely to gain attitude, while the crew muttered in confusion. Certainly, nothing had changed in shape or weight since the last simple takeoff. . . .

"I came out of hiding and saw Lotti in the middle of the plane," Schreiber recalls. "I looked out the side and I though, 'Oh my God, we've taken off.' We must have been four, five miles from shore. I hadn't heard any of the yelling. You couldn't hear anything because of the noise.

"In fact, when I touched Lotti on the shoulder, he brushed his hand like this, over the shoulder, thinking it was—I don't know—a fly, maybe. I touched him a little harder, and he turned at me and stared with open mouth, and he said something, but I couldn't hear him, either. He wrote me a note, and the first sentence on the note was: 'Are you an American?' "

"Lotti then took me through the catwalk, with gas tanks on both sides, to the front of the plane and motioned for me to stand there. He tapped them on the shoulder and, when they looked back to see me, I figured:

'They're now settling my hash.' It was the first time I had misgivings about the judiciousness of my act."

Some newspaper stories that followed maintained that Assollant had proposed dumping the stowaway into the ocean for endangering their lives and their mission.

"If he did, I wasn't aware of it," Schreiber says. "Later I learned that under the maritime law, they could very well have done that. If they really and truly discussed it, I'll never know.

"When I asked Lotti about it later, he just smiled, because Lotti was kind of a gracious guy, good sense of humor. He called me 'a devilish fellow.' If he was mad, he never showed it to me, but they must have been mad.

"Incidentally, the motion picture of the takeoff shows they took off in excellent attitude—a little slow, but in perfect attitude. Don't forget, the *Green Flash* nosed over on the same sand a few days later. There's been a few defenses, not by me, because I'm not qualified, but newspaper clippings said my added weight on the tail did no damage and probably even helped on the takeoff.

"Lotti told me later they had difficulty gaining altitude because they didn't have equipment like they do now. They didn't know about rate of climb, weights and balances. It was experimental. They were guessing. The technical parts of it I can't intelligently comment on, but I can say they showed me no animosity."

While Assollant still struggled to raise the plane further from the water, Lotti wrote out an agreement, in English, for Schreiber to sign.

"The note said, 'Whereas we were successful in the takeoff, we have decided amongst us that you are going to be one of us. We are going to assign you some duties. You will either succeed with us, or you are going down with us.'

"Then Lotti went over to a little cabinet and poured cognac into the caps of four Thermos bottles, and initiated me as a member of the crew. Now if that wasn't the peak of French elegance, I don't know what is."

Schreiber's first duty was to operate a slot for a wind-driven generator that powered the radio battery. He botched it up. The wind pressure from outside wrenched the metal slot from his grip, tossing it outward toward the tail assembly. For the rest of the flight, the cabin was chilly because of the opening, and the pilots prayed the metal segment had not damaged any vital part of the tail. Meanwhile, Schreiber was getting his full initiation as a transatlantic flier.

"We got past Newfoundland and night came quickly, flying east. The plane got into an electrical storm. They had three compasses on the plane, no two of which agreed. They tried to climb out of the storm, but the altimeter kept dropping.

"At one point, they ran into a downdraft and started to nose-spin. Lotti and I could see the needle coming down fast—from ten thousand feet to a couple of hundred feet from the water. Lotti grabbed my hand, and we clenched our hands together, figuring this was the end. We couldn't see a thing out the window, just the altimeter needle dropping. You can be sure, at that time, I wished I were back in Maine.

"I guess the man upstairs was smiling on us, because nothing happened. The next thing we knew, we got out of the storm, daylight was coming, and we were flying by the sun. But when they calculated the fuel, they realized they could not make Paris, because they had been driven south. We saw land and ships, and we knew we were passing the Azores, so they made plans for Portugal.

"They ran into another storm, not as serious as the first, and they tried to get back on course. This was the second day, nearly thirty hours later, and we're still flying east, long past due, but we hadn't found land yet.

"The sun was probably within an hour of setting when they saw land, which they later learned was Cape Finisterre, Spain. Fuel was getting critical as they looked for a place to put down. Just the greatest luck in the world, plus the skill of the pilot. They see the beach, near a rocky shore, and they come down lower to look it over, circle around, it's so remote, nothing around, the most beautiful landing. We all got out and kissed the ground. Literally.

"We were all smiles. Everybody. We had lived through it. They were more aware of the hazards than I was. I was oblivious, or I never would have gotten on. I'm not that great a hero. The four of us clasped hands, embraced each other, no difference among the four of us.

"After ten minutes, two kids on bicycles came up, and we tried to figure out what language they were speaking. I had a little Spanish in high school, so we found out there was a village six kilometers away. We borrowed bikes and pedaled to Comillas, a typical, picturesque little Spanish town of around five hundred, six hundred people, nice little plaza, everybody in town staring at us. With our luck, there was an English journalist on a little hiatus with a lady friend, and he spoke Spanish. He nearly flipped when he heard our story, and right away he got on the telephone.

"Now, everything was buzzing. They started to have a big fiesta right away, opening wine casks, everybody dancing and singing. We were having the greatest time, with no sleep at all, you understand, when we realized the plane was unguarded. Lotti was afraid souvenir hunters would tear the plane apart. I said I would stay with the plane all night, so this banker put a mattress in his big Buick and made a roundabout drive to the beach.

"They laid the mattress on the deck of the plane. There were some militia there, too. I was dog tired. I lay down on that mattress and, oh, boy, I conked out. It must have been around nine, ten o'clock. I don't know how long I slept, but all of a sudden I heard hurrahs and I saw lights—torchlights.

"Youths from that area made a parade to the airplane and wouldn't let me sleep. So they presented the belle of the village to me—a redhead with blue eyes, beautiful, and she wanted to come in the cabin with me. I said no way. I didn't know what the purpose was, but had some sense of propriety, and I just said no way, not with all the publicity. They stayed for about an hour, and then I motioned to them that I was so sleepy, so they left me alone.

"The next morning about daybreak, a plane landed on the beach, sent by the Spanish government to refuel our plane. I didn't know we had a water-cooled engine, and lo and behold, they put some water in the gasoline tank, and they had to drain out the whole thing, so we had to stay there another day.

"After they dried out the plane, we flew across the water to a little place on the French coast, then inland to a French air base at Cazaux, where the runway was lined with big, black Senegalese soldiers in abbreviated uniforms, just glistening in the sunlight, every ten feet. We refueled there and it was another five, six hours to Paris. By then it was nighttime when we landed at Le Bourget.

"The French crowds were nothing but gracious to me," Schreiber continues. "They carried me everywhere. They wouldn't let me walk. They were waving French flags everywhere, and somebody had an American flag, and I asked if I could wave that. They said, 'Of course, you're an American!' "

For four days, Arthur Schreiber was treated like a hero, just as Assollant, Lefèvre, and Lotti were. Because of several aborted flights from France in 1928, Lotti and his crew had been labeled as publicity-seekers by many French people. The French now made national heroes out of the three aviators, and the bureaucrats who had tried to ground them now kissed them and decorated them with medals.

While most of Comillas celebrates the arrival of four men from the sky, a handful of Spaniards guards the *Yellow Bird*. (*New York Times*)

The young American stayed, where else, at the Hotel Lotti on rue Castiglione, enjoying the parades and the banquets and the crowds. He turned down offers to write his story for the American newspapers, because of his promise to Lotti.

"In that note I signed, I agreed to consult them on any offers I received. I also agreed to split fifty-fifty everything I would make from the flight in the following year. One newspaper offered me twenty thousand dollars if I would write my story first, but Lotti told me to holdoff until his story had been submitted. Then my price went down to five thousand dollars, but I had no complaints."

When the parties ended, Schreiber boarded the steamship *Leviathan* and sailed to New York, writing an account of his adventure on the way. He was given a reception back in Maine—and disappeared from the headlines almost abruptly.

"I consider myself the luckiest guy that ever lived," Schreiber tells me. "I've tasted of life like few people that ever lived. I've had a dozen different careers—military, animal trainer, show business, deputy sheriff— and by the way I finally learned to fly after World War Two. Now I've just sold my jewelry-cleaner business to a national corporation, but I help them run it. I don't know what I'll do next, but I'm not finished."

His eyes still have that spark from the pictures of half a century before, that untamed look of a boy who is going to do what he wants.

The three Frenchmen allowed the stowaway to be honored at all the celebrations. In his leather jacket, Arthur Schreiber looked more like an aviator than they did. (*New York Times*)

"I've always been like that," he says, "In retrospect, I can see where people might interpret my actions as a dastardly thing to do, risking the lives of the people on that plane. I would have to agree with them that I did not act wisely, but it wasn't done maliciously, it was done ignorantly.

"Believe me, if somebody were to do what I did now, I would censure them just as strongly as I was censured, because now there is greater awareness. I've learned to avoid making anyone else pay for my adventures, but I'm still an adventurer. I've been married to four wives, each for at least ten years. The others were just trainees for me. Muriel is the best, by far.

"Did I tell you, we took our honeymoon visiting Lotti at his three hundred-year-old estate in the south of France? He grows grapes in the St. Emilion region. We were on our way to visit Lefèvre in Monte Carlo, where he retired after being an executive with Air France.

"But the morning we arrived in Monaco, he died. I guess you know what happened to Assollant. He was shot down by the British by mistake during World War Two.

"I still keep in touch with Lotti. By coincidence, his daughter married a fellow who lives here in Southern California, and I hear from her occasionally. I've always thought of him as a man of courage and determination. When I think of the way he treated me. I stowed away on his airplanes—and he toasted me with cognac."

21

Armand Lotti

Paris, France

Armand Lotti sounds like Rex Harrison. Slip him into the House of Lords and he could undoubtedly make a speech defending the Empire without being detected for the Frenchman that he is. His fluidity in English-English is evident as he comes bustling through the door, not only by his words but by his pip-pip accent.

"Sorry to be so late," he says. "But I couldn't find a taxi, so I had to change Métros twice."

Armand Lotti is nearly eighty. He has come from the other side of Paris for an interview in the Paris bureau of *The New York Times*. He seems thirty years younger than his age, his hair only streaked with gray, his footsteps lively. His right eye is a milky gray, from the hunting accident in 1928 that propelled him to fly across the ocean in 1929.

When I compliment Lotti on his youthful appearance, he responds: "I have two daughters in their twenties. They should be my grandchildren, really. It keeps me young, but it's a little hard at times. I don't have the patience that young parents have. But c'est la vie."

I thank Lotti for his excellent command of English. I had been prepared to use my basic French to interview him—my accent has made Frenchmen wince from Bayeux to Sète—but obviously that won't be necessary. Lotti learned to speak English fluently when he observed American hotels in the mid-1920s, and he perfected his English-English two decades later.

"I was a liaison officer in World War Two," he says. "I was sent by the Free French Forces to prepare for the landing of 1942, and one of my jobs

Jean Assollant and his bride, Pauline Parker, two days before the *Yellow Bird's* flight. Armand Lotti had to hide the bride so the pilot would be rested for the trans-atlantic voyage. *(New York Times)*

was to persuade the admiral from Australia that he shouldn't land at Bougie, but five miles farther down the coast. It helped to speak English like this. Keep it to yourself, please, but I've got your Legion of Merit award from President Truman."

The skill in English also came in handy in 1929, when he and his companions came to the United States with his airplane, the *Yellow Bird,* to attempt the first French crossing of the North Atlantic from mainland to mainland. He was the only one of the three crew members who could speak with the Americans—although his pilot, the war ace Jean Assollant, spoke English well enough to marry an American show girl two days before the flight.

Lotti recalls persuading the young woman that her new husband's life depended on him being well rested for the flight. Once she agreed to sleep apart from Assollant the night before departure, Lotti had her hidden in Portland, Maine, so the bridegroom couldn't find her. Assollant saw no humor in the separation, but today Lotti chuckles about it.

Lotti has described this incident, and hundreds of others, in his own book, *L'Oiseau Canari (The Yellow Bird),* published in 1968 by Calmann-Lévy. I tell Lotti how much I enjoyed his rather sharp observations about aviation in the late twenties.

"The book was a little sarcastic, maybe," he says. "But I think it was right."

He tells how he was raised in comfort, destined to run l'Hôtel Lotti on the Right Bank. (The family name is Italian, but Lotti was raised a French-man.) He was already seven or eight years old when dapper little Santos-Dumont conducted his first flights on the plains of western Paris, but Lotti has only a vague memory of being taken to an air meet at Juvisy and being squeezed among the legs of adults, with brief glimpses of the sky.

Aviation did not touch him until after he served as a motorcycle liaison officer during the first war and later spent nearly two years observing Ital-ian, American, and Quebecker hotel operations to prepare for his career as hotelier. He was nearly thirty years old when Lindbergh landed at Le Bourget in 1927.

"I had a friend, a dentist named Hipwell, who had connections with the U.S. Embassy," Lotti says. "He managed to get me in one day as Lind-bergh was meeting people. I caught sight of him from afar. I didn't meet him until two years later, when I got to America, and he gave me advice that would save my life."

Lotti saw other American aviators, including Ruth Elder, the Ameri-can, at his hotel in 1927–1928 but he did not think about flying until the ac-cident in 1928. He was hunting in a forest when another hunter's lead pellet ricocheted through the woods and destroyed his eye. When he rea-lized the damage was permanent, he searched for a way to prove himself, something perhaps even more dangerous than hunting.

"The Blériot people were very nice to me at their flying school," he says. "I had only one eye, but they let me go through my exams. Naturally, I couldn't get my license."

After making his first solo flight, Lotti realized he could never attempt a long-distance flight on his own. A friend of his—a Parisian hatter and "Renaissance man" named Willoughby—began putting him in touch with aviators. Eventually, Lotti teamed up with Jean Assollant, pilot, and René Lefèvre, navigator.

Although he was already thirty, Lotti did not want his parents to know he was investing his time and money in aviation. He invented excuses for disappearing each day, and he and his companions began testing the plane at Le Bourget.

After Lindbergh, pilots scrambled to conquer the many other routes of transoceanic air travel, including the dangerous east-west flight, against the headwinds. The excitement in the French capital seemed almost palpable: The smell of danger, of bravery, floated into Paris on the night air. At dawn, aviators would risk their lives on a "raid."

In one of the best sections of Lotti's book, he describes the tension at Le Bourget at dawn as the barflies staggered out to the field. (Dawn was the best time of all for flying because of the diminished breezes.) Lotti compares the spectacle to a public execution.

They have prolonged their nights, made the nightclubs, drank and danced, especially drank, then run aground at Les Halles, given the night-workers the sad spectacle of their idle banality, and performed the ritual of the onion soup. One of them, disordered in memory, has become the envoy of foresight, and has proposed: "Let's go to Le Bourget." "To Le Bourget, to Le Bourget," the excited voices have cried. . . .

In the next paragraph, Lotti describes how the night owls would rush to a telephone to describe a crash to their friends, and when bored of that subject, switch to the latest fashions of the rue de la Paix. He uses a wonderful word for these swells in their fancy clothes who come to Le Bourget to watch aviators die. "Poubelles," he calls them—garbage pails. Soon the "poubelles" would be coming to watch him.

The crowd gathered at dawn on September 3, 1928, to watch Assollant gun the bright yellow Bernard plane toward the New World. Lefèvre sat next to Assollant while a third crew member, identified only as "Monsieur Lévy," was hidden in the back. Lotti could hear the plane burst forward and lumber into the air, but then he heard Assollant give the urgent command to dump all the gasoline in preparation for an emergency landing.

After they glided back safely onto the field, Lotti was photographed by a man from *l'Intransigeant*. Within hours, his identity was made public at every news kiosk in Paris. At the hotel, his parents were horrified, but the aviators were horrified for a different reason: They learned the plane had faltered because a mechanic had mistakenly closed the tap from the fuel tank; when they landed, they had ten seconds more of gasoline.

The French press began to label the team as incompetents, and the insults got worse later that fall when the trio tried the southern route to America and the flight ended in Casablanca after engine failure. The press accused Lotti of publicity stunting, of not making a serious effort to cross the Atlantic. The military warned Assollant and Lefèvre not to try any more raids. Lotti's father put pressure on him to sell the plane and get back to the hotel business. And the government, under criticism because thirteen airplanes had disappeared in two years, ordered an end to all long-distance flights.

After all these attacks it is no surprise Lotti feels kindly toward the United States: In his book he contrasts the sniping French journalists and timid bureaucrats with the people who helped him when he finally reached America.

"Your people were more willing to give a person a chance," he tells me.

Forbidden to plan any "raids," the crew spent the winter of 1928–1929 arranging for a stronger Hispano-Suiza engine. The company could not officially cooperate, but promised to send a mechanic wherever the plane should appear. Engine companies were motivated by potential good publicity should one of their machines make a historic flight, but they were also eager to improve their product through constant testing.

In the spring, with the bureaucrats still forbidding transatlantic flights, Lotti made plans to fly to England. Once again, *l'Intransigeant* publicized his secret plans, but Lotti persuaded the manager at Orly to give him enough gasoline for two hours. Assollant flew the plane to Southampton, where they had arranged to put the plane on the ship *Leviathan.*

Fearful that the French might request the English to detain the ship at the dock, Lotti counted upon the traditional two-hour dinner break that any important bureaucrat would take. Sure enough, by the time the officials got back to their desks in Paris that afternoon, the *Yellow Bird* was at sea aboard the *Leviathan.*

Once in the United States, the pilots rejected Roosevelt Field, where Lindbergh had departed in 1927, because of muddy conditions. In New York they were taken seriously by the press and by other aviators, including the biggest aviator of them all.

"He came to visit us," Lotti recalls. "He was a very sweet fellow, not showy at all. I wasn't there when he arrived, so Assollant and Lefèvre didn't get much out of the conversation except that he found our instruments were very poor. We had a heavily loaded plane, six and a half tons. We didn't like the fields there, lots of chimneys surrounding the fields.

"I was inspecting the field when Lindbergh came a second time. He didn't have to say his name. I knew who he was. I thanked him for coming, and we had a longer talk.

"I didn't put this into my book in 1968, because it took me a long time to realize the value of the information he gave me that day.

"He said, 'Yes, I told your friends that your instruments are very poor,' and he suggested we buy a Pioneer gyroscope that showed the position of your plane on a small scale of the horizon. If you flew left, the figure went left. If you moved up, the figure moved up.

"He didn't have a Pioneer himself, he told me, because it only came out in 1928. He just had a level indicator. He said the Pioneer would be frightfully helpful, and I thanked him for his advice.

"He started to walk away and then he came back and said, 'One more thing I must tell you. If you ever take ice, fly low.' I put that in my mind, but I didn't think we could fly low because we had a very heavy machine. But I thought of it soon enough after we took off. We got over Newfoundland in bad weather and we had to go into the clouds. I looked at the strut holding the landing gear and I saw ice on it, so I went up to my companions and I said, 'You remember what Lindy said?' I went again and took another look at the struts, and the ice was becoming more and more thick.

"I said, 'There's one thing. We can go on to Paris and lose our lives, or we can go by way of the Azores, and meet the anticyclonic zones which are more favorable, because you can't dream of flying low with a heavily loaded plane.

"We weighed too much, which of course you know all about. If the plane got out of control, it would take us two hundred yards to get her up. We couldn't take risks, so we forgot Paris, and the next best thing was to save our lives and save the plane, so we planned to go by way of the Azores. But Lindy's advice and that Pioneer made a difference."

Lotti says he bought the Pioneer, an earth inductor compass, from Clarence Chamberlin, who had made the first mainland-to-mainland crossing after Lindbergh. But the Pioneer is not displayed with the *Yellow Bird* at the Musée de l'Air because "the Germans took it out during the war," Lotti says.

"They also took out the radio. I had the radio rebuilt, but I couldn't get in touch with the proper people for a Pioneer because the company had been sold."

Lotti tells how his first attempt from Maine ended because the fuel mixture was imperfect, causing Assollant to sputter back to the beach. At that point Lotti was afraid he was wearing out his welcome in America, too. Fuel was not easily purchased in 1929.

"The Hispano people neglected to tell us that the petrol in the States was at a more critical point than in France. The petrol people said, 'We'll give you another chance but we won't give you a third.' "

On the night before the final takeoff, Lotti recalls, he and the Hispano mechanic, Raoul Leroy, went out to inspect the plane for the last time.

"We saw a tube that was slightly leaking. I discussed it with Leroy, a charming fellow and a good companion, and he said, 'You can't go like this.' But I knew if we asked for another tube, we wouldn't have any money left, and we'd be out of luck again. We tied the tube the best we could, but it still leaked. We dumped one hundred liters of fuel, just not to take any chances with weight."

Perhaps the drop of one hundred liters made the difference on the morning of June 13, as the *Yellow Bird* lumbered down the sand at Old Orchard, with Arthur Schreiber hidden in the back of the plane.

The incident of the stowaway happened so long ago that Lotti seems to have no vestigial emotion left. His only mention of Schreiber so far has come in the discussion of the weight of the plane, as if the American boy had been a kind of natural phenomenon, like wind or rain. When I bring up Schreiber's role, Lotti seems to fidget. He has promised me an hour for the interview, and the hour is long exhausted. (We never even get to chat about the hour and a half in which he piloted the *Yellow Bird* on the second day of their trip: the reward for his efforts, the psychic payment for his eye wound.) He does say there was never any discussion of throwing Schreiber overboard, and he laughs at the gossip that the stowaway was a publicity gimmick.

"He's a nice boy and was very lucky to save his life and come across me," Lotti says. "We get together every couple of years.

"I live near Bordeaux now. I'm in the wine business. St. Emilion. I sold my share in the hotel in 1949. Oh, yes, it still exists, but my relationship has been cut. Those new businessmen are not very sentimental. They made a good bargain, and all they could think about was chucking me out. We keep a studio in Paris for when we visit here."

He is visiting Paris this week to help commemorate Lindbergh's flight fifty years later. At the ceremonies out of Le Bourget, I cannot help but no-

The four musketeers pose at a party given them in Comillas, Spain. Armand Lotti, far right, is carrying his pet crocodile, which shared the journey from Maine to Spain. (*New York Times*)

tice how he and Maurice Bellonte seem uncomfortable near each other, as if the tarmac at Le Bourget has room for only one national hero. To me, they are both heroes, and I ask Lotti the same question I later ask Bellonte about the Concorde.

"I recently took the Concorde to America," Lottie says. "For me, it was like a pilgrim entering the Holy City. I had always dreamed of the Concorde. The inside is decorated nicely. Beautiful and charming hostesses. Food—four stars. You hear this voice saying, 'Ladies and gentlemen, we are now flying at twenty-seven thousand feet. In two minutes we'll be flying at forty-six thousand feet.' And I kept thinking how our heavily laden plane would roam for hours before making three thousand feet.

"You know, a great deal has been said about the Concorde, and perhaps it is true, that it was not up to our financial means, especially after the war, which has ruined the country. But one thing: The Concorde has been built by the top engineers, by the most modest workmen, with care, with pride. It was the pride of our country.

"I was talking with friends of mine who don't understand the kind of dispute being made in America. One day you'll be preparing a super Concorde, and you can't avoid the noise. If you live around an aerodrome, you just put up double windows, and you can economize on fuel in the winter. You can't stop progress.

"For one hundred and fifty years we are destroying the world on which we live. Now we have found this out, all of a sudden. Ecology. When a human being finds out something, we will go on a pendulum, too much one way, too much the other way. We've gone too much on ecology.

"But even with the progress, I don't think aviation is the same today. Oh, the first time he is alone in the air, it is the same for a young pilot. It is always the same. But after that—what can you do? In those days, it was a show, a Roman circus. Today, you take a plane like you take a bus."

22

Martin Jensen

San Diego, California

Martin Jensen is talking about his trip to Hawaii—not the one in 1927, the murderous Dole Race when he flew the Pacific in twenty-eight hours and ten other people died trying, but the trip last year, when he played travel agent for his old friends in aviation.

"Some people wanted just the flight, and some people just wanted the hotel, and some people wanted both," he says. "It was three different trips in one."

He chuckles at the incongruity of an eighty-year-old pilot running a tour to Hawaii. Having Martin Jensen organize that tour was like having Joe DiMaggio showing people around Yankee Stadium, saying: "I played a few games here myself once."

As they crossed the Pacific in their four-engine jet, some of the tour members knew Martin Jensen had once glided into Honolulu with four gallons of gasoline left in his tank.

We are sitting around the Jensens' modest house, halfway up a steep hill in the Lemon Grove section in east San Diego. Martin and his wife, Doris, are showing me color pictures of the trip, of old Charlie Willard, the grand old man from Glendale, the fourth American to fly a plane, who took part in the Hawaii excursion just months before his death.

"It was so nice to have Charlie with us," says Doris Jensen.

The Jensens tell me about their garden and their fishing trips. ("A woman who likes to fish? I knew she was right for me," Jensen says.)

But the talk always comes back to the Dole Race. It has almost become part of his full name: "Martin-Jensen-Who-Flew-in-the-Dole Race."

Most people forget Jensen did not actually win the race; but surviving that horror show was prize enough.

Jensen, a Kansas farmboy who spoke only Danish when he was a child, joined the navy during the First World War to learn to be a mechanic by fixing planes. One day a petty officer said if Jensen was going to fix the damn things, he ought to fly in them, too. To a boy from the cornfields, just going out to sea was an adventure, but the petty officer kept saying, wait till you try the air.

"They kept after me, and finally I said, 'If you're going to kill me, let's do it.' The first ride was so impressive that I was just astonished. They let me hold the controls in return for my doing a little repair work on their automobiles. There wasn't a day that I wasn't ready to fly. I'd stay up at night because I was always ready to fly. I loved to work on 'em, but riding in them—that went even further."

He stayed in San Diego after he left the navy, working for Claude Ryan, getting his pilot's license, flying across the United States in a Jenny in 1925. One day a man bought a plane from Ryan and asked if Ryan knew anybody who might want to open an air service in Hawaii. Jensen dropped his wrenches and raised his hand.

When he arrived by ship in Hawaii on January 1, 1927, the plane had been nicknamed "Malolo," which everybody told him meant "Flying Fish." He kept wondering why natives were hesitant about getting into the machine, until somebody explained that "Malolo" had another meaning in Hawaiian—"impending death."

Because of that semantic problem, business was a little slow in the islands, and Jensen took whatever jobs he could get. One of his steady assignments was dropping newspapers and supplies into a leper colony. After Jensen left the private flying business job, another pilot took four passengers up in the "Malolo" and they all spun to their death.

"I guess the name meant exactly what they said," Jensen says.

He was still island-hopping around Hawaii in May of 1927 when Lindbergh flew the Atlantic, about the distance between California and Hawaii. But there was a basic difference: Between New York and Paris there are a few oases like Newfoundland, Bermuda, the Azores, Ireland, and England, where, with any luck, a pilot with engine trouble might touch down. Between California and Hawaii there was nothing.

"I've always thanked Lindbergh for making my flight possible," Jensen says. "No, he didn't give me extra confidence, because I knew I could fly the Pacific. I already had plans to do it. But within three or four days of his flight, everybody was all hopped up for these long flights."

On June 28, 1927, two young officers, Lester J. Maitland and Albert F. Hegenberger, made one of the most admirable flights in history, from Oakland to Honolulu in twenty-five hours and fifty minutes, knowing that if they missed by more than two degrees they would run out of gas in a huge ocean. They were helped by a rudimentary radio beacon, an overlapping beam that, when it functioned, told them if they were on target.

Two weeks later, Ernest L. Smith and Emory Bronte also traversed twenty-four hundred miles of open space, crashing safely into trees on the island of Molokai. The circus was on.

A couple of newspaper editors talked James Dole, whose family raised pineapples, into donating a prize for a great Pacific race between Oakland and Honolulu. Even though the nonstop crossing had been made twice, they felt a race would publicize aviation, Hawaii, and their newspapers. Dole decided to top the Orteig Prize of twenty-five thousand dollars, which Lindbergh had won, by also offering ten thousand dollars for second place.

"I went back to California and tried to raise money and a plane," Jensen recalls, "but nobody wanted to contribute to my demise. Claude Ryan let me have an airplane, but I couldn't get ready in time, so I turned it back. To be eligible you had to post a one hundred dollars fee ten days before the original start, so I gave them a fictitious wing span, length, and horsepower.

"Then I found an airplane up there that somebody had started but didn't have the money to finish, a monoplane built by Vance Breese in San Francisco. I worked night and day. They had no fabric or wires or propellers or wheels or cowling. I worked night and day splicing wires and covering fabrics on the tail surface and on the wings.

"Then they pushed back the start four days, which was perfect for me because I could not have started otherwise. It was set for the sixteenth of August. But four days before that day, they told me the rules and said I had to have a navigator, unless I could make celestial observations by myself, which I couldn't.

"Everything was going against me. I advertised in the paper for a navigator and got many applicants. One guy said he was a Boy Scout. I said, 'Well, can you navigate?' He said, 'Yes, sir, I was lost in the woods one time and I found my way out with a compass.' I told him, 'That's not navigating. That's not navigating.'

"Then I had a young girl that wanted to go. She said, 'I can get into the movies. That will make me.' Well, she was out. Then some old woman said, 'I would like to go out. I'll take my chances with you.' I said, 'Well, I'm sorry, but I won't take my chances with you.' She couldn't navigate at all, either.

"Finally, this fellow came along, Paul Schluter, who was a seafaring man, spent a lot of time around the Hawaiian Islands as a ship's navigator. Ben Wyatt, the examiner for the race, said he met all the qualifications for a navigator. I couldn't afford to pay the guy because I'd already mortgaged the airplane and the prize money in case I won, so there was no money for anybody."

The navigator said he didn't mind. After all, it would be his first flight in an airplane, so who was he to complain? Jensen says he wasn't concerned about trusting his life to a stranger who had never flown.

"He was trusting his life with me, too," Jensen says.

"I had planned on going by myself in the first place. I wasn't thrilled with that because I couldn't make celestial observations. But I did have a navy man chart my course for me—start out with two hundred and forty-eight degrees for two hours, then two hundred and forty-seven for two hours, then two hundred and forty-six and so on. That was called a great circle course.

"When they told me I had to have a navigator, I said, 'All right.' Then Ben Wyatt called me in and said, 'Martin, I was in the navy with this guy. I want you to promise me one thing.' I said, 'What's that?'

"He said, 'I want you to promise me you'll do everything that navigator tells you, even if you think it's wrong. If you do that, you'll get there, but if you don't you won't. It's that simple.'

"So I said I promise, but do you know he started out on two hundred and forty-eight degrees and never changed his course for twenty-four hours?" Jensen says, still unsure why Schluter did not follow the plan. "It's a good thing they made us carry ten percent extra gasoline, or I never would have made it. One of the other pilots came out there with maps showing two thousand and ninety miles to Hawaii—but that was nautical miles, not statute miles, which are an eighth of a mile less. That meant he didn't have enough gas to get there, until they found out." (The officials made the other pilot take on more gas.)

"The race committee tried to check everything. I was going to carry five-gallon cans of fuel that I could throw overboard when they were empty, but they objected because it would change the compass by removing a metal container, see? So we had to put in tanks two days before the flight, working all night and all day, really pressed for time.

"The night before, I slept just as well as I ever slept. It didn't bother me one iota. The navigator was pacing the floor all night, but I didn't know that until the morning. He said, 'How could you sleep the night before a flight like this?' I said, 'What do you mean?' He said, 'That flight coming up.' I said, 'For goodness' sake, I've been flying around Honolulu in the Pacific Ocean and thinking nothing of it. It's just as dangerous between islands if your engine quits as it is in the middle of the Pacific.' "

The race had originally been planned for the twelfth—the anniversary of the annexation of Hawaii, when there would have been a full moon. But the date was pushed back four days to allow the pilots to prepare their planes, and the field of fifteen began diminishing before it could reach the starting line.

By the morning of the sixteenth, the race had claimed three victims: Jimmy Giffen had crashed near San Francisco and survived, but George Covell and Richard Waggener had crashed near San Diego and were killed. Art Rodgers tried to bail out near Los Angeles, but the rip cord tangled with the plane, and he was killed. Four others dropped out by choice or for lack of equipment, leaving eight planes at the starting line.

For the remaining entrants, the order of takeoff was determined by drawing from a hat. Actually, it was a wastebasket; the symbolism was appropriate, considering the carnage that followed.

Norman Goddard and Ken Hawkins cracked up their heavy *El Encanto* on the runway, and were fortunate to get out alive. Livingston Irving's *Pabco Pacific Flier* couldn't lift its weight off the ground at all. That meant six planes took off, but three of them came back shortly with problems. One that temporarily returned was the *Miss Doran,* named after a schoolteacher from Michigan who was going as passenger, and navigated by Vilas Knope and flown by Augie Pedlar.

"He was a wing-walker, a daredevil," Jensen recalls, "but he wasn't the kind who could fly in a fog. You've got to know what you're doing."

When Pedlar returned, his plane was making evil noises, and the spectators clamored that Mildred Doran be removed from the plane before its daredevil aviators took off again. She insisted on getting back, however, and the plane was last seen flying toward the Golden Gate.

It was not the end of the deaths. Jack Frost and Gordon Scott, in their Lockheed Vega sponsored by the Hearst newspapers, were the favorites. They took off easily but were never seen again. And two days later, William Erwin and Alvin Eichwaldt took off to search for the others and try to fly to Hong Kong to collect another twenty-five thousand dollars.

"They sent a message they were in trouble. Then they sent a message saying they were out of the spin," Jensen says. "A couple of minutes later, their message got higher and higher in pitch, like wind in the generator, and all of a sudden it just stopped."

That added up to ten deaths connected to the Dole Race, and left just two planes in the race—Arthur Goebel and Navy Lieutenant William Davis in a Travel Air monoplane, the *Woolaroc,* and the Jensen-Schluter team.

"I was cruising before I got to the end of the airport," Jensen recalls. "I did not push my engine. I knew what a heavy load would do to you."

"I had to fly real low because the fog was right on the water for the first two hundred miles. One time I didn't see this ship until I was almost on it. I went right over it. I had to be near the water to see the difference between the water and sky.

"Of course, the navigator started out with two hundred and forty-eight degrees, and I figured that was all right, right on the button. But he never changed it the whole trip.

"Just before dark, I got scared because I was still in fog. I wanted to be out of the fog, see? I climbed to about four thousand feet and went into a diving turn. Nothing seemed to be working right. I had done a lot of night flying, and I knew what to do when I went into a spin.

"It's vertigo, see? No reference point. You can't even walk a straight line in the dark unless you have a reference point. You'll walk in circles. It's the same thing in an airplane. The more I pulled back on the stick, the faster I got going. To slow it up, you shut the engine down and pull it into a spin, so I'd know where I was at. That was good for seven minutes. Then it happened again, so I went into a spin faster.

"The fog was eight thousand feet thick, right on the water. I had a compass, but that didn't do me any good. I had a bank-and-turn indicator, but I didn't know how to use it. During the day, you have a reference point in fog, even some slight shadow. But I'd never been in total darkness before.

"I decided then that I had only five hundred feet left, not enough for another spin, so I nosed it down and leveled off around one hundred feet above the water. I said, 'All right, I'm going to do this all night—hold my foot pedals steady.'

"I held that thing for four and a half hours. That was a long time to sit there and not know exactly what's cooking. So when the moon came up, I got a slight band under the fog, then I relaxed. But I still had to stay within one hundred feet of the water, so the navigator could do celestial navigation. It was hard to tell our altitude because the altimeter was affected by the different air pressure.

"One time I hit the water with my left wheel and I pulled it up into a steep climb, and I got a negative G—tremendous pressure, things flying around the cabin, centrifugal force. The navigator lost his telescope somewhere in the plane. He was about six feet away from me. Some gas tanks were in the middle. We passed messages with a clothesline and a stick.

"After we landed, I went back to examine the damage we had done. I found a rip in the fabric, about a foot where the spray of the water had hit it. It was noisy, it sure did scare me, too. I didn't lose my wits. I knew what I had to do to get it back up again. It must have been just the top of the wave.

"I didn't sleep, and I didn't have any food, either. I was just worried about getting there. When you reach the point of no return, you've got to think you can do it. I set an endurance record of over thirty-five hours in 1929, and I had more trouble staying awake when I was going in circles.

"Was I frightened? I was, when we got a thousand miles from anyplace, out in the middle. The only thing that did bring me through was determination. I could have given up, but I had so much difficulty getting into the race, getting the plane, getting the money, that I was not about to just quit out in the middle of the ocean.

"At the end of twenty-four hours, we should have been within sight of land, considering we were averaging one hundred miles per hour. But we couldn't see land. I wrote a note back saying, 'Circle and wait for high noon,' so he could take a reading.

"When noon did come, he took three shots and averaged them out, and then he wrote me a note saying we were two hundred miles to the north of our course. I asked him if he had changed every two hours like we were supposed to. If he had, we would have hit it on the head."

Why didn't Schluter change his course? Jensen just shrugs.

"They always say I did eighty miles per hour on that flight, but when you consider all the time I was out there circling, I was doing one hundred most of the time. They said I was wandering all over the ocean—but there was a darn good reason for it. But the navigator didn't know where he was at.

"Well, I changed course and headed due south for two hours and then turned to two hundred and thirty-five degrees, and in five minutes we were right on course. Then I picked up the island of Oahu, in line with Wheeler Field, and wrote him a note saying he could sit down now. He wrote a note back saying 'Don't do any stunts, we're lucky to be here.' "

When Jensen touched down at Wheeler Field at 2:20 P.M., with four gallons of gasoline left on board, he learned that Goebel and Davis had landed shortly after noon, after flying twenty-six hours, seventeen minutes, and thirty-three seconds. The winners now richer by twenty-five thousand dollars.

Jensen's time of twenty-eight hours and sixteen minutes qualified him for the second prize of ten thousand dollars—all of it already mortgaged to other people. He was greeted by his wife, Marguerite, who was heard by reporters to shout: "Martin Jensen, where the hell have you been?"

The festivities were dampened when nobody else arrived out of the eastern sky in the hours that followed.

The newspapers, which had been printing so many stories about the heroics of aviation since Lindbergh's crossing in May, now saw the other side of early long-distance flying. The Philadelphia *Inquirer*, for example, labeled the Dole race "an orgy of reckless sacrifice." The Dole company offered another twenty thousand dollars in reward money for the missing pilots, but no trace was ever found of the seven missing people. A month later, a cruise ship paused midway across the ocean to drop a wreath into the water and play the spiritual portion of Dvořák's *New World Symphony*—"Going home, going home."

For Jensen and Schluter, the second-place money was just enough to quarrel about.

"When we got there, the newsmen asked the navigator, 'How much did you get?' and he said: 'NOTHING!' See, he told me he would do it for the glory, but now that they asked him, he said: 'NOTHING!' and they said, 'Well, how much did Jensen get?' and he told them ten thousand dollars. And they said: 'How much did you get?' And he said: 'NOTHING!'

"Well, hell, I was ten thousand dollars in the hole. I had borrowed so much money I still owed ten thousand dollars. But fortunately, I wrote my story for the newspaper and got paid fifteen hundred dollars and I borrowed another thousand dollars and gave him twenty-five hundred. And I'm still in the hole.

"People ask me if I would have done better without the navigator. That remains to be seen. But I know I would have flown above the clouds. I wouldn't have had any trouble there, if I had followed the course that navy navigator set for me.

"Another thing that happened from that race: For three days afterward, I couldn't hear a thing because of the exhaust, three feet from my face. That's all I could see at night—a yellow flame, turning blue."

There was one glaring benefit of the race, which Jensen acknowledges: When he returned to the mainland, he was a celebrity. The M-G-M movie

Martin Jensen ferried Leo, the M-G-M lion, around the United States until they had a rough landing in a lonely canyon. (American Hall of Aviation History, Northrop University)

people gave him a job flying Leo the Lion around the country in a Ryan Brougham with a cage in the middle. It was a lot of laughs, Jensen says, until he flew up the wrong canyon in Arizona and had to crash-land in the treetops. Fortunately, the plane did not split apart, putting Jensen and Leo the Lion into an early version of *Alive!* He stuck his extra sandwiches in the lion's cage and went off for help.

Soon after, Jensen moved to Long Island, where he flew stunts for Tidewater Oil, in an effort to get their brand name on the picture page of the daily newspapers.

"One time I offered the guy from the *Daily News* an exclusive picture if he promised to get the Tidewater signs in the picture. To make sure he did, I climbed out on the wing, up in the air, and took a wrench with me and pretended to be working on the engine. Of course, my copilot was at the controls, but still, it was a pretty exciting picture. They told me it was the first time they ever used the entire front page for a picture of an individual—except for declaration of war."

In 1928 and 1929, Jensen set endurance records over Roosevelt Field, sometimes joined in the air by his wife, Marguerite, and they became second only to the Lindberghs as America's favorite flying couple.

"My first wife gave me a lot of trouble," Jensen recalls now. "Always spending money. We broke up after a while."

The era of the endurance flights, sponsored by manufacturers, did not make Jensen rich. Seeking a more lucrative career, he tried organizing his own aircraft manufacturing companies in the 1930s and was talking about a plastic-and-mahogany airplane in 1941, two months before Pearl Harbor. Just before supper, he shows moving pictures of a small helicopter he designed that he wishes somebody would manufacture.

For the last part of his working career, Martin Jensen worked for one of the huge aircraft companies that had grown up during his flying lifetime.

He also became reacquainted with Doris whom he had known back in 1923 when he was working for Claude Ryan and Doris used to visit Ryan's

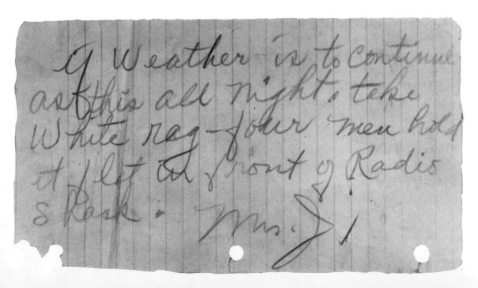

Right: Martin Jensen got a lot of publicity for his oil-company sponsor by pretending to repair his Bellanca monoplane while his copilot handled the controls. (The Garden City Archives) Below: Note tossed by Marguerite Jensen asking ground crew to signal weather forecast during an endurance attempt. (The Garden City Archives)

airfield. About ten years ago she saw Jensen's picture among some old-time pilots and she made inquiries to the Northrop officials if that was Martin-Jensen-Who-Flew-in-the-Dole-Race. Doris, who had worked for seventeen years for McDonnell and Douglas, discovered Jensen was living north of San Diego.

"When he started coming down, he didn't look like I remembered," she says. "I got fat living by myself," Jensen says. "Eating starchy foods." Doris has slimmed him down by feeding him meals like the one she serves to us this evening—meat loaf and fresh greens right from the garden. When we are finished, we stand up and talk about the Dole Race once again:

"I don't feel I'm somebody great, because I'm not. I'm just a boy who was raised on a farm, and they'll never take that out of me.

"How do I feel about surviving that race, when others were killed? I feel there is a superpower. I really feel that. I've done so many things and I always come out. I believe in God. I don't go to church because I have my own way of looking at it. And I never pray for Him to help me because, one of the things, God helps those who help themselves. That definitely got me through the race.

"People criticized that race because of the people that got killed, but I thought it was a wonderful idea. I knew my chances were very slim but I was willing to take the risk. Every pilot on that race, every navigator, knew the chances of them getting there was about one third. And that's what it worked out to be."

23

Viola Gentry

Westbury, New York

Viola Gentry wants to see the hickory tree that had such an impact on her life, that made her arms hang crookedly, that made her use "store teeth" for the rest of her life.

She wants to see the tree in the light of almost half a century, to remember the foggy morning when she was a prominent pilot trying for a world's record, and the hickory tree was the only large obstacle in a square mile of flatland.

"It was still standing a few years ago," she says. "I'd like to see it again. Didn't get much chance the first time."

The first time was in 1929, when she was known as the "Flying Cashier," a working girl who had become one of the celebrities at Roosevelt Field. Her specialty was the endurance flight, aviation's answer to the marathon dance—a test of will that kept people flying in circles until they ran out of gas. The goal was to test the newest aircraft, whose design kept getting better, but sometimes the pilots still died.

Today Viola has traveled north from Miami ("by bus, honey, so I'd have some money left for a beer") for the fiftieth anniversary of another marathon, Lindbergh's flight across the ocean. She was a friend and contemporary of his; she has visited his grave at Maui.

She wears a white knit sweater, even though the temperature has risen to nearly eighty degrees on this May 20. She keeps a lace handkerchief tucked in her sleeve and daubs her face every few minutes, her hands at an awkward angle to her forearms.

This disability is the souvenir of that moment when her plane came

smashing out of the heavy fog and slammed its way onto the front page of
The New York Times:

MISS GENTRY IS BADLY HURT,

HER PILOT KILLED IN CRASH:

RIVALS IN AIR BEG FOR NEWS

Viola Gentry was big news in 1929, her successes and her crashes, and
as we wait for the Lindbergh ceremonies to begin, she describes the route
that led her to that hickory tree.

She was three years old when the Wright brothers first flew at Kitty
Hawk, but people didn't notice the event in the hamlet of Gentry, North
Carolina, where the Gentry family had settled in 1658. Viola says she discovered aviation in 1910, "when Mama folded her wings" (an old aviation
term for dying) and Viola ran away to Jacksonville, Florida. She begged a
pilot, George Gray, to give her a flight—and her aunt in Jacksonville
spanked her for it.

When she was seventeen and on her own, Viola got a job on a troop
train heading to the West Coast.

"The boys were supposed to go to Vladivostok," she says. "My job was
to keep 'em on the train. I kept 'em singing all across the country, until we
got to San Francisco. Then I got a job in the Grand Hotel on O'Farrell
Street.

"One day they told me a plane was going to land on the roof of the St.
Francis Hotel. I told my boss, 'You take the switchboard, I'm going to see
that plane.' It was Lieutenant [Ormar] Locklear, doing some stunt for the
movies. There was chicken wire to stop him, but he stopped three or four
feet ahead of the wire. That got me really interested in flying."

Viola took lessons from Bob Fowler, a well-known pilot of the 1920s,
and learned just enough to regard herself as a pilot. When she heard of a
giant fair being planned in Philadelphia, she insisted that a woman pilot
would be a drawing attraction to the fair. But after traveling across the
country, to seek a flying job, she found the promoters hedging about the
job.

"That fair was a total flop," she says with a wink. "It would be a shame
to say I was glad, wouldn't it?"

But Viola was hooked. She moved to New York in order to be close to
the Long Island airfields. She got a job as a cashier at the Richelieu Restaurant on Fifth Avenue in New York, taking the train to Curtiss Field for lessons every morning with Roger Q. Williams, another major pilot. She
soloed on September of 1925 and became one of the regulars at the field.

On March 14, 1926, she rented a plane and, accompanied by a male
pilot, she flew under the Brooklyn and Manhattan bridges, getting herself
attention in the press. Then she switched to endurance records, setting a
mark for women on December 20, 1928, by staying up eight hours, six
minutes, and thirty-seven seconds.

Endurance records were dependent upon fuel supply, of course, and the techniques were just being developed. Some pilots tried oversized tanks; others took on cans of fuel from catapults on the ground, or from ropes hanging from another plane. Viola's friend and competitor, Martin Jensen, developed a device like a football goal post: The pilot would swoop down and grab the can with a hook. It was all somewhat risky. Inevitably, they tried plane-to-plane fuel hoses. When Elinor Smith pushed the record past twenty-four hours in 1929, it was obvious that endurance flights would need two pilots. The engine had been perfected beyond a single human's endurance.

Even though Elinor Smith and Viola Gentry had proved they could compete with men, a woman was not always accepted on the airfield.

"Sergeant Peterson was adjusting my parachute when I was going for the record," Viola recalls, "and he told me I should stay home and have children. Right while he was strapping on my parachute. He said the airfield was not a proper place for ladies. Today we have women pilots. Some women are qualifying for the astronaut program. Their reactions are better than a man, some of them."

Viola Gentry and Joe Jones in front of the Cabinaire biplane, 1929. A few days later, Gentry and Jack Ashcraft crashed in this plane while attempting an endurance flight in a thick fog.

When a pair of army pilots established an endurance record of 150 hours and 40 minutes, Gentry decided to stay in the air for a week, with a copilot. It was assumed the copilot would be a man.

"I got a lot of criticism for that," she says. "People didn't know anything about aviation. We didn't have automatic pilot. We had a Chevrolet oil gauge and maybe a compass, and that was all. What did people think we would do up there?"

Viola was anything but wealthy, so she obviously could not finance her own flights, but sponsors were usually willing to provide equipment for the testing and the publicity. Viola's Paramount Cabinaire biplane was supplied by Walter Carr, an Early Bird pilot from Saginaw, Michigan. The 110-horsepower Warner engine was supplied by that manufacturer, and gasoline was supplied by Richfield. Since most pilots, like Gentry, had to work at other jobs to support their habit, they were not always available. Charles W. Parkhurst, who teamed up with Gentry on a nine-and-a-half-hour endurance attempt, broke up the partnership when he got a full-time job elsewhere. Carr might have flown with her, but he developed a cold.

But Clyde Pangborn, a pilot and promoter, matched Gentry with Jack Ashcraft for the next attempt.

"I knew all about Jack Ashcraft," she recalls, politeness and awe dominating her voice. "He was a famous pilot with the Gates Flying Circus. A good reputation. Plus, my people were Masons and his people were Masons, and that made him my brother. I said I'd like to fly with him."

Ashcraft had flown during World War I and had seen his share of tragedy: In 1924, a passenger had been killed in his plane; in 1928 a bomb exploded at a fairgrounds in Macon, Georgia, killing Ashcraft's brother and best friend but sparing him; shortly afterward a passenger took a suicide leap while Ashcraft was flying him around.

Ashcraft, also known as the "Texas Cowboy" was famous for his "dead stick landing," in which he would wave both hands to the crowd as the plane made its final approach. When people got bored with that, he learned to play taps with a bugle while landing. He often told interviewers he wasn't afraid to die. When his time came, he said, he would "get it."

On June 27, 1929, Ashcraft and Gentry were ready to challenge the latest refueling endurance record of 150 hours and 40 minutes, set by an army team in their plane *The Question Mark*. The Ashcraft-Gentry plane was labeled *The Answer*. Also poised for a shot at the record were Martin and Marguerite Jensen and William Ullbrich in the *Three Musketeers*.

"We were taking off from the upper field, where Admiral Byrd's ramps were built," Viola recalls. "Just before Jack took off, he said he wanted to call his mother in Independence, Missouri, so he got out of the plane again. That call was the nicest thing he ever did, because the next time his mother got a call, he was dead."

The weather was good when they took off at 8:46 P.M., Ashcraft flying the first four hours while Viola rested in the back.

"We put a plywood board in the back where I could sleep. There was also a toilet in the back, just like in modern days. The gasoline tank was made into a seat, so we could hold more gas."

To give herself privacy from her various male copilots, Viola had installed a plywood divider between the pilot seat and the rear seat. After midnight she exchanged places with Ashcraft and wheeled the plane above Long Island.

"Around two o'clock the fog came in from the ocean," Viola recalls. "Dr. Kimball [the noted weather forecaster] thought it was going to clear, but the Mitchel Field water tank just disappeared below us. I knew once the fog came in from the ocean, it would never go away until noon, and I told Jack that."

There developed, in the gloomy night fog, a problem in group dynamics. Ashcraft was asserting himself and Gentry was deferring even though there was no official chain of command.

"Jack said I should put on a seat belt. He'd been flying with the Gates Flying Circus, and I was just a few years in the air. Sure, people asked me about that later. I knew the fog would last. But was I going to give him orders? Absolutely not. Anybody who had been in the air as long as he knew what he was doing.

"But I did ask him to land. He said, 'Are you afraid to fly with me?' I said, 'If I was afraid to fly, I wouldn't fly.' The doctor said later that was what saved my life—I wasn't afraid.

"We never thought about death. Almighty God put us on the earth. When your time comes up, whether you're in bed or in an airplane, your time comes up."

But—as the old joke goes—what if the pilot's time comes up?

To keep their bearings above the fog, they flew in squares for the rest of the night—five minutes east, five minutes north, five minutes west, five minutes south. Ashcraft was counting on two things: that the fog would lift soon, and his buddy from Hartford, Connecticut, would meet them above the field for refueling by 7:00 A.M.

Around 5:00 A.M., Ashcraft resumed the controls. At the same time, Lee Rockwell, another backer of the flight, sent a radio message that he would arrange for an emergency refueling if they needed it. But they said they had two hours of gas left, enough to hold them until Ashcraft's buddy, named Kincaid, flew down from Hartford. Rockwell was so confident that he left the field, but Kincaid was held up by the same fog across Long Island Sound, and would not arrive at Roosevelt Field until 9:00 A.M.

By 5:50 A.M., the night watchman at Roosevelt saw *The Answer* flying low. At 6:10 it returned, apparently sputtering, low on gas. By this time, Gentry says, Ashcraft was looking for a break in the fog. She had already dropped a weighted note that said "Need gas immediately," but the note would not be found in a gully until later.

"Jack ran out of gas," Viola recalls. "He told me to fasten my seat belt because he was going to jump the Westbury water tower and land in the potato fields."

The first meeting of the International Women Pilots Association, later known as the 99's, in Valley Stream, Long Island, 1929. Left to right: Mona Holmes, Mary Samson, Elvy Kalep, Ruth Elder, Mrs. John Reiney, Amelia Earhart, Elinor Smith, Viola Gentry. (Air and Space Collection, Nassau County Museum)

There were a lot of potato fields on Long Island in 1929; the lush flat earth kept the New York region supplied with hashbrowns and French fries until the parkways and the subdivisions swarmed over the land. In 1929, an aviator in distress could hope to land in the potato fields and do no more damage than grind up an acre or two of mashed potatoes au Cabinaire. Ashcraft certainly knew that as he glided down into the fog.

"I wasn't concerned," Viola recalls. "Jack didn't say much except, 'Hang on.' I woke up two or three days later in the hospital."

The powerless glide of *The Answer* took it into the Hicks Nursery, major supplier of shrubs to all the North Shore estates. The only tree of any size, too big to transplant, was a solitary hickory tree jutting above the seedlings. At 6:13 A.M., *The Answer* stopped dead at the hickory tree, at a gruesome right angle to the ground. Ashcraft was crushed by the heavy engine and Gentry thrown forward against the plywood partition.

"The woman was dazed and almost hysterical," Henry Hicks, owner of the nursery, was quoted in *The New York Times*. "It looked like the man was dead so we got the woman out first. She muttered something about her name being Viola Gentry, and finally I could understand the other things she was trying to say. She was telling me she was Viola Gentry, and that she wanted me to notify Bill Ullbrich, who was in the *Three Musketeers*."

Her friends and competitors, Ullbrich, Martin Jensen and Marguerite

214

Jensen, also seeking an endurance record over Long Island, dropped hand-written notes, inquiring about their friends' condition, while Viola Gentry was rushed to Mineola Hospital, near death.

"Almighty God gave me life," she says today. "It would have been easy to take it, right then. God told me when I was unconscious that I was to live, to help other people.

"For the next year and a half, I lived in the hospital. The doctors kept working on me. They put me in a body cast. They tried to straighten out my two arms. They made me store teeth. They gave me blood for my internal injuries."

The Flying Cashier had no money to pay her hospital bills, but her friends staged a dance at Roosevelt Field, and raised several thousand dollars. Later she was transferred to a New York facility with the appealing title of "Hospital for the Ruptured and Crippled." (It has since changed its name.) The doctors approached her case with enthusiasm, for rarely had they seen a patient, and a celebrity at that, so badly broken, so determined to recover.

"I wanted to fly again," Viola says. "At that time they were organizing the women pilots into the 99s. The doctors said they would only let me go if I found a nurse who would accompany me. Luckily, I found Mrs. Grogan, who stayed with me for months, and that's how I got out."

With the support of friends, Viola returned to flying several years after the crash. In 1932 she had another, less serious, crash with a pilot named Jack Warren, whom she had married secretly around the same time.

"His family thought I was a disgrace to women because of my flying," Gentry says. "His mother backed me up, but that was all. We were married five, six years and we had a ball. We had no children, thank God. I used to feel sad, but I feel better now, with all the problems today. Dope. Bad language. Bishop Sheen says you blame the parents, not the children, but I don't know."

Jack Warren died suddenly of pneumonia in 1937, and Gentry scattered his ashes from an airplane. For twenty-five years she worked as an assistant housekeeper at the Bellevue Clearwater Hotel in Florida, taking time off to fly in several of the women's long-distance races. At the age of seventy-two she was a copilot for Ruth Johnson on the *Powder Puff Derby*, keeping track of the checkpoints on the map, but not taking the controls. Soon after that, cataracts ended her active flying.

Now she travels around the country to as many reunions as she can afford—a gentle pioneer who does not care for addressing large groups, but who can charm a small audience. Today, at the Lindbergh ceremony, when Viola Gentry is introduced to the crowd, she waves timidly. But the young newscasters, with their persistent microphones and their limited knowledge of Gentry's history, find her a charming interview.

"The pilots today, they're all jealous of us," she tells a young woman from a radio station. "The astronaut from New Jersey, I always forget his name, he says we had all the fun flying.

"When I met him, I asked him the same dumb questions: Did you dream about going to the moon? He said the same answer I would have given about my career: He had to concentrate on getting the ship where it was going, not thinking about other things."

When the festivities are over, Viola and a few old-time friends decide to search for her hickory tree, just a few miles away in Westbury. They drive over to Jericho Turnpike and look for a sprawling nursery, but the Hicks' three hundred acres have dwindled to a few dozen, and the fifth generation business is now a retail garden shop.

Edwin W. Hicks, a man close to her age, comes out to greet her. Yes, he says, he remembers the wreck. It was his father who pulled her from the wreckage.

But the tree? Viola asks. What happened to the big tree that broke Jack Ashcraft's neck and put her in the hospital for a year and a half?

Hicks gestures to his left and right, at the cement parkways and the subdivisions slashing through the foothills of the North Shore. The tree, he says, was taken down a few years after the crash, to make room for Robert Moses' Northern State Parkway. That must be close to forty years by now.

"Oh my goodness," Viola Gentry says.

Viola Gentry tells the younger generation about the real flying, 1977. (Photo by William E. C. Haussler)

24

Maurice Bellonte

Le Bourget, France

In the Musée de l'Air Maurice Bellonte is signing autographs with a fountain pen. A wisp of a man, eighty-one years old in a gray striped suit, he seems even more modest compared to the garish red airplane hanging over his head, the first airplane to ever fly nonstop from Paris to New York. He was the navigator of that plane.

After signing his name in copies of his autobiography, Bellonte leafs through the book to locate a few printer's errors—fractions of time, a false date. With a neat flick of the fountain pen, he corrects each misprint.

"He is very meticulous," says his wife, Raymonde, a tall formidable woman who stands by him.

Bellonte is included in this museum for his navigational work on the first scheduled airline in the world—"La Ligne," between Paris and London—and later for bucking the brutal headwinds with Dieudonné Costes in 1930 to reverse Lindbergh's journey. He is visiting today after ceremonies honoring the fiftieth anniversary of Lindbergh's success. No event commemorated in the Musée de l'Air has happened outside the lifetime of this gentle man in the gray striped suit. When he was born, just north of Paris, there was no powered aviation at all.

Bellonte does not remember the first flight of the Wright brothers—he was seven years old at the time—but he can remember going to the flatlands at Bagatelle to see Santos-Dumont fly his Demoiselle, and the first planes of Gabriel Voisin at Issy-les-Moulineaux, both on the edge of Paris.

The French had just as many early heroes as the Americans. In 1909, when Bellonte was thirteen, a hot-eyed Frenchman named Louis Blériot, using crutches because of an injury, hobbled into his monoplane and crossed the English Channel at dawn—the first long-distance "raid" in history.

"In school the next day, we all made paper airplanes," Bellonte recalls. "We all knew the name of Louis Blériot. We went to see him fly at Bic. Then we used to go to the atelier, the little shop, near my house in Courbevoie, where Blériot was making his planes. We'd look through the spaces in the wall. For the privilege of getting inside, we'd go fetch gas in a wheelbarrow. Little by little, I went to work for Blériot."

At nights, after school, the young boy would do odd jobs, while Madame Blériot stitched the canvas wings and told the apprentices how her husband's Channel-crossing plane had been built *en famille.* One day they overhauled an engine that Bellonte recognized as the one that had powered Blériot across the Channel.

"I had my hands on that engine," Bellonte recalls with pleasure nearly seventy years later.

I ask Bellonte why he went into aviation. Was it the dream of historic crossings such as Bleriot's? Was it the desire to fly like the birds? Mrs. Bellonte, a former philosophy student, interjects with the pragmatic response: "He was not rich." There were six children in his family, and an apprenticeship with Blériot was a financial blessing. The glimpses of the Blériots were a bonus.

Bellonte saw combat during the war, but he brushes off his tours in Europe and Morocco because he was not a pilot. When he learned to fly in 1921, he did it by observing over the shoulder of the established pilots, long before he imagined himself crossing the Atlantic.

In the Musée de l'Air Bellonte walks a few paces to a cigar-shaped fuselage and pats it with affection. The name is *Goliath,* and it looks more like a trolley car than an airplane.

"It would resemble a plane with the wings on," says Bellonte, pointing to the place where the wings once fit.

Then he points to a picture on the museum wall, showing passengers in derby hats and sport jackets.

"It was like a garden," says Mrs. Bellonte.

"La Ligne," her husband says softly. "The Line."

In 1921 he was an airborne mechanic and radio operator for the Company Air-Union, the first scheduled passenger service in history, established between Paris and London after the war. The flying time was posted as three hours and twenty-two minutes.

"Sometimes there was only one or two passengers," he recalls.

People did not casually check themselves onto "The Line" for a hop across the Channel, not at first. They wanted to be shown it was safe. Henry Farman, the pioneer aviator, tried to promote the service by having his picture taken in the cabin, as if he were in a café.

"People were afraid," Bellonte says, as he and his wife chuckle conspiratorially. Then perhaps for the millionth time, he tells his favorite story of the lone female passenger and the twenty-four-hour trip.

He and Costes were a team by 1924, having made friends over the billiards table. One wintry day, they left Paris with one passenger but were forced to land at Poix in the Somme region because of oil problems.

"We had about eleven hundred kilos of freight," Bellonte said, "and it was snowing when we had to land. Then we continued to Abbeville and landed for fuel.

"The first time it was not so bad because the pasenger was taken to the farmhouse by the guardian of the land. Then as soon as the day came, we flew again, but stopped for petrol at Lympne."

By now they had crossed the Channel and were within an hour of their field at Croydon, on the south side of London, but: "Ten minutes after takeoff, one of the engines stopped, so we just had to land in front, the plane went on its nose. The passenger jumped out, as we did. This was in the snow, near Ashford. She took her little bag and walked away."

"She had enough," Raymonde Bellonte says, chuckling with vague disdain for the woman who had no faith in The Line.

One thing is apparent from talking to old pilots like Bellonte. Crashes were part of the business, to be handled as well as possible—and to be survived. They were not the multi-hundred disasters of the jet age, when crashes are fewer, but deadlier.

"If we knew we were going to crash, the passengers would go to the rear, the plane would land on its nose, the passengers would not be injured."

Bellonte turns his slight body toward the cockpit, which is on a higher level than the passenger cabin. There is room for only one pilot in the cockpit.

"I learned to fly by watching other pilots," he says. "But we had no double control on this plane. If the pilot left his control, he would get down from his place, and I would climb up. There would be twelve passengers if we were filled. They would see me climb up the ladder to the controls, but they did not know I was not a pilot yet."

"And you did not tell them," his wife says, chuckling again.

Bellonte recalls the rivalries on "La Ligne," how Costes and a British pilot named McIntosh used to race across the Channel, to see who could clear customs first. Occasionally, pilots on The Line were killed, but Bellonte says he and his partner never took risks, and the run soon became stable.

Aviation was moving to longer challenges by the mid-1920s, "raids" to the Orient, to the Americas. The French had hoped one of their pilots would make the first nonstop connection with New York, but when Fonck and Nungesser failed tragically, and Lindbergh made the historic crossing on May 20–21, 1927, the French reacted with admirable gallantry, considering their disappointment.

"I was at the field that day," Bellonte says. "I saw Lindbergh landing, although at the time I did not meet him.

"It was a daring exploit," he says. "We thought it was very important to the development of aviation. It was a starting point. We thought, if we had a plane able to do it, we would have tried it. It was rather difficult to get the plane that would fly the Atlantic. And flying eastward, with the tail winds, *The Spirit of St. Louis* was able to do it. But flying westward, we had to wait three years."

Bellonte recalls how in 1928 "a rich man, an industrialist" (Louis Breguet, the aircraft manufacturer) hired him to refine radio and navigation equipment. Costes had already left La Ligne to work for Breguet, and along with Joseph Le Brix had made the first flight across the shorter, less treacherous South Atlantic route. Hoping to be teamed with Costes on future "raids," Bellonte trained himself to use a sextant, to take sightings from the stars; Costes kept expanding the capabilities of their Breguet "Super Bidion" single-engine biplane.

They painted their plane a garish red because "There was already a *White Bird* [Nungesser], a *Yellow Bird* [Armand Lotti], and other colors," Bellonte explains. On July 13, 1929, they raced two Polish war aces, Idzikovski and Kubala, out into the Atlantic, both planes atempting a nonstop crossing, but head winds reduced ground speed to fifty miles per hour, forcing the Poles to crash in the Azores, where Idzikovski was killed. Realizing they could not reach the United States without refueling, Costes and Bellonte returned to Europe, covering 3,354 miles in twenty-eight hours, proof that their plane was durable, but no record.

"We could have crossed the Atlantic by stopping in the Azores," Bellonte says, "but we tried for a nonstop record instead."

The next venture was an overland flight to the Orient, but they had no way of knowing the garish red color would be as dangerous as the conditions of flying.

"We tried to fly to China nonstop," Bellonte recalls. "We could see nothing, above the clouds. It was hard to know where we were."

Mrs. Bellonte, whose English is excellent, helps her husband describe the adventure. They used Russian maps issued in 1847, communicated by hand-written notes over the throb of the engines, and ended up flying a record-breaking 4,910 miles in fifty-two hours before landing their red biplane in Tsitsikar, Manchuria—in the middle of a border war between China and Russia.

Their Chinese captors, on that distant frontier, reasoned that only a Bolshevik would be flying a red airplane, and Costes and Bellonte were held captive for several days until somebody contacted the French embassy in China. (The story of this flight to the Orient is told in his autobiography, *Le Premier Paris–New York* published only in French, by Plon, in 1976.)

On the way back, they took a side tour of the major cities of the Orient and Europe. The red airplane, hanging in the Musée de l'Air, has the names painted in white relief—Tsitsikar, Harbin, Moukden, Shanghai, Hanoi, Calcutta, Karachi, Alep, Athens, Rome, Marseilles.

By the time they got back to Paris, they were heroes. Bellonte gestures to a cartoon on the museum wall, showing two aviators using a red airplane for an outdoor pissoir. One aviator turns to the other and says, "Ah! Mon Vieux! . . . Depuis Paris!" (Ah! Old Fellow . . . Since Paris!)

"When we got back to Paris, we knew we could fly the Atlantic and survive anything," Bellonte says.

Raymonde Bellonte smiles with tolerance as she recalls an incident yesterday, when Giscard d'Estaing visited the museum. The young president had pointed to the large question mark painted on the side of the plane and asked what it meant.

The Bellontes were too polite to tell him that in 1930 everybody in France knew why it was called *The Question Mark*. So many aviators had died attempting long-distance raids that the government had banned all further expeditions. Armand Lotti and his pilot managed to slip their plane out of Fance to make the first French flight from west to east in 1929, while Costes and Bellonte worked so secretively that one reporter called their mission "a question mark." A few days later the crew painted a giant question mark on the red fuselage.

"We were planning to fly the Atlantic Ocean," Bellonte says. "We knew it was necessary to fly more than eight thousand kilometers even though the Atlantic was only six thousand. Because of the head winds, it was necessary for our plane to have more speed.

"*The Question Mark* was much faster than *The Spirit of St. Louis*. His maximum speed was two hundred kilometers, ours was two hundred and fifty. Our engine was rated for six hundred and fifteen horsepower, but in fact it was seven hundred and twenty. We were sure we could do it when the weather was right."

Without revealing their plans, Bellonte laid out a four-legged flight plan for 6,310 kilometers in thirty-six hours. On August 30, they got the favorable weather report they had been awaiting—fair weather and easterly winds early on the first of September.

"We were supposed to take off at five in the morning, but the weather was not good, and we did not take off until ten," he says.

"The plane was very heavy—six and a half tons—so if we took off with all that weight, we had to see where we were going, near the ground."

As they waited to attempt a feat that had killed so many other Frenchmen, what did Bellonte do?

"He slept," Mrs. Bellonte says, knowing the story by heart. "I did not know him then. I was studying philosophy in New York, but I met him a year later, when we were skiing in the Alps. Later he told me how he slept."

On the first of September, their colleague, Jacques Codos, surveyed the clearing skies in a smaller plane and at quarter to ten he gave the word to Costes and Bellonte: "You can go now."

Two minutes late, Maurice Bellonte and Dieudonné Costes complete the first west-bound Atlantic crossing from mainland to mainland. They quickly flew on to Dallas to collect the twenty-five thousand dollar Easterwood Prize, adding the names of a few more cities to their well-traveled plane, *Question Mark*. At their send-off in New York, Bellonte, left and Costes, right center, were greeted by Colonel Easterwood, left center, and Clarence Chamberlin, far right, another famous pilot. (*New York Times*)

Costes barreled the heavily laden plane down the runway, using thirteen hundred yards for the takeoff. Codos followed them for a while, over the Oise and the Seine, but waved farewell as they headed for the English Channel at St. Valèry.

On this day, nearly fifty years later, Bellonte does not have the time to tell the details again, how he made seventeen different astral sightings to keep the plane on perfect course, how their year of planning produced a flight with no terror and no surprises.

"It is all in my book," Bellonte says, tapping the copy of his autobiography. "You see the picture here. We had no phones on the plane, and Costes and I were exchanging notes. You see, a full box of notes. Costes asks me, 'You recognize?' and I say, 'yes.' A few minutes later he says, 'Sea gulls.' "

The Atlantic passed on schedule. The weather was bad at dawn off Newfoundland, but the plane was lighter, and handled easily. They were sighted several times, and word was passed to the new Curtiss Field in Valley Stream, Long Island, where they planned to land. But at Curtiss Field memories persisted of the celebration in 1927 for Nungesser and Coli, who never appeared out of the ocean mist. All day on September 2, Costes worked his way down the coast, thirty-seven hours and twenty-four minutes of flying time ("We were two minutes late," Bellonte says, but that was pretty good.") until he made an ordinary landing and the partners were carried on the shoulders of cheering Americans. It was only a fair exchange for the gallantry shown to Lindbergh in 1927.

Bellonte recalls their first words being broadcast to crowds waiting, around midnight, all over France, as the band at Curtiss Field played the "Marseillaise." He also recalls one special person waiting for him in the relative tranquillity of the hangar. Lindbergh had been forced to drive to New York after his own plane had conked out in Pennsylvania.

"He said he never would have missed our landing," Bellonte recalls. "He greeted us so warmly. He said Paris to New York was much more difficult than New York to Paris. That is what he said. I never forget that."

There was little time for a triumphant tour of New York because the flight was technically a run from Paris to Dallas, to collect a twenty-five-thousand-dollar prize that had ben put up by a Texas millionaire. The aviators rushed to Dallas, qualified for the money, then toured American cities for another swath of names to be painted on the flaming red sides of *The Question Mark*.

He touches briefly on his career after that—engineer for Hispano-Suiza, decorated for working in the underground during the war, chairman of the French Safety Commission from 1950 to 1961. Costes died in 1973, so Bellonte receives all the honors now, whenever Frenchmen celebrate aviation.

In 1977 the Bellontes were flown by Air France to America for the fiftieth anniversary of Lindbergh's flight. They crossed by Concorde from Paris to Washington in one-twelfth of their time in 1930.

"You do not even have time to be tired," Bellonte says.

I ask about the complaints about noise and expense of the sleek Concorde.

"We do not hear any difference on the ground. They all make the same noise," Mrs. Bellonte says.

There is a trace of wistfulness in the old navigator as he thinks about the jump from *The Question Mark* to Concorde.

"I think there have been many big progress," he says. "But it is not the same. We had to make it ourselves, from our own experiences. Now everything is programmed. All this progress. It should have made the people of the world closer together. But I don't know. This is what I wish."

As Bellonte signs an autograph, I chat with Raymonde Bellonte, referring to her husband as "Monsieur Bellonte." An impromptu look of concern crosses her intelligent face, the look the French use when the onion soup is too salty, or some American abuses their language.

"We do not call him 'Monsieur Bellonte,' " she says academically, but not crossly. "He is 'Maurice Bellonte.' He is a part of history now."

V
The Industry

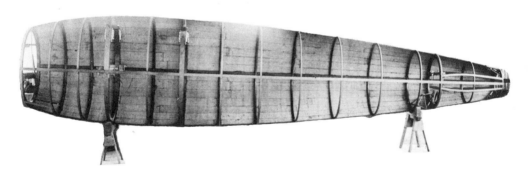

Airplane pilots received most of the attention in the late 1920s, since they were the ones who put their bodies inside the flying machines, but competition among the builders had its own tensions, its own intrigues.

From the very beginning, the builders learned and borrowed from each other, to the point of nasty legal struggles between the Wright brothers and Glenn Curtiss, or the broken partnership of Claude Ryan and B. Franklin Mahoney.

The friendship and contacts intertwine regularly in aviation, like a subplot in John Dos Passos' *U.S.A.* In chapter 25, John K. Northrop describes how he first worked with the Loughead (Lockheed) brothers, then worked for Donald Douglas, then formed three separate companies under his own name that were eventually absorbed by giant corporations. Yet Northrop always retained his reputation as one of America's most creative engineers, designing sleek new machines such as the Vega and the Alpha.

By the time Jack Northrop hit his prime, builders were no longer designing planes for itinerant stunt men and free-lance taxi pilots. They could see a market developing for scheduled air service, based upon the efforts described earlier in these pages by Maurice Bellonte, Harry Bruno, and Claude Ryan. After Lindbergh came back from Paris, he and his young bride made long flights to the Caribbean and North and South America to test the routes for Pan American. Other top pilots explored routes for the fledgling companies, particularly for sixteen firms that gained government contracts to carry the mail.

In chapter 26, one of the epic airline captains, Dick Merrill, recalls ferrying the mail in the night fog above the rugged Piedmont mountains. He had almost none of the equipment available today and would have to seek out remote grassy fields when he could no longer stay aloft. The growing companies were now able to provide systematic instruction for their pilots. New careers for enterprising young people began to open up, as George C. Dade recounts in chapter 27. But too many inexperienced private pilots were killing themselves and endangering others, so the federal government sent inspectors out to the fields to try to limit the accidents. At Roosevelt Field on Long Island, the federal representative was Dome Harwood, who recalls the joys and the perils of his new job in chapter 28.

A new airplane-related career emerged in 1930 when the fledgling United Airlines decided to put stewardesses with nursing training on the Chicago–Cheyenne–San Francisco run. In chapter 29, one of the original eight United stewardesses, Harriet Fry Iden, says her job was not merely "coffee, tea, or milk."

In the 1930s, while still a distinct minority around the airfields, women continued to prove they could be the equal of men, just as Elinor Smith and Viola Gentry had shown in the late 1920s. When the men pilots were called into service in World War II, women handled most jobs in the factories, and they also took over some of the airborne roles at home. As a high-ranking officer in the Civil Air Patrol, Nacy Hopkins Tier (chapter 30) trailed submarines along the Atlantic coast, learning after the war just how vital her role had been.

Somewhere along the line, the day of the pioneer was over. Today, the surviving Early Birds might claim that the only true pioneers were those who flew before World War I, but others would insist the Lindberghs and Doolittles and Elinor Smith Sullivans were pioneers, too. Still others will put in a claim for the cosmonauts and astronauts as pioneers, and the black Americans and the female Americans now in the aerospace training program. In many ways they are all pioneers.

But by 1930 a real border had been crossed from when the Montgolfiers and the Wrights took their first flights; from when Cal Rodgers buzzed across the United States and Harriet Quimby gave up her writing career in order to fly. The age of the individual is long gone; achievement and airplanes are no longer of human dimension. In chapter 31, George C. Dade describes how the Long Island Early Fliers felt putting their hands on an airplane fifty years old, seeing it emerge from the rust and the dirt, re-creating with their hands an age of personal triumph that has largely vanished.

25

John K. Northrop

Santa Barbara, California

Northrop is one of those awesome corporate names like Lockheed or Douglas or Boeing. You know they are out there winning massive government contracts and building more airplanes, but they only intrude on your consciousness when something extraordinarily good or bad happens to them.

Unless you happen to depend on your income from one of these behemoths, names like Northrop are hardly as personal as other American manufacturers. You don't exactly shave every morning with your trusty Fairchild razor, or drive to work in the family Grumman.

But these aviation companies are also named after people—men who tinkered in garages and basement workshops, who were born to the last echoes of stagecoaches and grew old to the roar of space rockets. To aviation buffs, these people are famous for what they contributed to the industry. John Knudsen Northrop, for example, is known for his sleek, simplified body structures.

The name Northrop became personal to me in the spring of 1977, when I visited France to interview Maurice Bellonte and Armand Lotti, two of France's early aviation heroes, and was asked by my newspaper to file a story on the Paris air show.

Just an hour earlier, I had been eating the cassoulet at the Beaux Arts Restaurant, a dish I understood perfectly, every last bean and sausage of it. I had been feeling very eighteenth centuryish in the narrow streets of the Left Bank. Now I was on the broad plains of Le Bourget, and felt like the last human among space-age mutants.

Frightening machines were roaring overhead; giant halls were crammed with computers and engines and models of new airplanes. Customers speaking a dozen languages had spent the equivalent of lunch at the Beaux Arts for a ticket to wander among all this technology.

Did you know there are airplane freaks as fanatic as baseball fans? English buffs wore denim jackets with souvenir patches from every air show in the past generation; they knew the dimensions of the latest Airbus from France the way a bleacher bum in Wrigley Field knows Bobby Murcer's slugging percentage.

I was confused by the massive display of aerospace hardware, and it struck me that the only way I was going to understand the industry that created these machines was to zero in on one company. A Swedish businessman told me one of the hottest planes at the show was "your own Northrop F-18 fighter." I had never thought of Northrop or any other aviation company as "my own," but I sought out the Northrop hospitality suite, a prefabricated chalet at the edge of the runway, with pots of flowers and lawn furniture set outside, so people could watch the hardware fly. Inside, a company official put a glass of wine in one hand and documents in the other hand, so I could read all about the F-18 Hornet, a naval strike fighter with Sidewinder missiles.

One page described the six-minute routine the pilot would perform—a "half Cuban eight," a "wave-off Immelmann," and ten other maneuvers to impress every premier, dictator, president, troika, junta, and shah from the Potomac to the Suez.

Most maneuvers would take place over the field, so any crashes would stay among the family, as it were, rather than injure any Frenchmen working in the fields outside Le Bourget.

This was no idle precaution. Four years earlier, people told me, a Soviet Ilyushin TU-144 had crashed at the bottom of a low maneuver, killing five crewmen. The day after my visit to Northrop, a Fairchild Republic A-10 would slip out of synchronization on its six-minute routine and crash at the bottom of a loop, killing the pilot.

This potential of death created a tension in the Northrop chalet when the F-18 prepared for takeoff. The friends of the company crowded forward to watch, all drinking, eating, talking, and breathing suspended for the next six minutes. The plane roared over the observation area, looped and flipped and wiggled its wings, turned and roared back upside down, turned again, dived and climbed and flashed back to the runway, six minutes later, and everybody commenced to breathe.

A few minutes later, there was a commotion as Hank Chouteau, the test pilot, strode into the room, still wearing his flight suit. People applauded and patted him on the shoulders. I glanced at the Northrop literature describing Chouteau as part Osage Indian, part French. Chouteau had designed his own coat of arms—"The Lance and the Lily"—combining his two proud heritages.

Chouteau drank a beer and admitted he was "a little dehydrated" from his minutes of tension in the oxygen of the cockpit. In a low-key technical way, he seemed as professionally proud as any athlete I had ever met after a good performance. For six minutes, he had carried the hopes of that giant corporation—their reputations, people's incomes—in his hands. Now he was going to look at films of the maneuver; there was so much he had missed "while I was absorbed in details."

In that half hour the aviation industry became more personal to me. Then Bill Schoneberger, an official from Northrop, casually mentioned that John K. Northrop himself, famous for designing the Vega and Alpha airplanes, might be willing to be interviewed. I made my request on the spot, since I knew that the company, now a sprawling giant, had once been nothing larger than the dream of one engineer from Santa Barbara, California.

A few months later, I am driving north along Highway 101, with the Pacific Ocean on my left and rugged bare brown mountains on my right.

The handsome, secluded apartment building in Santa Barbara faces east, toward the continent. His rooms seem quite orderly, the apartment of a meticulous person who has plenty of free time for straightening up. Then I remember being told that his wife died earlier in the year. "Jack" Northrop is tall, slender and sandy-haired, and reserved, as I explain my hopes for this book.

"You're talking to a very old-timer who has been retired for twenty-five years now," he says. "This company is doing a lot of interesting things today, but I'm more or less out of date. I can tell you a little about how I started, however.

"My family moved to Santa Barbara from Nebraska in 1904, so I'm almost a native, but not quite. I was nine years old.

"My earliest recollection of aviation is going down to Los Angeles to see a Frenchman named Didier Masson.*

"My interest was really stirred by the Loughead brothers, Allan and Malcolm, who later changed their spelling to 'Lockheed.' They had a two-passenger seaplane that they used to carry passengers to the San Francisco World's Fair in 1915. At the conclusion of that fair, they moved back to Santa Barbara.

"They were running a seaplane down a ramp to the water and carrying passengers out, and then I found they were actually building planes here in Santa Barbara. I was attracted by it, and I tried to get a job. They were working in Rusk's Garage, where I had worked as a mechanic, three blocks from the ocean. I saw the two-passenger plane they brought down from San Francisco, but the airplane I worked on was a seven-passenger flying boat that was designed to carry more people and make more money faster, and was built here. Allan Loughead was a promoter-pilot person and not an engineer, basically. Malcolm Loughead was a very high-class mechanic,

---

* Masson was an American, who commanded air strikes against Pancho Villa in Mexico in 1913, and later served in the Lafayette Flying Corps.

but also not very good with any engineering training. When I went to work for them in 1916, they were pretty well complete, but they needed somebody to design the wing structure. I'm not a college graduate, but in those days Santa Barbara High was a good one and I had a natural knack for math and geometry and physics and chemistry and mechanical drawing, so I was probably as well prepared for the work as some college graduates.

"I did the designing of practically everything they built from the oceanfront for about a year, before they decided to make a transcontinental flight. So we changed it from a float plane to a land plane, by modification of the body and additional landing gear. But the first flight ended in a nose-up accident in Arizona.

"When the war came along, I was drafted into the army, but the Lougheads got a contract for the building of two Curtiss HS-2L flying boats, and they got me to come back to assist with those.

"After the war, they wanted to build some sort of an airplane that could be sold as a continuing product, so I designed for them a small, single-place sport biplane, with folding wings. It had a nice clean fuselage—something I used later in my work.

"Up until that time, airplanes had been built any which way as far as aerodynamics were concerned. Right from the start, I was interested in making the airplanes efficient aerodynamically. That carried right through my whole life as an airplane designer. I could see the whole world waiting for a plane that was just a little better, a little more efficient, than the planes of that time."

From the beginning, Northrop was concerned with designing sleek, light craft that cut through the atmosphere with less resistance than the earlier, bulkier enclosed craft.

"So I designed the S-1 sport biplane, and Allan Loughead was able to build a nice little two-cylinder engine of about twenty-five horsepower and he flew this engine very well. However, it was priced at two thousand five hundred dollars, which was so much more than you paid for a used Jenny at the cessation of World War One—certainly no more than three hundred dollars. So the Lougheads went broke in 1920, and I went to work for my father, a building contractor.

"But my father had undertaken a building too big for his background, and he was out of a job. Needing a job desperately, I went to Santa Monica and got a job with the Douglas Company, a very important period in my life. The first week I spent in the carpenter's shop, building ribs for the Round the World Cruisers, and then I had the opportunity to move up to the engineering department.

"I have such an outstanding memory of going to work in the engineering department. I was told to design the fairing for the fuselage, an outside structure designed to reduce drag. There were clips that would be fastened to steel tubes—but in all my work with the Lougheads, I had done nothing of that sort.

"I was at my wit's end because I needed a job desperately, and here I was falling down with it. I fooled with it and fiddled around for a whole morning, getting scareder all the time. I took my lunch out of my lunch bag, and tried to eat it—and really did get sick. Then I went home, feeling I had probably lost my job. Well, it didn't turn out quite so badly. When I came back, somebody else had been assigned to do the fairing, and I was told to do the gas tanks.

"This, I knew how to do. I worked with Douglas under very happy circumstances for three years and learned a tremendous amount."

As Northrop discusses the people with whom he worked, it becomes obvious how much crossbreeding there was in the California aviation industry. Douglas had emerged after the First World War as an early builder of mail and passenger planes, and Northrop, with his proclivity for design, would observe how Douglas ran his own firm.

"Don Douglas himself was the primary salesman of the organization and did a certain amount of directive work in the engineering department, but I never considered him a designer of aircraft. He was a wonderful friend and highly capable and had a good relationship with possible military customers. But the times he actually worked with the drafting board were few and far between. He depended on the individuals in the engineering department and had a general idea what he wanted to accomplish. When he had to cut back, he sent a wire saying, 'Let all the engineers go except two,' and one of them was me.

"My work at Douglas was a conventional two-seater, with external bracing and skin on the fuselage. As I learned more, worked more, I began to see the tremendous possibility in cleaning up the airplane, making the fuselage smoother, getting rid of brace wires. Get rid of what we call parasite drag—everything sticking out in the air that isn't exactly contributing to the lift.

"In the fall of 1926, at home, I laid out the outlines of the Vega," Northrop says. "It was a radical design in those days, far removed from the more conventional types that Douglas was building, and I felt he would not be interested. Also, I wanted to own a share of the company which built it, which was impossible in the Douglas Company.

"You don't sit down one night and design an airplane. You sit down for a couple of months. At that time they were comparatively simple to what they are today. They were ridiculously simple. My early design was a drawing, a few details. The fuselage was a monocoque."

As Northrop explains it, a monocoque has a single-layer fuselage, as opposed to most airplanes which have an internal structure covered by external plates for strength. Most explanations of "monocoque" use an eggshell as the best example of single-layer strength. Several Frenchmen had applied the theory to airplanes, but Northrop was one of the first to do extensive practical work with it. His other contribution on the Vega was reducing the external structures.

"I wanted to build a full cantilever wing without any braces—and put the strength in the wing itself. We were living in what I call the golden age

The single-layer fuselage, known as a "monocoque," which John K. Northrop helped prepare for the Lockheed Vega, the premier plane of the late 20s and early 30s. (Anthony Stadlman)

of aviation. We knew we could fly. There was no doubt about that, but the world was still your oyster when it came to improving the structure.

"I had a big argument with Allan Loughead who said, 'You'll never sell it as long as you live unless you have braces on the wings.' In those days, that was a logical argument. I hung on for the full cantilever—and it was built that way.

"Allan Loughead was selling real estate in Los Angeles, and I said I thought the Vega could be very much better than anything else, and how about starting a company to build it. He had a friend named W. K. Jay, who had good association with financiers. The present Lockheed Company was founded at that time."

Northrop describes the way the work was divided in that company:

"If there was any socializing, Allan Loughead did it. He was the hail-fellow-well-met. He knew all about Hollywood, and he would show them around if there was any socializing after business. I was the one and only engineer until shortly before I left. I'm a loner anyway. I'm an unsocial person, not antisocial.

"I met the pilots, of course, They were the customers, once the job had been done. They would look at the plane, decide if they wanted to buy it. But the pilots never had much to do with the design, except our own test pilot, of course.

"I can't give our test pilot too much credit. Eddie Bellande was the test pilot on all our early tests. He was absolutely invaluable to sense what was happening.

"I had a private license and did a certain amount of solo flying for my own education, but I was primarily a designer and aeronautical engineer. I never really had a yen to fly on my own. I went along for the ride, and to

John K. Northrop with his longtime test pilot, Eddie Bellande. (American Hall of Aviation History, Northrop University)

learn what I could, and to improve the plane. When we were working on the Vega, I never took it off or landed it.

"Eddie Bellande said it would wobble a bit. It didn't have quite enough fin—the fixed vertical tail surface, which terminates in the rudder to the rear. Well, I increased the fin area and reduced the rudder area a little."

The Vega began to appeal to some of the biggest names in aviation—Roscoe Turner, Art Goebel, Wiley Post, Hubert Wilkins, and Amelia Earhart. In 1930, Ruth Nichols set the record for a flight between Los Angeles and Roosevelt Field—thirteen hours and twenty-two minutes. From June 23 to July 1, 1931, Wiley Post and Harold Gatty flew a Vega monoplane, the *Winnie Mae*, for the first round-the-world flight, beginning and ending at Roosevelt Field. Their actual flying time was four days and ten hours and six minutes and the feat was a great boon to the Lockheeds.

"It was life or death to the company. If the plane was selected by one of them, it would establish records almost from the first, and would be a tremendous boost to the company.

"Wiley Post did a tremendous job. He set I don't know how many world's records. Earhart, too. Hawks, another one. All these people were interested in the most efficient airplane, and it so happened that we built it."

Lockheed sold 141 Vegas over a few years, an excellent sales record—

"an indicator that it was worthwhile cleaning them up," Northrop says, but he was not comfortable with the makeup of the company.

"Please don't stress this," he says, "but Allan Loughead had a friend who came out of Chicago, in whom Allan had a great deal of confidence. He went around after a few weeks saying, 'You can't do this, you can do that.' He said we absolutely had to make a dual plywood fuselage. W. K. Jay and I decided life was too short, and we raised the money in late 1928." (It was not until later that I realized Northrop was talking about my Czech friend, from an earlier chapter, Tony Stadlman. When I wrote Northrop asking him to tell me a little more about his relationship with Stadlman, Northrop sent back a note saying: "Stadlman was shop superintendent both in Santa Barbara and with the first Loughead Company in Burbank in 1926. He lives in the San Francisco area and we have not kept up an active contact." Neither man would explain the coolness of so many years ago, although Stadlman, in the earlier section, was more expansive than Northrop.)

In 1928, for the first time, there was a product with John K. Northrop's own name on it, even though the company was called Avion.

"It was really well known that I was the designer of the Lockheed Vega, so my name was of some value for the possibility of advance in aircraft design. Nobody knew the name of the financial people. In fact, you couldn't name an aircraft company after a list of stockholders. It was related to the reputation of the designer."

Did Northrop think he was taking a risk in starting a new company?

"There was enough interest in aviation at the time, it was possible to raise the money and get started. I don't think the monetary end ever concerned me. I guess it should have. I was spending somebody else's money so many times. But I had a knack for knowing what would turn out all right—to take advantage of the golden age of aviation, to make a better airplane, make a stronger airplane, that would climb faster."

When asked to name his most important contribution, Northrop says it was the first plane developed by the new company—the Northrop Alpha.

"I had experimented with a wooden monocoque before, but now I developed a smooth-skinned metal monocoque. This was the Alpha that is now hanging in the Smithsonian, because it was the first of its type with the thin skin of the airplane carrying the structural load."

Northrop takes a sheet of the Santa Barbara newspaper and batters it with his hands.

"Once it buckles, it has no value at all. Through a certain amount of research, we found that thin-skinned metal, plus stiffeners, made the stress-bearing value completely practical. It eliminated what nobody wanted to have—a sudden failure.

"We had not only a very durable metal structure, but a practical one from the standpoint of strength-weight ratio, and ease of manufacture, and that type of structure which developed on the Alpha was really the pioneer for every airplane in the sky today as far as the structure is concerned.

"They differ greatly in detail, but they all employ thin metal stiffened in various ways to carry the load, instead of steel tubing or something strung outside the structural strength."

Did people criticize his idea? "They probably did, but not to any great extent where it would discourage me from doing what I thought was correct. Of course, the Ford Tri-Motor was early metal, but it was corrugated. We gave thinnest structure.

"Of course, we knew the Alpha was a success long before we put it in the air. We used bricks as the static test. We loaded bricks on the cantilever wing until we had a number of pounds per square foot—the maximum load of an airplane. That's how we knew the structure was adequate."

The Northrop Alpha was purchased by National Air Transport (later merged into United Airlines) to replace its old biplanes. Later, TWA used it for its first night flight on the airmail routes.

The Alpha was such a success that William E. Boeing, who had been building planes since 1916 at Seattle's Lake Union, purchased the company from Northrop's financiers.

"They all sold out to Boeing," Northrop says. "After a couple of years they wanted to move it to Wichita, Kansas. This was in the thirties when there wasn't a lot of money and it was a perfectly logical move, but, remember, my family came from Nebraska to California, and I wasn't about to move to Wichita, Kansas.

"I went back to work for Douglas a while, worked on design and construction, more business than they could handle. I set up my second company in 1932, and perhaps it was too successful because Douglas acquired fifty-one percent of the stock in 1938. A year later the present Northrop Company was started, at Hawthorne in the Los Angeles area.

"The thing I tried to do with the third company was a continuing quest for simplicity and low drag, resulting in the design of the flying wing. This was the ultimate in my quest for simple, cleaner airplanes. There's nothing but the wing. It's a perfectly straight-lined structure—no booms to hold the tail, no breaks in the structure."

Northrop takes out a glossy aviation yearbook from the late 1940s and points to a B-49 Flying Wing, which looks like a spaceship—a continuous mass, no long wings projecting out, a droopy tail like a dolphin's hindquarters. By conventional wisdom, it looks like something that should be under the sea rather than flying over it—but we all know about conventional wisdom.

"It was a highly efficient plane—two to three times as good as conventional designs flying today. The cost per pound would be no more than seventy-five percent of the conventional plane because it's so much more simple.

"Look, here's a bunch of them at the factory. We built models of them—a one-hundred-seventy-two-foot span airplane, with enough space so men could walk around in it. It was designed for bombs and reconnaissance. We had sixty pilots fly small models—one thousand hours for the small model, five hundred for the large model, with no adverse reports."

Why don't people know more about the Flying Wing today?

"In 1948 we were ordered to scrap them all," he says. "Our company was very young and inexperienced, and we didn't have our politics straight, and somebody decided they wanted somebody else to have the business. It was canceled from a purely political standpoint. The forces that canceled it were so strong, it appeared wise to cancel it for the good of the company. I'd like to play this phase of it down, but actions were taken toward this company so somebody else could have the business.

"I still think one of these days somebody will pick it up and go with it."

We have been talking for over an hour now, sitting in the same chairs as when we began. I have the feeling both of us are waiting for somebody to bustle in from the kitchen to serve coffee or tea. Quickly, I switch the subject to the massive brown mountain looming out the back window.

"There's a golf course out back, and I walk on it most days," he says. "It is beautiful in Santa Barbara. Mrs. Northrop and I moved back here about twenty years ago. Mrs. Northrop passed away five months ago and I'm still trying to get used to it."

Northrop says he retired not too long after the disappointment of the Flying Wing. He says he still does "some consulting work" for the present Northrop Company, but it's not the way it used to be.

"I loved looking ahead, planning," he says. "The chance of being in it at the point of it happening. When I left Northrop, we knew everybody by sight. We established human relationships. Today, everything is done by committee.

"In the old days, one or two military people would talk business. They were real gentlemen. Now, the rules and regulations are so great. My experience was so great, I don't see where you could have it today."

26

Dick Merrill

Fredericksburg, Virginia

It is a picture-postcard day in Virginia, spring blossoming everywhere, people congregating at the old churches in the center of town, which are all red brick and iron grillwork and white shutters. Is this really neon-and-aluminum America, these old brick colonials being renovated by real people, or are we in the middle of a big outdoor museum?

Just south of town, where the highway speeds up again, is another living museum, and here the old Spads and Mailwings are poised in an open-sided hangar. The signs warn not to touch the propellers, because most of the planes are ready to fly, but you can walk up to them, stick your head into an open cockpit, and fantasize what it must have been like carrying the mail—in the dark—over the Piedmont, before radar was invented.

The museum has one living feature few museums can match. Suppose, for example, when you visited the Rodin museums in Paris or Philadelphia, you could take your questions to a side office, where the elderly sculptor was at your disposal?

Here at the Shannon Airport Museum the curator is in residence. He is Harry Tindall ("Dick") Merrill, who has logged more official miles than any pilot in history. He is eighty-three years old now, as wrinkled as he is tanned, and his hoarse southern chuckle is bothered by shortness of breath.

He is an original. He is one of those pilots who supplied the glamorous image of airline pilots for a generation of the American public.

"I've flown over fifty thousand hours," he tells the autograph hounds and the antique-plane buffs when they drop into his office. "They credit me with forty-four thousand one hundred eleven hours and twenty-nine minutes for a scheduled airline, but when I flew privately, I was never logged. I'd fly one hundred and twenty-five, and one hundred and thirty hours a month in those days. I built that up. The limit is eighty-five hours now. Nobody will ever get those numbers I flew."

It wasn't just the hours. It was the survival of accidents in three different decades; it was the fires he detected from the air, the sick babies he rushed to hospitals, the races across the ocean, the presidents he carried, and the sacks of mail he ferried through the mountain fog. Not only that, he was good copy.

When Dick Merrill opens his scrapbooks, I realize I have read about him a hundred times before, even if I did not remember the name. He was the darling of Broadway columnists when New York was glamorous; he was a Stork Club regular; he ran around at night with Walter Winchell, and popped up in Ernie Pyle's first articles about aviation.

1930. New York *Daily News*. Ed Sullivan's column:

Pilot Dick Merrill, greatest of the mail transportation aces, made a two-point landing on some scallopine of veal (in Mamma Leone's restaurant).

These were the blurbs, the items, the escapades, that formed the image of airline captains. In an age when we thought presidents had wisdom, when we assumed doctors could cure everything, when all clergymen had a direct line to the Maker, we also believed that airline captains led exciting lives. And the reason we believed that was Dick Merrill.

"On one trip to Europe I met Churchill, King Albert of Belgium, and the Earl of Granada, then flew into New York and went to the Stork Club. Winchell, Damon Runyon, Bob Considine, about three o'clock in the morning, back in the Cub Room, all these characters would meet back there. Jake the Snake, Mike the Bike, Weaver the Cleaver, and they'd all want to fly down with me, but they'd never ask me to do one thing wrong. I'd go back to the Cub Room and Runyon would say to me, 'Merrill, I want to tell you, you're a helluva guy. You've gone from royalty to the Mafia in one week.' "

On this graceful southern spring day, Merrill is much closer to his roots than when he was hanging around with Winch and Jake the Snake. Before he met those New York sharpies, he had earned his reputation by flying in every state Robert E. Lee defended, and a couple Lee fought against, too.

"All the captains today were my young copilots," Merrill says. "Whenever I fly Eastern now, they announce that an old pilot is on board, and if he were the type to boast, he would tell you how he taught the Wright brothers how to fly. Heck, young stewardesses don't even know who the Wright brothers were. Well, I did teach Wilbur, but Orville learned by himself—heh-heh-heh.

"I grew up in Memphis and New Orleans, and the first time I ever saw a plane was 1914 at the Mississippi State Fair in Iuka. Katherine Stinson was the pilot, doing stunts and loops, and that intrigued me. I went to France in 1917 and flew about six or seven hours at Issoudun, but I didn't learn anything. In 1920 I flew a Jenny with the Stinsons in San Antonio. That's where I learned to fly.

"I bought an old Jenny in Columbus, Georgia, for six hundred dollars, and went barnstorming. I was always the pilot. I never even learned how to fix the plane. I flew sixty years and couldn't change a spark plug. The stunt man was always the mechanic, and later the airlines had mechanics. Barnstorming was a rough business. If it rained Saturday and Sunday, you couldn't afford a hotel.

"I flew for the Gates Flying Circus for a while. There was a fellow named Bugs McGowan who advertised, 'Come out and see a man jump from a plane without a parachute.' He'd put on a helmet and shoulder pads, and the pilot would come down low over the grass fields, going twenty, twenty-five miles per hour, go into a landing stall, and Bugs would hang off this ten-foot rope, hit the ground, and roll over. Later he was killed, but not doing that."

As he barnstormed the South, Merrill gained a reputation as a bachelor who never drank or smoked but enjoyed making a wager from time to time. A couple of the sporting people of New Orleans even toyed with the idea of bankrolling him for the Orteig Prize between Paris and New York.

"There was this gambler called Nick the Greek, who had a hot night at the tables and said he was going to finance me," Merrill says. "I knew I could do it. But that night he went back to the tables and lost it all. Then a colonel was going to bankroll me, but people started calling it a suicide attempt, so he backed off. I forgot about flying the Atlantic until much later.

"I met Lindbergh a couple of times, but to me, he was always a weirdo. I talked to fellows who went to flight school with him. He bailed out four times, when other pilots would go right in, through the fog.

"His statements, the things he did after 1936. See, most of my friends have been Jewish. I go to them first if I need friendship. In my heart, I couldn't like him, after the things he pulled."

After Merrill gave up competing for the transatlantic prize, he joined the exotically named Saint Tammany-Gulfcoast Airways, an airline formed after the U.S. Air Mail Service was dismantled, which flew the mail between New Orleans and Atlanta. In 1928 he joined Pitcairn, the forerunner of Eastern, which had four Mailwing airplanes running between Atlanta and New York.

"The banks were using it because the mail could leave Atlanta by eight o'clock at night and be delivered in New York in the morning. The post office and the army couldn't fly at night. They killed off all their pilots. It's a little bit different at night. You have a forced landing at night, you can't just pick out any spot to land. That's why you got paid twice as much.

"To give you an idea why we liked it, you got five cents a mile flying days, and ten cents a mile flying at night. There was no training. You just

1928 - Capt. Henry T. (Dick) Merrill - 1976

Dick Merrill, as a night-mail pilot in 1928 and handling a modern jet in the late sixties. (Shannon Air Museum, Fredericksburg, Virginia)

started out and did it. You weren't supposed to fly unless the weather was good, but at eight o'clock in Atlanta, you wanted to go, regardless of the weather ahead."

The Pitcairn Mailwing PA-5, which Merrill used at first, had been specially built in 1927 to carry mail, with compartments for 500 pounds of mail sacks in front of the pilot. Soon he switched to a PA-6, he says, which could cruise at 110 miles per hour, land at 50, and had a range of 600 miles.

"It had a needle that kept you from going from one side to the other. Years ago, they didn't have those instruments, in the early days of flying, and that's why so many pilots were killed. The minute they'd get in the clouds, the airplane would get away from them. It would spin right in. When you're in a darkened room, you have no reference on the horizon. You have to rely on instruments.

"Fortunately, I had some experience, so it wasn't totally strange to me. We got very proficient with our instruments, but we wouldn't trust our luck too much. If it got too bad, every thirty miles there was an emergency field."

It sounds easy from fifty years' distance, but in 1929 to fly blind was to venture where the human race had not yet been.

"There was always an element of risk about the engine quitting at night," Merrill says, "because you couldn't see anything. In the daytime, at least you could see to miss a tree. But at night, if your engine quit before you got to one thousand feet, you'd get your name in the papers—but you wouldn't get to read it yourself.

"After one thousand feet, you could jump out. Lindbergh would go up to one thousand feet and jump out, but Art Smith, flying right behind him, would go a little bit lower, down to three hundred feet, and see the field, and land on it. Lindbergh deserves all the credit he got, but the Rubertson brothers couldn't afford to have the mail burned up, so they almost fired him.

"When I flew that North–South route, the other pilots would say, 'You'd better get going, Merrill's coming tonight and he's not going to stop.' If some pilot landed and didn't want to fly the weather, they'd say, 'Look out, Merrill's going to throw you down a sandwich.' That meant I'd fly over somebody. A little competitive. That was my claim to fame. I was one of the best bad-weather pilots in the country."

But even legends had to find an open space in the countryside sometimes, and Merrill's scrapbooks are bulging with his escapes:

• The beacon was out in Greensboro, and Charlotte was socked in with weather, as Merrill circled the Carolinas on the night of January 8, 1929. When he realized he would have to bail out, he could hardly squeeze out of the narrow cockpit. He fell more than a thousand feet before the parachute opened, and he sprained his ankle hitting the ground. But, Merrill notes, "I got the mail off on the morning train," then, he adds, he stayed over in Shelby, North Carolina, nursing his injuries with a lady friend.

- Buffeted by a northeast wind over Williamston, North Carolina, Merrill found himself making no headway. He made a perfect landing with the help of flares, in the face of gale winds, and put the mail on the train.

- Safe landing in a fog in Royston, Georgia.

- When the motor quit on him near Amelia, Virginia, he had to slip over the telephone lines, then drop heavily onto an emergency farm field, planting furrows with his airplane and cutting his forehead on the instrument panel.

- Landed through dense smoke from a fire near Spartanburg, South Carolina.

- Caught in a private plane in a lightning storm, he made an emergency landing at Hopewell, Virginia.

- Emergency landing at Appomattox Courthouse, Virginia.

"I don't think I ever canceled out but one time," Merrill says. "You can't do that today. The rules are tighter now. The romance is gone out of it today. In those days, the people in Spartanburg and Greenville and Richmond would say, 'Let's go out to the airfield and watch the mail plane land.' That was at one in the morning, I'm talking about. You'd put your lights on, dive at the crowd. Today nobody can even get in the cockpit unless he's authorized."

The reason for the tighter supervision comes out in Merrill's next statement. Of the first forty pilots hired to fly the night mail for various airlines, thirty-one died in accidents before they had a chance to grow old.

"We lived in Richmond, had a little place at the airport," Merrill says. "There were four of us on the Atlanta–Richmond run. Two would sleep in Atlanta and two would sleep in Richmond.

"Sid Malloy stayed with me at Richmond. He hit a tower in the fog at Fort McPherson, Georgia, on Friday the thirteenth of September 1929. John Kytle of Hapesville, he was bringing the mail into Atlanta one night, ran into Stone Mountain and didn't get a scratch. About two months later, we had a stratofog all up and down the East Coast, he ran smack into the Blue Ridge.

"Another fellow, Glenn Fields, flying down from Memphis, I guess around 1929.

"His wife and children are waiting for him. He's on top of the clouds all the way down, just about out of gas, and he has to come down. He's twenty miles out of Atlanta. Five more minutes and he'll be home. I remember it as if it was yesterday. There's not but one mountain within twenty miles of him, that's Kennesaw Mountain, and he runs right into it. That just shows you fate. Five more minutes and he'd have been down.*

"The rest of us were just lucky we lived because at some time or other, the airplane would get away from us. Then we learned to use what we had.

"The needle, that was the important thing, to show if you were turning left or right. We didn't have the sophistication we have today, but we could keep it going straight with that needle. It was like a gyroscope, you could judge by three hundred and sixty degrees, by how long it took you to turn. You could turn one hundred and eighty degrees and go back.

"Then we had the airspeed to keep you controlling up and down. We had an altimeter. The bad thing about that was, if you were at Richmond, which was practically sea level, you knew where you were. But you'd get to Atlanta, it was one thousand feet high, and you had to compensate because of your altimeter. You couldn't just stay one hundred feet above sea level. No, sir. You had to know where you were.

"Of course, we didn't have contact with the ground. We heard the government weather reports, but we didn't have a transmitter. Later we had a receiver, a low-frequency range, if you got on the right side of it, dash-dot, but if you got on the other side, dot-dash. If you flew it right down the center, where you should, it was a T.

"The only thing was, if you got any rain at all, you couldn't get it. Static would drown it out. They had these Department of Commerce stations every hundred miles."

All well and good for staying in the right direction. But how did Merrill know when he was over a landing field in the middle of a cloudy night?

"Every field had a code, like Richmond was RD in Morse code. There was an antenna, signals were sent, two, three miles from an airport. If you got right over the station, you'd get a cone of silence."

Fine. Now you were over a field—still unseen. How did you get down?

"You knew, no matter how bad the weather was, you'd see a beacon, always one thousand feet from the field, and then you knew you were ahead of the runway. You'd set up a certain airspeed, hit the ground, and hope you stayed right-side up.

"Sometimes when you landed, you couldn't see enough to taxi to the hangar. I used to take off night after night when you literally couldn't drive a car or mail truck. I've landed when I couldn't see the ground. Lots of times.

"Later they had instrument landings where you could go straight down the runway. You did that in a DC-3. I checked out [tested] Arthur Godfrey in a DC-3. Made him land with a hood over his head."

---

*This took place a few months after Fields gave flying lessons to George Dade on Long Island.

As Merrill perfected the art of blind flying, his fame began to spread around the country. Part of it came from the heroics: buzzing a burning home until all eleven residents were awakened and saved; flying a sick baby from Asheville, North Carolina, to Johns Hopkins Hospital in Baltimore.

It did not take journalists long to discover Merrill's colorful life-style. In the early thirties, aviators were celebrities, just like ballplayers and movie stars. The young Washington columnist and later a war correspondent, Ernie Pyle, once did a whole column about Merrill wearing a bathing suit on the daytime Atlanta run because of the hot sun on the open cockpit. (Snow was no problem in the open cockpit, Merrill says, because the snow "just went right on by.") Other writers discovered that Merrill carried a pet squirrel in his shirt pocket on all flights. Later he carried a lioness on a few night runs.

Eventually, the night flights were discontinued because of accidents, and Merrill began flying passengers when Pitcairn became Eastern Air Transport, now Eastern Airlines. During the racing season, he managed to balance his flying schedule with quick sorties to Saratoga.

He got a reputation as the pilot who wouldn't die. In 1933 he crash-landed an Eastern Curtiss Condor in Dacula, North Carolina, without injuring his three passengers. In 1936, both engines quit in Eastern's Douglas DC-2 over Port Jervis, New York, but he landed "right on the side of the mountain" and all eleven passengers survived.

The planes kept getting bigger, and the stakes higher. In 1947, Merrill was flying one of Eastern's Lockheed Constellations off the Atlantic coastline when a propeller sheered off, slashing through the cockpit window— three feet from his head—killing a flight attendant. But Merrill got the plane back to an airport without injury to any of his sixty-eight passengers.

"Lockheed said I beat a ten-million-to-one chance," Merrill says. "But it wasn't that bad. I just outlucked everybody, I guess. I could name a hundred nights when I should have been killed. The Good Lord's keeping me around for something. Everybody was getting killed, but you'd say, 'It won't happen to me.'

"I built up such a feeling, I didn't think an airplane could hurt me. I may get killed walking across the street someday, but those airplanes have had so many chances to kill me, I don't think they can.

"I may be wrong, I may get killed someday, but then, could there be any better way to go? Fly right into the side of a mountain and, bing, get it over with, instead of being sick and lingering like poor Roscoe Turner did."

Merrill talks about one other famous flight. In 1936, he teamed up with Harry Richman, a pilot and popular entertainer, to attempt a record for crossing the Atlantic from New York to Europe and back again. Flying a Vultee with forty-thousand ping-pong balls planted in the wings for flotation, they reached Wales in sixteen hours and were barreling back near Newfoundland, when the instrument panel indicated some kind of problem.

Dick Merrill and his pet lioness, Queen, on an early Eastern Air Lines mail run. He started with pet squirrels, just to keep him company on those foggy nights over the Piedmonts, but when the squirrels kept getting lost, he found a pet that wasn't so easy to lose. (Photo: Eastern Air Lines)

"He was the owner, but technically I was the pilot because he didn't have the experience in bad weather. His manager told him, 'Harry, we know you can fly, but here's a guy making a living flying an airplane. Before you do anything, ask Merrill.'

"We get near Newfoundland, if he'd asked me, I'd have said, 'Nothing wrong, Harry, just our airspeed is out,' but, bing, he reaches out and dumps four hundred and forty gallons in the Atlantic Ocean. He just goes berserk.

"We landed in Newfoundland, got more gas, came into New York, but we would have gone nonstop if he hadn't dumped the fuel. People asked me to write articles, to write books about it, but what does it mean now—the guy's dead. We could have set a record that would have held until the jets came in, but that's water over the dam now."

Merrill flew press charters during the presidential campaigns, and he flew Dwight D. Eisenhower many times, and even though he retired around age sixty, he continued to fly for nonscheduled companies into his seventies. He hasn't handled a plane in the past year because he hasn't been feeling well, he says, but he uses the airlines regularly to commute from Miami Beach, where he lives with his wife, a former Goldwyn Girl.

"I'm eighty-three now," he says. "How lucky we have been to fly. People are earthbound, yet we've been able to go beyond that. I've heard Jimmy Doolittle say he wouldn't like to live his life all over again because he didn't think he'd be as lucky next time. Well, nobody could be as lucky as I've been. There might be a few bad nights I'd like not to live over again. But if I could, I'd like to go out tonight, out of Richmond at one o'clock in the morning, and do every bit of it again."

27

George C. Dade—II

Glen Head, New York

"During my teenage years, the emphasis in aviation shifted from the individual to the age of corporations," says George Dade, sitting in his home-basement museum, where he is building a scale model of the Curtiss-Roosevelt Field complex. That field was where he spent his childhood and later developed a thriving airplane packing business.

"When my father went to work for Glenn Curtiss on Long Island in 1921, most pilots were still making airplanes by themselves, step by step. By the time I got out of college, you had people like Dick Merrill flying for new airlines, never touching an engine himself. That's in the space of a decade.

"I was right there, watching it happen, and getting caught up in the growth. That kind of specialization meant hundreds of new careers in aviation for people like me who happened to be in the right place at the right time.

"When we first moved to Curtiss Field, right next door to Roosevelt Field, I was happy just to help set out kerosene pots to mark the runway at night. A little kid tagging after the adults, scampering around an airfield. But every year I stayed there, the field got more built up, and more jobs were available. I started varnishing planes, selling tickets, working the public-address, and before you knew it, I was in business for myself, packing airplanes to go overseas during World War Two.

"What kind of jobs were available? My first full-time job was selling tickets to people going up for their first flight. It was a big adventure. Casey Jones, a famous pilot, had a flying service at Curtiss Field. My main

task was to convince people it was safe to go up. I got so tired of hearing people say, 'I don't mind how high I go, as long as I can keep one foot on the ground.' Later I operated the public-address system like a disk jockey, playing John Philip Sousa's 'Stars and Stripes Forever' until I wore out the record."

In addition to persuading people to try a short flight, Dade also pointed out the prominent aviators on the ground and in the air.

"On this job, I wore mechanic's overalls, just like the other employees, although as a ticket-seller, I didn't get very dirty. I stuck out like a sore thumb, with that spotless uniform, so I used to visit the big drum behind Hangar 16 where they tossed the oil rags, and I'd rub one of those rags all over my overalls.

"This was about the time Lindbergh came back from Europe and started flying exploratory routes. Needless to say, we paid more attention to him by this time. One day Lindbergh was having trouble putting on his parachute, and I just happened to be hovering a few feet away, so I rushed over to give him a hand. Louie, from Court Commercial Photos, took a picture of me adjusting Lindbergh's parachute. That's probably my prize souvenir from those days.

"Nowadays people ask me if that picture was taken just before he flew the Atlantic. I'd like to say yes, but too many people know it wasn't. If you

The crowds inspected the latest in aviation, 1928, at Curtiss Field. (Air and Space Collection, Nassau County Museum)

look at the picture carefully, you can see a few swipes of oil on my overalls, to show I was a big-timer.

"I got to see a lot of Lindbergh in those years, when he was making all the observation flights for the airlines. Curtiss gave him a twin-seat Falcon with four hundred horsepower. He was always afraid of taxiing over to the hangar because people were so crazy, they'd just rush over to his plane. He was afraid somebody would get killed by the propeller. The press would announce he was due at the field, and five thousand people would show up. It was just unbelievable. A couple of times I'd drive out to the end of the runway and he'd get in the car, and we'd slip away from the crowd.

"I was even present at one of the few times in his life when Lindbergh got bawled out for the way he flew. This was in 1928, when Floyd Bennett went up to rescue the German pilots in Canada and caught pneumonia. Lindbergh volunteered to fly serum to Montreal, but in his haste he took off without clearance and with the wind at his back—both against all rules. It didn't help, either, since Bennett died right after that.

"When Lindbergh came back a few days later my boss the manager of Curtiss Field, (Mazel 'Merry' Merrill)—just a grand guy—called him quietly into his office. I put my ear to the wall and heard him dress Lindbergh down such as you've never heard.

AIR CRASH KILLS
JIMMY COLLINS

The late Jimmy Collins, famed test pilot, examines prop on plane before recent flight.

CRASH KILLS FAMOUS TEST PILOT.—The fate he often mentioned in his "Flying Stories" in The News caught up with Jimmy Collins yesterday. As he swung in to land near Farmingdale, L. I., on what he said would be his last test flight, the motor ripped off his Grumman fighter, the ship crashed in cemetery.

"He said: 'Not only did you disregard your own life, but you risked that airplane and the safety of others on the end of the runway.' This went on for fifteen or twenty minutes. Lindbergh took it humbly. Didn't say a word.

"Merry Merrill was another of my heroes. On August 25, 1928, I wrote in my diary, 'Never had a better boss in my life.' Three days later he took off for Buffalo to ferry Lindbergh's Falcon back home to Long Island. I remember going out that night and turning on the beacon, but he didn't show up. A few days later they found his plane in the woods upstate. I was heartbroken at my boss' death, but he wasn't the first or the last.

"That was the other side of aviation in the twenties. There was the romance, the excitement, the pioneering, but there was also the price of it—the blood. I used to keep this diary every night before going to sleep. I'd make a list of all the pilots who had been killed, but I stopped counting when the list reached one hundred.

"From hanging around Bert Acosta and a lot of the other famous pilots, it was my observation that they didn't talk too much about dying. They were sorry. They missed their friends. But death was part of flying. Maybe for fifteen minutes they'd think 'It could have been me,' but then they'd go back up again, get it out of their system.

George Dade knew over one hundred pilots who died in crashes, including his family boarder, Jimmy Collins, in 1935 (The Garden City Archives) and a pilot named Flannigan in 1929. (George C. Dade)

"I got that way myself, because I lost so many friends. My folks used to rent out rooms upstairs to aviation personnel. The most famous tenant we ever had was Jimmy Collins, an early test pilot for Grumman. He was called 'Nine-G' Collins because he was one of the first pilots to dive an airplane and pull it back and feel the force of gravity to nine G's.

"He was a very studious man, not the daredevil type at all. Very polite, very considerate. At one point, I was sweeping out the house, but he treated me just like his brother. Of course, he wasn't making much money himself, now that I realize.

"While he was living with us, he was making a dive with tremendous stress on the plane, and the plane disintegrated in midair and he was killed. Not only did I feel awful for him, but I had to go back to his room and put together all his things and ship them back to his family. He had very few belongings outside of some clothes. Several times I had to clean up after pilots who died, but this was the only time in my own home.

"With all this carnage, it was no wonder my parents didn't want me to go up in a plane. They had an absolute rule, but my desire was stronger than their prohibition. One day Johnny Wagner was teaching a friend of mine to fly, and he asked, 'Do you want to go along?' So I did. Being in the air was everything the pilots told me it would be.

"Now I was stuck. Every night I would write down all the trivia of my life—what I had for dinner, who I spotted at the field. But here was something special to me—my first time up in a plane—and I didn't dare put it down in my diary. Suppose my mother had seen it?

"So for that day—May 16, 1928—I simply wrote the initials 'W.U.' That stood for 'Went Up.' I must have done that half a dozen times before my parents found out.

"The way it happened, Johnny Wagner took me up for another ride, but as he slipped back to land, I saw my younger brother, Bob, standing next to the fence. I knew if he saw me, he'd go back and tell my parents, so I ducked down in the cockpit, hoping my brother would leave.

"Unbeknown to me, my brother had seen me take off, so he knew I was there. After a while, he came over and put his foot on the wing and got in the front seat and said, 'George, aren't you going to get out?' Well, I thought I was in for trouble, but apparently I survived, because my diary shows I went up many times after that. I think my parents knew I was going to fly, no matter what.

"I begged rides from anybody who was going up. One day Ellie Smith asked me to accompany her on a flight to Wilkes-Barre, where she was performing at the opening of the Wilkes-Barre airport. Looking back now, I can see why my parents were so upset about my wanting to fly. I was only fifteen and Ellie only sixteen. Sure, she was already an excellent pilot, but still, we were just a couple of teen-agers. Imagine today, letting a fifteen-year-old go with a sixteen-year-old to the Poconos. I don't mean a boy-girl thing. I mean flying.

"On that flight we ran into bad weather when we got into the moun-

Seeing so much death did not deter seventeen-year-old George Dade from making his first solo flight in 1929, becoming one of the youngest pilots on Long Island at the time. (George C. Dade)

tains. The altimeter said we were three thousand feet high—but we were only clearing the mountains by a few feet, and the weather was getting lower and lower. Finally, Ellie looked for a level field, which is not so easy in the mountains. She made a landing in a farm field, but there was a rut, around four feet deep, and she banged up the plane. I was just happy we survived.

"The funny thing was, this was the time when Lindbergh was courting Anne Morrow, and all the press was right on their tails. I was about Lindbergh's height, was wearing helmet and goggles, and Ellie was smaller than me, and had her helmet on. We could not convince those farmers we were not Lindbergh and Anne Morrow until we made a telephone call back to Curtiss Field, to arrange to get us home.

"I was flattered by the comparison. I used to tag around Lindbergh when he came to the field, and I made up my mind I was going to be a pilot, too. I got a job with the Roosevelt Flying School, which took over the field when Curtiss moved to Valley Stream. Working for the school, I could learn to fly at reduced rates.

"My diary says I took my first lesson on July 9, 1929, with Lieutenant Glenn Fields, just out of Army Flight School in Texas. We spent thirty minutes practicing banks and turns, and on my third lesson we did takeoffs and landings. I had around five hours of dual flying time, but I still wasn't thinking about a solo on July 19, when Glenn Fields said to me: 'think you could do it all by yourself?'

"Now I've heard many pilots describe their first solo as carefully as their first kiss. For me, the outstanding recollections of my first solo were not any overwhelming fear of being up alone, but the emptiness of that front cockpit. It seemed so huge without Glenn Fields sitting in front of me. I could even see his control stick moving when I would activate the dual control in the rear cockpit. Almost as if he were up there with me. Maybe that helped me get through my first solo, who knows?

"When I landed, I was one of the early solo students of the Roosevelt Flying School. I got my private license at the age of seventeen, after a test by a federal inspector named Dome Harwood, who was like a god around Roosevelt Field. Somebody wrote at the time that I was only fifteen and that I was the youngest pilot in the United States. The press liked to exaggerate things about flying. I still have those clippings, but there were several pilots around Long Island who were younger than I.

"Before long, Glenn Fields moved south to fly the airmail, and flew into a mountain in Georgia.

"People made a fuss over my being a pilot. It helped me get through Hempstead High School, I can tell you that. I was always looking for excuses to run over to the field, so I'd cut a class here and there, but I would give speeches about aviation in my Science or English class. I developed enough poise that I had the lead in the school play, and I even gave the address at graduation, though somebody else was the valedictorian.

"I used to tip off my teachers when Lindbergh was coming to the field, so they could get a glimpse of him, or I'd get his autograph for their copies of We. Sometimes if there was an extra seat on the company plane, I'd let my teachers get on. I'm not saying that's the only way I got through Hempstead High School—but it didn't hurt.

"I never had time for extracurricular activities at Hempstead. The only thing I did for the football team was at our big game with Freeport. I flew over the field in my own plane and dropped out a banner with our school colors. It was a bedsheet my mother never missed. The kids at school all knew me as a pilot. That was a big thing. In my high-school yearbook, they called me 'Our Lindy.'

"I never quite made it to be a Lindbergh. By the time I got my license, the Depression was just starting, and the age of air stunts was ending. But there were many specialized jobs in aviation, even with the Depression, and before I knew it, I was in business for myself. It started this way:

"One company made announcements from a huge airplane that flew low over populated areas. They had two big speakers in the center, but the plane had a very low, gliding angle, so you had to talk fast. One day the regular announcer was sick, so the pilot, Randy Enslow, asked me to do it. I was strapped in the tail, in a wicker chair, next to three lights—red, amber, and green. We flew to Bridgeport, Connecticut, into the wind, with the red light on. When the light turned to amber, that meant get ready. The pilot would cut the throttle, go down at a sharp angle, and put on the green light, which was my signal to talk:

"'At your grocer today—a free dish towel for two boxes of Silver Dust—Silver Dust—the housewife's delight.'

"Then I'd push the button, because by that time we were right over the treetops. He'd jam that throttle forward, and we'd roar out of it, back to our altitude, repeating this over and over again. We also would throw out paper circulars. We'd get fifteen, twenty dollars an hour to throw circulars over Freeport or some town. Imagine the flack you'd get today, but nobody talked about pollution then.

"My next step to my own business was to buy my own plane from a student at Brown University. It was an Aeronca C-2, not much more than a power glider with a thirty-horsepower engine. It weighed only seven hundred pounds, and had thin tires, and a top speed of fifty miles an hour, even though it was rated for eighty. I remember I took it off from a ball field in Rhode Island, just getting over the outfield fence.

"It had just the right specifications for making money. I got a job with the RKO distributor to plug their latest films. I'd get a megaphone and fly along the beaches announcing, "Now playing at your local theater—*Dixiana* from RKO.' The cockpit area was so small, and I was around six feet four by then, that I'd pilot the plane with my knees while holding the megaphone.

"These little bicycle tires had an advantage, too. The plane was so light it wouldn't stay on the ground when you tried to land. So you'd have to reach out and grab the tires and hold them, like brakes. I remember one time coming back in a wind, the plane kept blowing back in the air, so I grabbed those tires and burned the insides of my hands.

"My business began on a trip to Boston to work the beaches for RKO. The ceiling kept getting lower and lower over Long Island Sound, but I pushed ahead against a twenty-mile-per-hour head wind, which meant I was gaining only twenty-five miles per hour.

"The plane didn't have any radio, and no instruments except for a compass and an altimeter. This was in 1930, and you didn't dare fly above the weather. It was like holding a gun at your head. Today's private airplanes—well, they're like another world. Like Buck Rogers against Daniel Boone. Anyway, the farther I went, the worse things got, and I knew I had to stay close to the ground.

"I kept going because I didn't want to go back over the water, figuring I'd find a small field. As you probably know, the farms in New England are pretty rocky, so the farmers take all the rocks and make a stone fence around the fields. When I saw clouds coming right over the next hill, I decided to slip into this field and wait out the storm.

"But I came in too fast and was heading directly for a stone wall. The prospect of hitting the rock wall was not too tasteful. In the corner of my eye, I saw a haystack. All I had to do was veer over fifteen degrees and I'd hit the haystack. I had never read anything in the textbooks about using a haystack to slow down, but it seemed like a good idea at the time.

"What I didn't know was, this farmer was a lazy farmer. Instead of pushing all his rocks to the perimeter of the field, he had made a big pile in the center and covered it with a foot of hay for the cattle. Well, I went into this thing expecting to be cushioned, and—whap! The wings came right around and almost dropped off, but I was lucky. I only had a nosebleed and a pretty good headache.

"Still, I was mad because I'd spent my last three hundred seventy-five dollars for the plane, and I figured my career was over. I called my brother, who drove up with a truck, and we cradled the plane and took it back to the field. Whenever there was a wreck, of course, people would come over to take a look."

As bad as it seemed, Dade's accident led to his new career.

"Apparently, people were impressed with the way we had cradled the plane on the truck, because pretty soon we got calls: 'George, I just turned my Waco over in Kingston, could you come up and get it?' And they'd pay us—fifty dollars at first, then more.

"In those days, you'd suffer ten times as much damage from moving the plane as from the crash. They'd pack the plane like you would a piano—tie it down as tight as you could. That's all right for a piano because it has a short truck, and couldn't twist. But an airplane would twist and be damaged. You might as well throw it away.

"I designed a biaxial support system, where you'd bolt it down in two directions, but not the third. That way, it could vacillate, without bearing the torque on its structure, but still be held in place. People began to patronize the Dade Brothers Company set up by my brother, Bob, and my father.

"Around 1935, when the Interstate Commerce Commission came in, we were qualified to carry wrecks in seventeen states. I personally had picked up wrecks as far away as North Platte, Nebraska. Sometimes if you made the mistake of getting to a wreck too fast, you had to cut the bodies out yourself.

"Later we got the idea of putting planes in packages for long-distance travel. The first plane was Al Williams' Gulfhawk, II but the way it happened was strange. He was supposed to fly in one of Lord Beaverbrook's air shows in Europe. As a publicity stunt, the Gulfhawk was going to be carried to Europe in the *Hindenburg*.

"Naturally, we got the call one afternoon that the *Hindenburg* just blew up. They still wanted to ship the Gulfhawk, so they made a quick call and discovered the *Queen Mary* was leaving New York City the next afternoon. The owner of the Gulfhawk called the New Jersey police for an escort to Lakehurst. We got in our truck and picked up the police, who led us through fields, on back roads, going so fast that we developed a regular convoy of three tow trucks, two ambulances behind us.

"Meanwhile, somebody called Grumman on Long Island and got the size of the plane, and we had a big box and platform made. We took the Gulfhawk to a pier, Al Williams packaged it, and put it on the *Queen Mary*. It got to the show on time and won the aerobatics competition.

"People paid attention to the safe way we packaged that plane to go overseas. All the companies were having trouble shipping planes. They'd put a rope around it, bend it every which way, get tremendous damage. Even before we got into World War Two, I was shipping planes to France, South America, Iceland, Finland, Sweden.

"I wanted a contract from Seversky, so I made up a model of the Seversky P-35 fighter, showed how I would pack it, just laid the package down on the president's desk. We sent two hundred, three hundred of them to Sweden. I got a contract to send one hundred Grumman Wildcats to France. Then when we got into the war, we worked for Douglas and Lockheed on the West Coast. We shipped Lockheed Hudsons from New Orleans. I had plants all over the country.

"The services insisted we work three hundred sixty-five days a year, round the clock. I remember one old general wouldn't even give our women off on Christmas Eve. This was in a Negro neighborhood in New Jersey, where the people were very religious, but the general said, 'Make 'em work.' I was afraid they wouldn't show up, but Christmas Eve, all one hundred women worked the entire shift singing Christmas songs, not the way you'd hear them in a white church, but with a gospel tempo, in harmony. One section would sing a bar, then another section would chime in. It just filled the hangar. Oh, I stayed until three in the morning, just listening to them, and I can still hear that music.

"By the end of the war, I figured We'd packaged thirty-three thousand planes. We did a business over fifty million dollars. We also built the wings for the gliders that landed in Normandy. They had our name on them, and even today, men will come up to me at an aviators' meeting and thank me for making those gliders so sturdy that half the men survived the landing.

"In 1945 I was named one of the 'Ten Outstanding Young Men of the Year' by the U.S. Junior Chamber of Commerce. Some of the others were Henry Ford II, Charles Luckman, Robert Ingersol.

"After the war, there were no more airplanes to package. We closed down most of the plants, and I tried getting into prefab housing, but the unions wouldn't cooperate. Lately my whole life has been putting something back into aviation. I've made a personal crusade to purchase old airplanes, and now I want to see an air museum on Long Island, right where I grew up.

"Something else aviation did for me. I was already a pilot when I attended New York University. There was a convention of student-council presidents in Boston, and I flew my own plane up there.

"At this convention I met a tall, very attractive southern girl—Edith Gorman from Winthrop College in South Carolina. Her parents were so concerned about her going north to this convention that they made her take a special train that skipped New York City entirely, so she wouldn't have to set foot in the big city.

"Well, they would have been shocked, because I promised her a ride in my plane during the convention. I picked a brutal Boston day to offer it. Sleet and wind coming down. It was a foolish thing to do, of course. I got on the runway and saw this Curtiss Condor just manage to take off. Later I found out it crashed on the way to Albany. We took off at a forty-five degree angle, doggone lucky we didn't land in the harbor. She must have liked her first ride in an airplane because she married me eleven months later, which is the nicest thing aviation ever did for me."

28

Dome Harwood

Francestown, New Hampshire

Since his wife died last year, Dome Harwood has lived in the woods by himself—but he doesn't exactly lack for company. Three times on this rainy fall afternoon the telephone rings: neighbors wanting to say hello, invitations for supper or drinks or both. Then there are the young women who live farther back on the unpaved road, who send him boxes of candy, wrapped in *Playboy* centerfolds, to thank him for plowing away the snow last winter.

"Thirty-one inches of snow on April Fool's Day," he mutters, in weary New England tones. "I've got a backhoe and a bulldozer, and every few feet I had to stop and push a huge mound of snow off the road, but I got 'em out."

Not bad for an eighty-year-old man with cataracts, living by himself in a farmhouse. Not surprising to the pilots who knew Dome Harwood when he was the first federal inspector at Roosevelt Field. Even today, there are many pilots like George Dade who remember Dome Harwood as a lower-case god, the enforcer who came to crack the whip when the government realized it would have to regulate the characters who were filling up the skies.

"Geez, we had people coming in with three hundred, four hundred hours, and they couldn't even make a turn," Harwood recalls. "You'd turn guys down and they'd stand there with their mouths open. They'd say, 'But I've been flying for ten years,' and I'd say, 'You're just lucky you didn't kill yourself yet.' "

When Harwood came to Long Island to police the airfields, the madcap days of aviation were getting to be a nuisance. Flying was actually safer than it had been a decade earlier, but the land around the airfields was becoming crowded with houses, the roads were filling with cars, and the bigger, faster planes did more damage when they had to ditch. People were flying airplanes for serious business now, for commerce and tourism; it was time to cut down the stunts.

The smart ones adjusted, like Dome Harwood, even though it was his own youth that was being banished. As we sit around his comfortably cluttered living room, he tells about his own route from stunt man to enforcer.

"I was a professional motorcycle racer, used to race them around Illinois. That's how I got my nickname, 'Dome,' from riding around this wooden track, called a 'cycle-drome,' which got changed to 'Dome.' It had nothing to do with me losing my hair early. Grew up in Galesburg, where my father was an engineer on the Burlington Railroad. Used to see Lincoln Beachey riding around the racetracks, flying that old pusher-type airplane.

"Saw a sign, 'Join the Army, Learn to Fly,' and figured I'd come home from war in an airplane. Like a damn fool, I put down all this motorcycle stuff on my record, so they made me a dispatcher in France, carrying messages for General Pershing at Verdun. But I'd take lessons from this instructor. Most of the pilots in the army didn't even know how to come out of a spin.

"Got out of the army, back in Illinois, I was a mechanic, fixing up planes for the barnstorming groups. Most came in with their uniforms on—RAF or whatever. I got so I could fly these damn things and then I was the first guy they'd ever seen standing up on a wing of a Jenny, doing stunts for Fox Movietone News.

"These damn cameramen would think of stunts for me to do. Standing on the wing while it looped. Rope ladder hanging down over a gravel road, guy goes off the rope at sixty miles an hour, hits the ground, black and blue all over, but didn't have a broken bone. Me? I rigged up a big belt, feet fastened so the yokels couldn't see you putting the contraption on, so I was all right.

"We were rebuilding Jennies at this airfield, but in 1926 they came out with the Waco-9. My boss signed a contract to take twelve airplanes and he was scared to death he was stuck with 'em. Geez, we sold one hundred of 'em. All we could get. Later on we took over the airport in Waterloo, Iowa, and this guy comes through and says, 'Hey, why don't you get out of these woods and go to work for the government?' "

The government had become involved in aviation in 1926 when lawmakers grew concerned over the number of accidents, and created the Aeronautics Branch of the Department of Commerce. (Later it would become the Bureau of Air Commerce, then the Civil Aeronautics Board in 1940, and in 1958, it evolved into the Federal Aviation Administration.)

"I talked it over with my wife and we decided we would do it because it paid thirty-two hundred bucks a year, which was more than I was making selling Wacos. In the winter I had to drive a taxi in Chicago, which was more dangerous than flying any time. I went to Washington for two weeks to a so-called school where they told you what to do and then I went to Roosevelt Field and they said, 'Don't sign any leases because you probably won't be there more than six months.' Hell, I was there for eighteen years.

"I don't think in history there's ever been an agency like this. See, they made this thing, and they sent these inspectors out, and I'd come up here and say, 'Look, I'm going to take away your license for two weeks.' Well, you had no recourse whatever. If I wanted to fine you, you had to pay one hundred dollars or they'd take away your license. The inspector was the law, the judge, the jury, everything.

"I was an aeronautical inspector. My job was to inspect pilots, mechanics, and airplanes. For a long while I was the only damn inspector at Roosevelt Field. I even covered Boston and Albany. It was illegal to fly without a license. You'd get a student permit by taking a physical exam, and that would allow you to take lessons and also fly solo as long as you didn't carry anybody with you.

"When I first started out, the exam for a pilot's license was after you had ten hours of solo time. Then you had to make three landings, a spiral from two thousand feet, one hundred eighty degrees to a spot, and three hundred sixty degrees to a spot, couple of figure eights. Then the limited commercial license—fifty hours, you could carry passengers within ten miles of the airport. That was so you could make a little money by taking people for rides.

Dome Harwood tested many celebrities for their flying licenses, including movie actor Jimmy Dunn, center. Dunn is pulling a switch of licenses with Scotty Begg, a Nassau County police officer who was a regular on the Roosevelt Field beat. (Photo by John Drennan, courtesy of the Begg Collection.)

"Then you had the commercial license. You had to do two turning spins, two turns each, come out the same way you went in it. If you were heading north, you had to come out of it heading north. Three spot landings, vertical banks, figure eights, anything you wanted to do, stalls of course. The inspector went with you.

"That was always good for laughs—the inspector at the dual controls of an old Jenny or Waco or Travel Air, giving a test to a World War One pilot who had barnstormed halfway across America, thrilling crowds and making his living, but who now had to impress a federal inspector to keep his right to fly.

"There was one guy who was just sliding around up there, eight hundred feet in the sky, skidding so bad it would almost blow your helmet off. He didn't know how to bank the plane at all. I just cut the damn throttle and came right in. I said, 'I'm sorry, son, but you'd better learn how to fly.'

"I wasn't one of those inspectors who thought you had to turn somebody down. A lot of people thought if you passed four, five guys in a row, you weren't doing your job. Well, that was a lot of crap, because you might have four, five people in a row that could fly. The next time you might turn down five in a row.

"You can always tell if a guy can fly the airplane. There's a million things you see. He could do all the things on the test, but you can tell he shouldn't have a license. But you know, even though I turned down people, I don't think I had an enemy at the field, and I wasn't obligated to anybody.

"Some of those inspectors would hide in the bushes and watch people fly, and grab away their licenses, but that was strictly against the ethics of the old CAA. We didn't go around sneaking, most of us. There was one airport manager in Sioux City who wired the CAA that if this duty-struck inspector came to his field one more time, he'd punch him in the mouth. He didn't care if they took away his license or not, he was going to beat the hell out of the inspector. But nobody ever punched me or threatened me.

"On a couple of occasions, there would be a ten- or twenty-dollar bill taped on the stick. I'd just get out of the plane and say, 'You come back in ninety days and we'll try this again.' I didn't dare do anything like that. Sometimes the women knew I was the only guy in New York giving out licenses, they'd invite you to dinner, to some nightclub or something, but I never got involved like that. I was very friendly with everybody, run around with anybody, regardless of whether they wanted their license or not."

One of Harwood's friends was Lindbergh, whom he used to know when Lindbergh was flying the mail around Chicago. They met again after Lindbergh's marriage, when Anne Morrow needed a license to continue flying.

"This was at the Aviation Country Club on Long Island, a very snooty place," Harwood recalls. "But he was still my friend, still called me

'Dome,' which all my friends did. I didn't have to go up with her because she already had ten hours of solo time, but I had to watch her from the ground.

"I remember, Lindbergh sat next to me on the wing of a plane, every move she made, and told me, 'If she doesn't pass this one hundred percent, she's going to get turned down.' He was tough on her. But she did it perfect. When she came in, you were supposed to cut the motor, make a complete turn and land, not using the throttle unless it was necessary. Theoretically, if you landed behind the line, you cracked up the plane. She set it down three times within fifteen feet of the front of the line. Perfect glide path, didn't have to slip down. Perfect."

Sometimes the celebrities were more of a problem, particularly when they became world-famous pilots first, then applied for a basic license.

"Ruth Nichols, she was one of the best pilots around. Just set a record from L.A. to Roosevelt Field in a Lockheed Vega, but she didn't have a rating on it. Two days afterward she said, 'Dome, I want to get a rating.' Now I'm a son of a gun. I told her to go up there, cut the gun, and land without using the gun.

"Well, I'm a son of a gun, but three times she comes down, and three times she's short. Once she comes in short of the damn telephone lines and she has to give it the gun just to get out. Each time she lands short of the test line. What the hell could I do? People were standing around and they don't know whether I'm going to give her the rating, or what.

"I'd look pretty stupid turning her down when she just set a speed record from L.A. to New York. She came into my office and shook her head and said, 'I can do better than that.' I sat down and gave her the rating. What in the hell was I supposed to do?

"It was just as bad with Clarence Chamberlin, the second guy to fly the Atlantic, right after Lindbergh. He let his license run out, and somebody in Washington didn't like him, so we got orders to give him a test at Roosevelt Field. They had this damn pressroom here, all the reporters, dozens of them hanging around. Now here come the newsreel cameras and the photographers, a great big hullabaloo because Clarence Chamberlin is taking a flight test.

"The whole damn thing was ridiculous because obviously the guy could fly an airplane, but the fact of the law said if your license ran out, you had to take the test. So he and I went up for a couple of minutes, fooled around, and when he landed I gave him the license. All the papers had big write-ups about it. Big deal.

"But then you had things that really went wrong. One time this guy in Port Washington had a seaplane he wanted to fly to Alaska. All the neighbors were complaining about the noise on the bay, but this guy said, 'I chased the Indians away to move here, and I'm not going to stop testing my plane because of a little noise.'

"Well, he wanted a test, so he could leave, and I asked in my office, 'Who wants to go to Port Washington and test this flying boat?' Nobody volunteered, so I appointed the inspector who worked at my office and I said, 'OK—you're it.' About an hour later, I get another call, and on my way to the telephone I knew what had happened. With those seaplanes, you'd get a leak, water under the floor, the water runs around, you can't get the nose down, and it stalls. The pilot and inspector, both killed. It just couldn't have been pilot error. I never got over sending that inspector over there, damn it.

"Lots of times I'd have to go to the crash. Awful? Oh, geez. One night we were over at my boss' house in Westbury, my wife and I, when I get a call, bad crack-up at Roosevelt Field. We go over there, this experimental airplane built in California, there were three guys in it, coming in for landing, they just spun in, geez, all three guys burned up. We go back to my boss' house, his wife is upset because we're late for dinner, and we walk into the dining room and what does she have on the table but a great big roast beef. I took one look at that, and that's all I could stand. I'd just been looking at these bodies all burned to a crisp.

"I've seen so many crashes. One day at the country club, my wife was with me, this guy cracked up and burned right there. I said, 'Now, look, you stay there, and so, Nosy, she had to follow me over there. These two bodies still in the iron seats, but there was nothing to them. Arms about half the size, eyes, lips still . . . She took one look at it, and that almost cured her of ever getting in an airplane. Lot of them, the bodies would still be in there, you'd have to help to get 'em out.

Harwood says his job became more complicated after Roosevelt was elected in 1932, and government commissions proliferated geometrically.

"Somebody discovered this thing was illegal, all these inspectors and no rules, so they organized the Civil Aeronautics Board [in 1940], with members appointed by the president, and they made a rule that everybody was entitled to a hearing in a little courtroom.

"We also had to put down the cause of every accident. The head of the CAA was mad because he figured we'd go broke, so he said: 'Here's what to do. Say it was caused by a collision with the ground.' Well, our legal department said you couldn't get away with that. We had to go back over our records since 1927 and make a report on every fatal crash."

Harwood says he never had a real crash as an inspector, but he avoided a few by skillful landings when the wheel assemblies failed. He is most proud of his ability to diagnose problems before they resulted in crashes—although people would not always listen to him.

"This Fairchild plane had a bolt three eighths of an inch in diameter. I asked them a dozen times, why in hell did they design a plane with such a little bolt in it. The engineer said, 'Oh, it's plenty strong.' But a month later their chief pilot was killed because the bolt busted. Then they made it bigger.

"Another time I was giving a guy a test for a commercial license. I was a nut on vertical landing, making him do a ninety-degree turn, where your controls are reversed. There is a lot of gravity on the pilot and I could hardly see the guy. I could hardly move the stick, with all the G-force.

"I realized something was wrong, and I put the plane in glide, pulled back, stabilized, and landed. See, this guy's seat had busted in the vertical, with a pretty good G on him. In my mind, the same thing had happened in the same kind of airplane in Pennsylvania six months before, two guys killed, and nobody knew what happened. I reported this seat to Washington, and they checked it out, and the company fixed it.

"That's the part you liked, correcting something. And all the people I met. Jockeys. Alicia Patterson, the founder of *Newsday*, a great woman. Show business people. Guy Lombardo, Leland Hayward, Ginger Rogers, Jack Teagarden. Dutch Schultz. Lots of guys from the underworld. The first Catholic priest ever to fly. An Indian chief, Buffalo Child Long Lance—was he popular with the women! Paul Gallico used to come around. It was a great time, very personal for the entire 1930s.

"About 1939, it got so damn big that we had our own office at La Guardia and then we moved into the city, had two floors in some office building. In 1945 I wanted to make some money and went to work for an aviation company, selling planes on Long Island. Within two years we just couldn't sell 'em, all the airplane factories shut down. I was sick of aviation by that time so I moved up here, worked as a carpenter, building houses, and never had anything to do with it.

"But I think of all the people I passed. Hundreds of 'em. You ask me if I ever made a mistake? Well, one guy failed the test and he came back ninety days later and was borderline again. I told him, '———, you'll never make a pilot!' But I passed him. Later he became chief pilot for one of the big manufacturers on Long Island. I was certainly wrong about him."

29

Harriet Fry Iden

Glendale, California

In the early months of the Depression, while many Americans were being laid off from jobs they had considered secure, eight young women were creating a new job category—airline stewardess.

By now, the very word "stewardess" evokes an invariable ritual—sell some whiskey, serve some chemicals-called-food, pass out headsets—but in 1930 the first eight stewardesses had to improvise their roles, just as the airlines were improvising passenger service. They were as much pioneers as the stunt pilots and engineers were.

The eight originals worked the Chicago–Cheyenne–San Francisco run for Boeing Air Transport, which later became United Airlines. A photograph of all eight shows the women swathed in capes and pullover berets that look like shower caps, standing alongside a Boeing 80-A biplane, and squinting in the sunlight. In the photograph they look forever twenty-four.

"The uniforms were wool," says Harriet Fry Iden, second from the right in the picture. "They made up wool suits because when we started, it was only a three-month trial. If we made a success of it, all right, and if we didn't, all right, but they didn't want to make two sets of uniforms."

She recalls these details some fifty years later, while puttering around her apartment in modern synthetic slacks and blouse. She is comfortably a senior citizen now (stewardesses grow older, just like pilots), but she can talk for hours about those first eighteen months when she helped create a career that thousands of women and men have followed.

"It really wasn't a matter of me being interested," she says. "They called me. I was a private-duty nurse working all over Chicago in the hospitals, some of them closing down because of the Depression. One day the registry called me and asked if I'd be interested in being interviewed by a Miss Ellen Church from San Francisco, who was looking for nurses to be attendants on transport planes.

"Well, you know how private-duty nurses are taught to be careful about going into houses where you don't know people, but my supervisor said, 'This is something entirely new, it's never been done before. I wish you would go down and meet her. She would like to interview you because they've already seen your picture.' "

Ellen Church was a nurse herself, but she had been beguiled by the advertisement outside the Boeing office in San Francisco, proclaiming passenger flights to Chicago. One day Church dropped into the Boeing office and asked for a job—perhaps even as a pilot.

This should not have been an outrageous request, considering what Amelia Earhart, Elinor Smith, Viola Gentry, and many other women had accomplished by 1930. However, Steve Simpson, the district manager, was not prepared to hire Church as a pilot (it is not clear whether she had ever flown a plane). He was looking to attract passengers for Boeing's system, and he was aware that Lufthansa of Germany had experimented with male couriers as early as 1928.

"Don't you think it would be good psychology to have a woman up in the air?" Church asked him. "How is a man going to say he is afraid to fly, when a woman is working on the plane?"

In an interview shortly before his death in 1973, Simpson recalled that Church was "obviously intelligent, competent, and friendly," and how he arranged for her to recruit seven more women—all nurses, because of their training and poise. Three were recruited in California and four more were needed from the Chicago area.

"I met her the next morning," says Harriet Iden. "She had already interviewed four hundred nurses, but she picked four of us, and we were measured for our uniforms. The next morning we had breakfast and were supposed to go for our introduction flight to Cheyenne, to meet the other girls.

"The pilots, of course, didn't want us. Nobody wanted women on planes. It was, you know, like having a woman on board ship. Forget it. There was fog and motor trouble, so we sat around till eleven o'clock, then we ran into a storm and the pilot paid no attention to us. We always stopped in Iowa City to refuel, two hours out of Chicago. They told us: 'Don't get out of the plane. Don't let anybody see you.'

"We stopped at Omaha to pick up another pilot, Jack Knight, and he took one look at us, stuck his flying gear in the rack, turned around in disgust, and walked into the cockpit. That was the last we saw of him that flight."

For all of the recruits, this was the first flight ever.

"I was disappointed. It was not the feeling of going fast," Iden says. "When you're driving fast in a car, you've got the telephone poles going by, but there was certainly no sense of speed for me.

"We ran into a line squall, a terrible storm, around Lincoln, and one of the girls got sick and we didn't want Miss Church to know it, so we took the little airsick carton and wrapped it in a newspaper and hid it in the girl's bag, so nobody would know."

After the meeting in Cheyenne, the women split up into teams and began working the daily flights to Chicago or San Francisco. At first they were called "flying nurses," but this was fought by the nursing association, Iden says.

"They turned their noses down at us. There was even talk of kicking us out of the registry. Then there was an argument between 'hostess' and 'stewardess,' and the word 'stewardess' hung on."

The women's capes were modeled after nursing outfits, with large pockets to contain screwdrivers and wrenches. The stewardesses were expected to aid in refueling, transfer baggage, mop floors, make sure the passenger opened the washroom door rather than the main door leading to the outside. When the pilot was forced to set the plane down in the countryside, the stewardesses had to help find food and shelter for the passengers.

"It's very hard to make people understand what those planes were like because we're so accustomed to those nice, bright, shiny planes with air conditioning and galleys. Those planes were all canvas on the outside, and the wings were wrapped in linen and they were glued down by something called 'dope.' Every so often, this would start coming loose and you'd have to set down. This happened to me once in Lincoln, Nebraska, when it was one hundred and nine degrees—and you know in that Missouri River valley it can get humid and awful.

"The only air we had were little things along each window, a little grille. You could push that open. Pressurized cabins? Oh, no. That wasn't even heard of. The cabins were very hot in summer but very cold in winter. There was supposed to be heat in the wintertime and there was, a little. In comparison to today, they were really prehistoric.

"They were very safe. We didn't fly in bad weather. If there was a bad storm, he'd simply sit the plane down in a cow pasture and wait till it passed over.

"Our nursing training wasn't used that often. Holding hands, that was about all. We didn't have passengers traveling that were ill. It was only airsickness. People got more airsick then because you'd have an air draft this way, then the other way. You're up on one wing, then on the other. It's like riding the ocean waves.

"We landed at Omaha one time, got hit by a freak tornado, plane on this side, like this, passengers getting sick and I'm holding their heads, looking at the ground one second, next second looking up at the sky. You don't know that kind of feeling in planes today.

"The passengers were not hysterical very often, but sort of a quiet desperation. They would think: 'I have started this. I have bought my tickets. I am on this flight. I will sit here.' Once they got in the air, it was usually

The original eight stewardesses, all registered nurses hired for United's routes between San Francisco, Cheyenne, and Chicago. Upper left: Ellen Church, the originator, and Alva Johnson. Lower left: Margaret Arnott, Inez Keller, Cornelia Peterman, Harriet Fry, Jessie Carter, and Ella Crawford. (United Airlines) The five surviving "originals" at a United reunion in 1975: Left to right: Jessie Carter Bronson, Cornelia Peterman Tyson, Inez Keller Fuite, Margaret Arnott, Harriet Fry Iden. (United Airlines)

fine unless we hit some rocky weather, which would upset their stomachs.

"We had a container in front of every seat, even then. We would hold their hands and give them some Amytal for sedation, put them in a reclining position. See, a lot of them were frightened on a plane and expected to get sick. I never got sick. One of the pilots, Johnny Cable, took me up while he was testing a 40-B one time in Cheyenne, and he tried all kinds of turns and spins to make me sick, but he couldn't."

"Some of the pilots were nice and some weren't. People were encouraged not to walk around the plane because the weight had to be stabilized. The pilot had a crank that he would turn whenever the plane would shift. Well, sometimes we were a little cross with the pilot, and if we had no passengers, we'd run back and forth just long enough to let him stabilize it. Then we'd run back again.

"Actually, that first summer, we had very few passengers. It was the mail that kept the line going. Now and then I see the Kraft Cheese commercials and I think of J. H. Kraft, the cheese man, who traveled so much with us. He had red hair and a red moustache, wore glasses, was a Methodist and was very interested in youth groups. Jay Gould from New York would fly coast to coast. Will Rogers, Peter V. Kine, a novelist. It was mainly for wealthy people, really, at first.

"But in the fall of 1930, they put on a night flight that gave us two planes in both directions each day. The air was very clear sometimes and the westbound would pass the eastbound and they'd tip their wings to each other."

By the fall of 1930, the first three California stewardesses had resigned, with Ellen Church remaining. When Steve Simpson went out to recruit more nurses, several hospitals banned him from their grounds.

"It was hard on your health," Iden says. "Several times girls had to check into hospitals because they were dehydrated, losing weight on the long trips. There wasn't anyplace you could stop for a hamburger or anything. It would take nine, twelve hours from Chicago to Cheyenne sometimes."

The newspapers of the day made flying seem romantic. One Cheyenne newspaper reported the presence of "eight beautiful young women, gowned in uniforms of gray green. Their presence at the Plains Hotel has attracted much favorable comment and curiosity."

Iden remembers it a little differently. She remembers taking a cut in pay in her new career:

"We were paid one hundred twenty-five dollars a month for flying. Nursing was seven dollars a day for a twelve-hour day, so if you worked every day you'd get around two hundred dollars a month. This was a difficult cut for us. We were allowed six dollars a day expenses away from home. Of course, the pilots could afford to stay anyplace. They didn't care. We stayed at the same place the pilots were. They were paying four dollars a night.

"When we first traveled, we had our names embroidered on our pocket. We'd get in the elevator and there were a lot of drummers and what-have-you, and they would call us by name, and they would call our rooms. Miss Church was making a trip with us and we got stuck in Omaha and we got in the elevator and somebody called her 'Miss Church' and read her name and called her room and then we were allowed to take our names off our pockets.

"I said, 'I will not stay in this hotel anymore,' so we went to the Fontinelle, where it cost me six dollars, the whole six dollars, out of my own pocket, but I figured it was better to pay out of my own pocket than to . . . But we made it up on our swindle sheet. We got paid for the cleaning of our uniforms, so we just had our uniforms cleaned a little more. And the pilots would usually take us out for dinner, but we didn't save any money."

Did the pilots, or any other men, regard stewardesses as fair game because they made their living on the road?

"No, no, no, no. We were all nurses. Men tried to get fresh. That was an occupational hazard. We could handle that. We didn't date passengers. That was a rule. We didn't date pilots, either. You didn't get caught. It was the same rules and regulations as a hospital, where you didn't go out with doctors or patients.

"I remember one time I had dinner with a very nice man who was going to New York, but he had to wait overnight in Chicago. He prevailed on me to have dinner at an Italian restaurant in the Loop. I said good night and I went home. He was very nice. I can see his face today, but I cannot remember his name. I think that's the only time I had dinner with a passenger.

"Most men were gentlemen in those days. There was one college professor from Iowa City, and he got to the place where he was chasing me around the plane, and I finally got mad and slapped his face. Then I went up and stayed with the pilot and copilot. When we got in, I knew I had to tell Uncle Frank Caldwell, the head of operations, what I had done. I figured I was going to get fired for this. Anyhow, I told him, and he said, 'Well, if you slapped his face, I guess he had it coming.' "

Iden takes out a pamphlet she used to distribute to her passengers in 1930. It describes the Boeing 80-A biplane as a ten-passenger craft weighing eight and three-quarter tons, fully loaded, fifty-five feet long, with upper wings eighty feet long and a lower wing span of sixty-five. The interior cabin was supposed to resemble a railroad coach, with plywood walls, and the cabin was only five feet, four inches wide.

"We gave out blankets and pillows right away and we were assigned a certain number of ashtrays that we had to collect. People were allowed to smoke cigarettes but no pipes or cigars. They made a little one-legged table that fit on the floor and clipped into the wall, but the vibration was so great, we had to use a nursing trick to put a pillow in the passenger's lap.

"They actually used china and silverware and glasses that first year. We served a cold lunch from the Palmer House out of Chicago—fried chicken, pickles, potato salad. This was during Prohibition, but we did

The early passenger trade featured china dishware and silver coffee pots. (United Airlines)

serve a brandied fruit cocktail. We served either coffee, tea, or bouillon— no milk, because we had no refrigeration. The Palmer House made such strong coffee, we always had to add a little water to it."

To keep me from getting the idea that the stewardess business was all work, Iden takes out her scrapbook and shows photographs of a couple of men and women taking a picnic on a Wyoming mountainside in lush summer weather, the crew on a break between flights in and out of Cheyenne. She says the pilots began to appreciate the stewardesses, and invited them into the cockpit.

"I never flew a plane by myself," Iden says, "but we all used to fiddle around when they had no passengers. The copilot would be right there on the controls, of course. I was always scared I was going to do something to turn the thing over. But I guess Johnnie got very proficient at it. She was a beautiful girl. Blond. Blue-eyed."

Johnnie was Alva Johnson, Iden's roomate in Chicago, who died in an automobile crash out west in 1931.

"After that, things were just not the same," Iden says. "New girls were coming in constantly. I got pneumonia and I wanted to get back to nursing. We felt we had had it. Nobody dreamed, when they put in the night plane, that flying was going to be as popular as it has become. Don't forget, there were a lot of crack-ups. Some of the gals and pilots I knew were killed in crashes. No, no, I never had any regrets. It would have been a terrible thing to be flying back and forth all those years."

Harriet Fry went back to nursing after eighteen months of flying, married William H. Wisner, the editorial art director for the Chicago *Tribune*, whom she had met while he was a patient. He died in 1963, and two years later she married Howard Iden, a friend of hers and her first husband.

"United invited us back for the thirty-fifth anniversary in 1965. Ellen Church and I actually worked a DC-8 Mainliner, first class, from Chicago to San Francisco. I poured the champagne and she poured the coffee and we both got paid ten dollars and forty-five cents. People got a big bang out of it.

"Not long after that, Ellen died in a horseback riding accident. Both she and Johnnie died from hitting their heads in accidents—those two girls in that picture there. They named a building for Ellen at the United terminal in Chicago.

"Another strange thing is that none of us had any children except Connie Peterman down in Corona del Mar. She's a grandmother now, but the rest of us, no. We still see each other from time to time.

"At one of the reunions, I met Joy Geddes, who came along after us, and has been a stewardess for thirty years. I asked her, 'How in the world did you stand it for thirty years?' She does mostly charter flights now, to Europe, when she wants to. Her answer was, 'Well, it's different today.'

"Personally, I think it's harder today. You have so many more passengers and they expect so much more. And of course they serve all you want to drink, and I think sometimes those passengers get a little obnoxious, a little demanding.

"I have never pushed a bell for a stewardess in my life. If I want a magazine, I go up and get one. If I want a drink of water, I get it. Maybe it's the times. People feel, 'I've paid for this and I'm going to get the most out of it.'

"I never thought of myself as a pioneer until one day I picked up a history of aviation in a bookshop and saw our picture. I couldn't believe it. We just thought of each flight as just another nursing case. Who knew in those days what flying was going to be like?"

30

Nancy Hopkins Tier

Glen Head, New York

Nancy Hopkins Tier is furious. She has just spent two and a half hours driving down from Connecticut, stuck in the middle of the weekend drivers, when she could have been soaring over their heads.

"Oh, that Hutchinson River Parkway, mile after mile with another car right beside you. All I wanted to do was pull back on the throttle and take off, just sit in the air, look down at the glorious earth until you get to your destination. But I had made up my mind to drive, and it was too late to change it then."

Well into her sixties, this robust woman still flies regularly, as do thousands of other pilots of that age. But she was an unusual pilot in three other decades—in the twenties, when she was one of the first women pilots around Washington, D.C.; in the thirties, when she was one of the few women in the Ford Reliability Tours; and in the 1940s when she was one of the highest-ranking women in the Civil Air Patrol, during the hazardous surveillance of the Atlantic coast.

As we chat on this lovely spring afternoon, I ask Tier why she was able to move into a world that did not encourage women.

"I suppose you could say I was ignorant, naïve, and trusting—confident, you might say confident, because I never thought of being anything else but successful.

"I was very fortunate, living with my father at the time, because he went along with it. I often wonder, with children of my own now, how relaxed he really was at the time. I mean, flying was challenging. You knew there were going to be forced landings, you knew there were going to be motor failures, and there were, and you had to meet them.

"Today, the engines are so reliable, if they're properly taken care of, but I always could take care of machinery because I'd taken a shop course in high school. Don't ask me why, but I just felt it would come in handy, which it did.

"Ever since I was in high school, I had just one determination—to fly. I don't know why, either."

She says she didn't get much encouragement from the all-male staff at the flying fields, who may or may not have known she was a niece and namesake of Lady Astor. When she made her first flight, a perfect landing in the crosswinds across the Potomac, the social reporters and Ernie Pyle all wrote features about her. Later she moved to the Old Curtiss Field on Long Island, working in the same office as George Dade, and taking more lessons in her spare time.

Tier became so good that she was invited to fly in the 1930 Ford Relia-

Nancy Hopkins was the only woman among thirty-five entrants in the 1930 Ford Reliability Tour. She had two motor failures, made the repairs by herself in open fields, and finished fourteenth of nineteen to complete the tour. (Nancy Hopkins Tier)

bility Tour, one of the most famous air events of this decade of development. Edsel Ford of the automobile family was trying to prove that airplanes—particularly Ford-produced airplanes—were so dependable they could keep a regular schedule. The tour was first held in 1924, and by 1930 it had been expanded to a five-thousand-mile marathon around the United States, with a daily itinerary that had to be maintained.

"You started in Dearborn, Michigan," Tier recites, "flew on to Kalamazoo for lunch, then flew to Chicago and stayed overnight. Milwaukee, Eau Claire, Wausau, you kept going for sixteen days, regardless of weather. You were trying to show you could maintain your pace despite the weather. Down the Rockies. Great Falls. Sheridan. Colorado Springs, Cheyenne, Garden City, Kansas.

"I had a forced landing in Arkansas," she continues. "She really blew at four thousand feet over the Mississippi, forty miles from Memphis. I just made a big circle—I was used to landing in small fields. I landed in the back of a little shack, tree stumps all around, hit an irrigation ditch and blew a tire.

"But the main thing was to see what was wrong. I pulled the propeller, checked out the cylinders, found the problem, went to work with a screwdriver and some wire, and it started right up. All I could think about was that great shop course back in Central High, and how glad I was to take it."

The twenty-two-year-old pilot kept her schedule that day, despite the breakdown, flying out of the stump-filled field, and finishing fourteenth out of nineteen pilots. A year later she married Irving Tier, who owned a fleet of planes in Connecticut, and she did not compete in races after starting a family.

But she did join the Civil Air Patrol after it was founded on December 1, 1941, with war in Europe already blazing and war in Asia closer than most people imagined. The CAP was begun in New Jersey, by a writer named Gill Robb Wilson, who felt the United States would need civilian help to match Germany's air power. As the United States joined the war on both fronts, the CAP installed coastal patrols and other observation duties. Tier was made a lieutenant in the new outfit.

We are talking in the late 1970s, when women are taking over more jobs in the armed services, getting closer to the front lines and the path of missiles, when there is still some official queasiness about women killing and being killed.

"The way I saw it, if you're going to worry about it, you don't volunteer," Tier says. "There's always the possibility you might get killed, but the people who think about it stay out of danger. After fifty years of flying, people say to me, 'Aren't you afraid?' Imagine doing something for fifty years that you were afraid of.

"The word came around that women were not to fly missions over the ocean, since there would be bad publicity if they were lost," she says. "There were planes going down all the time due to malfunction. But I could see that private pilots with expertise were going to be desperately needed in the war.

"By January of 1942, pilots with private radios began patrolling the New Jersey coast, where our shipping was being sunk, within sight of land, by German subs. So we flew down to Atlantic City, which dropped the sinkings almost eighty percent in the first month, just by our being there. We could report the location of the submarine, and they could plot a course to find it.

"We didn't carry weapons at first, but after a year they gave us a one hundred fifty-pound bomb, and fastened it on. We had only planes of one hundred fifty horsepower or less, since they put everything else into the service, so we couldn't carry much, but we designed our own bombsights.

"If it had gotten out that we were almost totally unarmed, the submarines could have blown us out of the air, but they always submerged upon approach of an airplane that could identify their position. We did a great thing. A great thing.

"We lost two men with motor failure in February. They couldn't have survived fifteen minutes in the water. We were so pitifully unprepared for the war, so far behind the times. Billy Mitchell had shown he could bomb the daylights out of old ships, but he got court-martialed for it. The navy. The precious navy. We had to live through the war, sinking one ship after another."

By the end of the war, the Civilian Air Patrol was given credit with bombing fifty-seven German submarines and destroying at least two of them. When asked why the U-boats had stopped their attacks along the coast, one German officer said after the war: "It was because of those damned little red-and-yellow planes."

George C. Dade—III

Glen Head, New York

"I was in for a shock when World War Two ended. I was still a young man—in my mid-thirties—and I realized that aviation had progressed from Glenn Curtiss to the threshold of the jet age since I was a boy. I looked around Long Island and saw jet fighters taking off just a few miles from where Bert Acosta took off that first day I arrived on Long Island.

"I kept waiting for Roosevelt Field to "get back to normal," but of course it never did. All that flat space that made Long Island 'The Cradle of Aviation' was now being used for housing developments. We heard that William Zeckendorf was going to plow over the old airfield and put up a shopping center at Roosevelt Field. I pleaded with them to save Hangar Sixty—the old Moisant hangar where I used to live—to keep it for a museum, but nothing doing. They just tore it down and put in a parking lot.

"Ever since then, I've been kicking myself that we didn't find some way to buy Hangar Sixty to establish our air museum. Then I joined the Long Island Early Fliers Club, where you bring around your old pictures and talk about the old days. When I became president in 1973, it occurred to me that if we presented Nassau County with a restored antique airplane, they'd hurry to build a museum to house it. Makes sense, no?

"Then we got lucky. The greatest aviation hero ever to set foot on Long Island was Lindbergh, in my opinion anyway. Frank Strnad, who is one of the most knowledgeable aviation historians around, located Lindbergh's first airplane, an old Curtiss Jenny. When Frank told us, I felt a tingle all over me. Forty-six years after I first saw the man, he was still my greatest hero. I remember reading in his book, *We,* how he purchased the old JN-4 in Americus, Georgia, and barnstormed for a couple of years before selling it.

"Now we might have a chance to buy it. Frank Strnad told me the Jenny had crashed in a field in Iowa in 1927—just before Lindbergh came to Long Island to prepare for his big flight. An old barnstorming farmer, Ernie LeClere, had bought the plane for the spare parts. Ever since then, the parts had been sitting in LeClere's barn in Coggon, Iowa.

"To my mind, Lindbergh's first plane, fully restored, would be a treasure for a Nassau County Museum. Of course, we had no idea what shape the plane was in.

"I knew I couldn't come on like some big-shot New Yorker, eager to make a deal, so I wrote a casual note to Ernie LeClere on our Early Fliers stationery, asking if he wanted to sell the Jenny.

"He wrote back saying it was definitely Lindbergh's first plane, but, no, he wasn't interested in selling it. He said the Smithsonian, the Minnesota Historical Society, and the Iowa National Guard had all expressed interest in buying or renovating it.

"Now I've always been a pretty good salesman, so I picked up the phone and asked for Coggon, Iowa. This was on a Friday afternoon. I said, 'Ernie, just by coincidence, I'm going to be in Cedar Rapids tomorrow. Are you going to be home?' He said he was. I said, 'Thanks, Ernie, I'll see you tomorrow.'

"I packed up my aviation scrapbook, got an early flight to Cedar Rapids, rented a car, and drove to Ernie's farm. He was a very nice guy. We talked for a while, and then he took me out to see the plane. What a mess. It looked more like scrambled eggs than an airplane. Just a bunch of parts lying on the floor. He said the cows had eaten the fabric off the plane years ago, because they liked the taste of the banana-oil dope. And generations of pigs, chickens, ducks, and cows had created quite a stench.

"This was it. I wanted that plane. I knew I'd have to sell myself to Ernie, so I got out my old scrapbook and went through it—how I was raised on Curtiss Field, lived in a hangar, knew all the old pilots including Lindbergh, had my picture taken with Lindbergh. Still, my posture was that of a city slicker trying to take away the farmer's goodies. Then I remembered my father had been born in Iowa, so I talked about that for a while. I must have talked for two-and-a-half, three hours, before Mrs. LeClere brought out a raisin pie, and of course it was the best raisin pie I ever had.

"Then Ernie brought out the biggest scrapbook I had ever seen, and for the next five hours he talked about his career, how he was president of the Flying Farmers of America, everything. I listened and listened and listened and listened, and after five hours, Ernie had sold himself to me. I was perfectly willing to buy the airplane from a guy with his perfect credentials. Then we went through another piece of raisin pie, and I could sense he was softening.

"I said, 'Look, Ernie, you're seventy-one years old. You've had this plane for forty-six years. If the National Guard was going to fix up the plane, they'd have done it by now. You want to see this plane restored before you die? What kind of deal do you want?' We agreed on a price and, as a clincher "I promised him and his wife round-trip tickets to New York as my honored guests when the restoration was completed. By now it was well after dark. The trip to New York seemed to make the difference because he signed the papers, and I gave him a check for twenty percent.

"I had a meeting in New York on Monday morning, so I told him I'd be back in two weeks for the parts. But that night, in a motel in Cedar Rapids, I couldn't get to sleep. I kept thinking that the first thing Monday morning, Ernie was going to tell his old flying buddies, and they were going to say, 'You mean you sold that Jenny to the skunks back in New York?'

"So on Sunday morning, I drove all the way to Iowa City, rented the only truck in the whole city, turned in my rented car, drove back to Coggon—by now it was pouring rain—bought a pair of overalls and boots, sloshed through all brands and sizes of manure, eighty little pigs squealing under my feet, back and forth a dozen times to the truck in the rain, gave Ernie the check, and took off for Chicago. My son, Steve, flew out to Chicago, drove the truck back, and I flew off to New York for my meeting. Yes, I changed out of my overalls and my boots somewhere along the line.

"When I got home to Long Island on Monday night, Steve was already home. He said, 'Dad, did you know there are initials, C-A-L, carved on a wing rib?' I got so excited, because to me this proved it was the plane. I'm sure Ernie didn't know that, or he would have charged twice as much.

"I started calling all the members of the Long Island Early Fliers, and before long we had a group of forty-three people working at my house every Wednesday night. Our target was getting the plane ready for the Bicentennial in 1976.

"For many of us, it was just like early aviation all over again. We had to think for ourselves—cleaning up the old parts, making replacements for the missing parts. We put duty charts on the wall, broke the assembly into crews. When we ran out of room in the basement, we added another section to my garage, then we expanded a breezeway into another workroom. We called our group 'The Jenny Works.'

"All our neighbors were very good about it. We'd have thirty cars parked on the narrow street every Wednesday night, but we'd park only on one side, and we tried to never block a driveway.

"We had so much skill and experience going for us—Erwin Hoenes, who learned his mechanic's trade with Tony Fokker right after the First World War; Hank Anholzer, the facilities planning manager for Pan American; people from Grumman and Republic and Sperry; June Bartlett, whose father used to fly the old Junkers at Roosevelt Field. So many others. We'd work hard for three hours and then Edith would put out the doughnuts and the coffee and the cider at ten o'clock, and nobody wanted to go home because they could see history emerging from the rust and the dirt and the raw material.

"We wrote all over the country asking for spare parts to Jennies. We got a stabilizer from Pensacola, Florida, a new strut from North Carolina, a rudder from Minnesota, a radiator from Kansas City, an engine from Thousand Oaks, California, and a propeller that Lindbergh had stored with his father in Minnesota. We got so many extra parts, we were able to build a second, uncovered, fuselage with a center section and tail assembly, radiator, engine, and propeller, to show the inner workings of a Jenny.

"When it began to take shape, we let Lindbergh know what was going on, and on November 9, 1973, he drove down from Connecticut to take a look.

"It was the first time I had met him in thirty-three years. I was still in awe of the man, but this time we talked as man-to-man, not as teen-ager to hero. He seemed happy to recognize the parts of his Jenny.

"I wanted to make sure it was really his first plane, so I mentioned about finding initials carved in the outboard rib of the lower right wing.

"You know how precise Lindbergh was. He said to me, 'That would be fifty years ago. I cannot honestly say I remember carving my initials. But I will say this: If I did it, this is the way I would have done it.' Then I asked him to stoop down under the wing, and look at the initials.

"He said in his mind there was no doubt. Later he wrote us a letter confirming the identity of the plane. His last sentence was: 'Your records of ownership sequence are clear.

"I think that was the last time he ever visited Long Island before he died. I just wish he could have seen the plane finished.

"I also wish he could have seen the stamp the government issued in 1977 on the fiftieth anniversary of his flight. I was chairman of the anniversary program for Long Island, and it took five years of lobbying by Charles and Ruth Dobrescu from our club to get the Postal Service to issue a stamp. They said they could not honor a person who had been dead for less than ten years—even a hero like Lindbergh—so finally we got them to agree to honor the flight, rather than the individual. They set up a special issuing office at Roosevelt Field for the ceremony. But he never saw that, or the finished Jenny.

"As the plane neared completion, somebody asked me if I was tempted to fly it. Well, there were a couple of good reasons why I hadn't considered it. First, I had let my pilot's license drop years ago. Second, the FAA would never have given us permission to take it off the ground without rigid tests. But the more I thought about it, I had this insane dream of putting on my aviator goggles and the World War One scarf and the leather coat, and sneaking the plane to a secret grassy field, and just gunning it for the sky. To fly above Long Island in Lindbergh's first plane. . . .

"I thought about it for thirty seconds before reality hit me. If somebody tried to take it up, he might destroy the plane, and himself, and all the work we had put into it. Jenny would never fly again.

Left: In 1928, Charles Lindbergh
had a little trouble adjusting his
parachute at Curtiss Field, and
young George Dade eagerly rushed
over to help the hero. (Photo by
"Louie," Court Commercial Studio,
Mineola, courtesy of the Garden City
Archives) Right: Forty-five years
later, Lindbergh visits George Dade's
basement to inspect his initials in the
old Jenny, being rebuilt by members
of the Long Island Early Fliers.
(George C. Dade)

"We got her together for the Bicentennial air show on Long Island in 1976. Then because the plane had been purchased in Georgia, we were invited to the Inauguration Parade for President Carter in January of 1977.

"We strapped the Jenny on a flatbed truck—just like in my old business days—and took it down to Washington in the middle of that horrible cold spell—snow and ice everywhere. They stuck us at the end of the parade, but I'll never forget the privilege of sitting in the pilot's seat as we passed the reviewing stand, moving pretty fast at the end of the day, and thinking the president was watching us, just for a second. I know that Walter Cronkite gave us a nice mention on CBS.

"Now we're on our way to a Museum, Nassau County has given us two old hangars from Mitchel Field and I've been appointed the dollar-a-year director to get it opened, working with a professional curator, William K. Kaiser. At least we know this special period in history will not slip out of memory.

"Whenever we old-timers get together, we gab about those first generations of flying—the Lindberghs and Earharts who were real people to us; the Bert Acostas and Len Bonneys, who have been forgotten by almost everybody. We're always telling stories about these men and women, and somebody is always saying: 'We should put these stories down on paper.' Now we have."

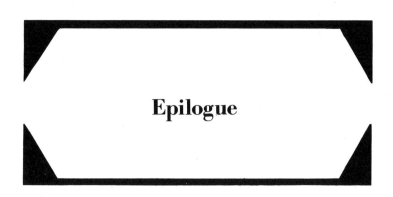

Epilogue

In writing a book about aged heroes and heroines, the "glory of their times," by definition, took place long in the past. All my friends of this book have seen close friends die suddenly in their youth, and outlived many of their loved ones over the years.

As familiar as death may be, it is always an intruder. Since these chapters were concluded, tragedy has intruded on some of my friends.

Harry Bruno, who kept promising me a tour of the museum in his summer home, was never able to keep that promise because of doctor's orders, and his heart finally gave out in March of 1978.

Frank Tallman, that skillful flying star of so many movies, who gave the Early Birds such a nice reception during their convention in October of 1977, crashed and died in his own modern plane during a thunderstorm in April of 1978.

The San Diego Aerospace Museum, where Walter Ballard had helped rebuild an old Jenny, was an acknowledged firetrap, yet it took an arsonist to set the blaze that destroyed the museum, the Jenny, and a thousand other artifacts in February of 1978.

I had been scheduled to meet Sir Thomas Sopwith, the ninety-year-old builder of World War I planes, in England in 1978, but the death of his beloved wife, Phyllis, on May 13 of that year understandably kept Sir Thomas from our appointment.

One of my most faithful correspondents has been Henry Newell, from his retirement home in Virginia. On July 22, 1978, Henry wrote me a letter clarifying a few details about the Aero Club of Long Island, and mentioning that he was spending a few days in the infirmary. Henry passed away nine days later.

The last time we spoke, Tiny Broadwick suggested she might be gone the next time I called. The feisty old parachutist died peacefully on August 25, 1978.

My prayers go out to these, and all other aviation people, whose lives have enriched so many others' lives.

Index

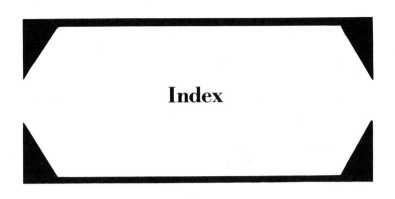

Index